1st August d. 15ᵗᵗ

LEGIONNAIRE

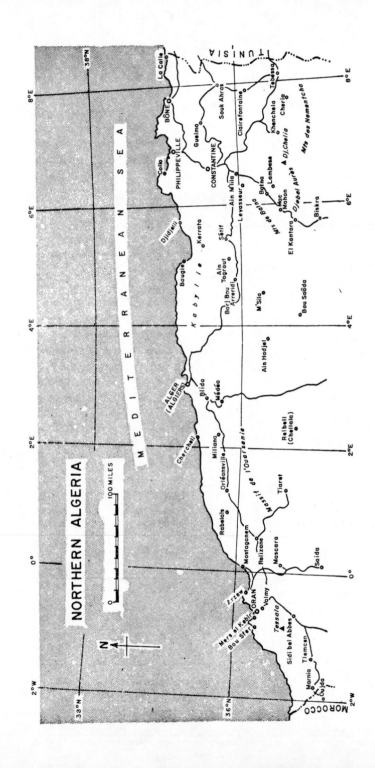

NORTHERN ALGERIA

100 MILES

N

MEDITERRANEAN SEA

La Calle
BÔNE
PHILIPPEVILLE
Collo
Djidjelli
Bougie
Kerrata
Kabylie
Sétif
Ain Taghrout
Bordj Bou Arreridj
GUELMA
CONSTANTINE
Souk Ahras
Clairefontaine
Khenchela
Cherig
Mts des Nementcha
Tabessa
Ain M'lila
Batna
Lambese
Mac Mahon
Mts de Batna
Djebel Aurès
▲ Dj.Chelia
El Kantara
Biskra
Levasseur
M'Sila
Bou Saâda
Ain Hadjel
Reibell
(Chelala)
Médéa
Blida
ALGER
(ALGIERS)
Cherchell
Miliana
Orléansville
Massif de l'Ouarsenis
Tiaret
Rabelais
Mostaganem
Relizane
Mascara
Saïda
Arzew
ORAN
Valmy
Mers el Kebir
Bou Sfer
Tessala
Sidi bel Abbès
Marnia
Tlemcen
Oujda
MOROCCO
TUNISIA

LEGIONNAIRE

My Five Years in the
French Foreign Legion

SIMON MURRAY

Times
BOOKS

Published by TIMES BOOKS, a division
of Quadrangle/The New York Times Book Co., Inc.
Three Park Avenue, New York, N.Y. 10016

Published simultaneously in Canada by
Fitzhenry & Whiteside, Ltd., Toronto.

First published in Great Britain in 1978
by Sidgwick and Jackson Ltd.

Library of Congress Cataloging in Publication Data

Murray, Simon.
Legionnaire
1.   France.   Armée.   Légion étrangère.
2.   Murray, Simon.   I.   Title.
UA703.L5M87   1978   355.3'5 [B]   78-14215
ISBN 0-8129-0798-1

Manufactured in the United States of America.

TO JENNIFER

'The grandest assembly of real fighting men that I have ever seen, marching with their heads up as if they owned the world, lean, hard-looking men, carrying their arms admirably and marching with perfect precision.'

FIELD-MARSHAL VISCOUNT ALANBROOKE

CONTENTS

CONTENTS

(Illustrations follow page 160)

INTRODUCTION

I joined the French Foreign Legion on 22 February 1960. I was nineteen years of age at the time and I stayed for five years. During that time I was never without pen and paper and I recorded the events of each and every day with very few exceptions. In this book I have extracted from those diaries what might be of interest and left out, I hope, much of the boredom. There were long periods of boredom in the Legion and sometimes that was the hardest part of all. I have picked out the characters at random and none receive undue attention because that's how it was – we were all loners at the end of the day – and I have highlighted the incidents which have left the deepest impressions on my memory because they mark the stepping-stones of my journey through those five long years.

When I arrived in Paris so many moons ago and stood in front of the Legion gates on that cold wet day in February, I was in a very uncertain frame of mind about it all. I knew that this was going to be something very different to what my somewhat sheltered life had shown me so far. I was not exactly classic material for the Foreign Legion although there had been a commitment to military affairs by my family in the past.

I had an elder brother who was an officer in the Scots Greys and a father, a grandfather, a great-grandfather and a great-great-grandfather who had all served as officers in the army in such fine regiments as the Black Watch and here was I about to become a second-class private in the Foreign Legion.

I had been to one of England's oldest public schools and was the product of good middle-class stock that had made some money from the Industrial Revolution and stockbroking and finally lost most of it through the follies of my spendthrift grandparents. Nevertheless, the traditions of the family and school combined to instil in me the values that were, and indeed still are, considered as those befitting a young gentleman about to make his way in the world.

I had read Wren's *Beau Geste* as every Englishman has and I held the traditional English view that service in foreign armies in foreign lands was an acceptable way to begin life – crusading it used to be called! What I did not know at the time was that Wren had painted a picture of the Legion that was not all that inaccurate and I was about to step into a very hard way of life indeed for which I was totally unprepared. It could not have been less romantic and as a recruit I could not have been further away from normal intake.

Many people have asked me why I joined the Legion and whilst there is no great mystery there is no clear answer. A perceptive mind may draw conclusions from these diaries – there was a girl called Jennifer, but it was more than that. I think it was still in the days when there was less of a rush through life. We had more time to sow our oats and have our adventures. Life was longer in those days.

I don't think the reason is that important anyway; what matters is that I went, and this is what happened.

SIMON MURRAY

PART ONE

Incubation

22 February 1960 – Paris

I was awake long before the dawn this morning and by the time there was a greyness in the sky I had finally made up my mind to go. By eight o'clock I was in the Métro heading for the Old Fort at Vincennes – the recruitment centre of the Foreign Legion. There were few people about and those who were had grim Monday-morning faces, probably reflecting my own.

From Vincennes station I walked through the streets and eventually arrived at the massive gates of the Old Fort. On a plaque on the wall there was a simple notice: *'Bureau d'Engagement – Légion étrangère – Ouvert jour et nuit.'*

I hammered on the huge doors which swung open in response and I stepped into a cobbled courtyard to be confronted by the first legionnaire I had ever seen. He was dressed in khaki with a blue cummerbund around his waist and bright red epaulettes on his shoulders. He wore a white kepi on his head and had white gaiters and I thought he looked quite impressive. I was less impressed with the archaic-looking rifle at his side. He slammed the great doors shut and beckoned me with his head to follow him.

I was ushered into a room on the door of which was inscribed *'bureau de semaine'*, which I assumed meant general office or something similar. It was a primitive enough chamber with a bare plank floor and a wooden table and chair. One or two old and tired-looking photographs depicting legionnaires holding the regimental colours, men driving tanks through the desert and others marching down the Champs-Élysées hung limply on the wall.

There was a sergeant sitting behind the table who looked me up and down and said nothing. I broke the ice and said in English that I had come to join the Foreign Legion and he gave me a look that was a mixture of wonder and sympathy. He spoke reasonable English with a German accent and asked me 'Why?'

I said something conventional about adventure and so on and he said I had come to the wrong place. He said five years in the Legion would be long and hard, that I should forget the romantic idea that the English have of the Legion and that I would do well to go away and reconsider the whole thing. I said I had given it a lot of thought and had come a long way and eventually he said 'O.K.' with a sigh and led me upstairs and into an assembly hall.

As I walked into the hall I was confronted with about forty people sitting on benches around the walls. Eighty eyes immediately focused on me and my own swivelled round the room in a flash. There was not one single face on which my eyes could come to rest and I could say 'He is like me' or 'We are the same in some way'. I knew instantly that I had not the slightest thing in common with any one of them.

I took an empty place at the end of one of the benches and contemplated my feet, but I could feel them all staring at me. They were an incredible mixture, dark, grey, white, brown, beards, moustaches, bald and shaggy, wearing an unlimited array of different garments, but they all looked tough and unkempt and totally different from me. I was wishing to hell that I had worn a pair of jeans and an old pullover instead of a three-piece suit with a double-breasted waistcoat, of all things.

A couple of them were sniggering on the other side of the room and I kept my eyes averted although I could feel myself getting hot. We sat for a long time until at last an officer arrived with a couple of men with white coats and we were told to strip down to underpants.

One by one we were called forward and given a series of medical tests. This took two hours and after it was over we were again left sitting on our benches. The medical had loosened a few tongues and people were chatting away to each other in different languages, mostly German. I kept myself to myself at this point and I was wondering whether I would be in time to catch the six o'clock flight from Orly back to London.

An hour passed and the officer reappeared accompanied by the sergeant who had been in the *bureau de semaine*. He made an announcement in French, from which I gathered that they had need of only seven of us and the rest could go. They read out seven names and mine was one of them.

The seven of us were called forward and led out of the room leaving behind the rest who were being herded up for departure back into the welcome arms of Paris.

We were taken along a series of dark passages and up several flights of stone stairs to a magazine at the top of the old building where we were handed battledress and trousers, a pair of boots and a greatcoat. Then we were given some food in a dingy little room with metal tables and stools. That dining-room was known as the *réfectoire* – at least that's what it said on the door.

Nobody spoke a word during the meal and when it was over we were ushered into a small room and made to listen to a tape-recording, repeated in several languages. In the room there was a single 40-watt naked bulb dangling from the ceiling on a long flex and the atmosphere was sinister. With me were two Germans, a Spaniard, a Belgian, and two Dutchmen. Everybody was tense.

The tape played in English and I was informed that I was about to sign a five-year contract and that when I had signed there could be no turning back. The voice that came over the loudspeaker was solemn and had all the gloom of a judge pronouncing sentence of death. I wanted to talk to it, I wanted to talk to anybody who was English, but it was a one-way dialogue and it was decision-making time. We listened in silence and nobody said anything, nobody started shouting to get out, nobody cracked or lost their nerve or gave way to rising panic. Then we filed through into an office one at a time and signed the contract. It comprised three enormous tomes of unintelligible French. Attempts to read it were discouraged and would have been pointless anyway.

I feel as though I have signed a blank cheque in favour of a complete stranger. Night has fallen and we are in a dormitory. Metal beds with straw-filled mattresses and a blanket. A bugle sounds 'lights out' in the night, faint and loud against the mood of the wind. It is the end of my first day and the beginning of a new adventure. I think that sergeant was right; it will be a long road and a lonely one. I am in the heart of Paris but it feels like the mountains of the moon.

The Next Day
We were awoken early with a bouncy bugle shattering cosy sleep and after a cold-water rinse and a mug of coffee we were put to peeling potatoes, sweeping floors and other general chores, called *corvée*, around the fort. There is very little talk primarily due to the language problem. The day passed quickly and tonight we are catching the train to Marseille. The journey begins.

24 February 1960
There was trouble on the train last night and I have already made an enemy. There were not enough seats and it was first come, first served. During the evening I left the compartment for a pee and returned to find a Spaniard had pinched my seat. I didn't like this situation at all. I tried very slowly to get across to him that he was in my seat and reading my magazine, but he affected deafness. It was early days to be getting into fights but it was even earlier to be running away from them, and I knew quite suddenly that I would have to make a stand.

In one move, before I had time to talk myself out of it, I grabbed him by the lapels, yanked him to his feet, and threw him the length of the carriage.

We were both quite surprised: he by being thrown so violently and me by throwing him. I am quite small and I am not used to throwing people about!

However, his surprise quickly gave way to other emotions and he came charging at me. Our greatcoats and the lack of space hampered active movement and neither of us got the better of the other, but I think I gave a good account of myself. Eventually the others in the carriage got bored with it and we were dragged apart. Public opinion came down on my side and the Spaniard was shoved out of the compartment back into the corridor. He went out with wild eyes glaring at me, screaming Spanish oaths and what were obviously threats of vengeance. I shall have to watch him.

We arrived in Marseille mid-morning and were driven in trucks to a fort overlooking the port. It is called Saint Nicolas. There are some three hundred Legion recruits here and they arrive in batches of about thirty a day from the various recruitment centres at Strasbourg, Lyon, and Paris. About half are shipped to Algeria every ten days or so.

The first move was to issue us with denims in exchange for our battledress uniforms. The denims are dirty and torn, without buttons, held together with bits of string. Obviously the other gear was just for the train journey and for the benefit of the general public so that they would not feel they were travelling with convicts, because that is now what we look like.

The central courtyard of the fort looks exactly like the kind of prison compound that one sees in movies; groups cluster together looking furtive, others sit on the ground leaning against the wall, somehow everybody is whispering – or is it that I can't understand what they are saying? The N.C.O.s look tough and they probably are. Why the hell do they look like prison wardens?

The atmosphere inside the barracks is cold and gloomy. The sanitary conditions are unbelievable. In a room which looks like an empty horse stable on a winter's morning, there is a solitary tap protruding from the wall, under which there is a sort of trough. The tap runs icy water, there is no window and no light, and this is the washroom for a hundred men. The lavatories are holes in the ground with foot-stands each side. Looks like a bad place for backache. In the dormitories bunks are three high, with the width of a man's body between them both vertically and horizontally. It reminds me of a concentration camp I once visited in Belgium that had been preserved as a macabre reminder of the Occupation. The food by contrast is good, if you can get it. The emphasis is on first come, first served and it is a self-service operation with no limits.

It is the evening and I am lying on my bunk with people all around. I am totally unnoticed, which is comforting. Card games are in progress around the tables in the centre of the room; the whole place is a complete fog of smoke and the sound is a perpetual jangle of different tongues jabbering in a million languages, none of which I understand.

Outside it's raining and the wind is blowing hard. Earlier this evening I walked along the battlements of the fort which overlooks the harbour. One can see the Count of Monte-Cristo's Château d'If and I think I know how he felt. Strange sensations and emotions as I looked at the beckoning lights of Marseille's night-life. The boats idling on their moorings waiting for the summer sun looked tempting.

It seems impossible to believe that I have been here for only one day. I feel much more a prisoner than a soldier. I really have cut the old lifeline this time: this is a long way from home and a long way from anything I have ever known. To think, if things had gone the way they nearly did and Fate had played a different card I would probably have gone into the British Army, been commissioned like my brother Anthony in the Scots Greys, and now be in a very different situation. I don't feel lonely but I feel cut off, totally disconnected from my own people. That's a bit frightening somehow. I could go down the plug hole tomorrow and there's not one single person here who would turn a hair.

It's going to be a long time before I see my friends again, or drink a pint, or go to the National, or play cricket. Didsbury Cricket Club will be in a terrible state next weekend without me. Anyway, I suppose I'll get used to it. They say one gets used to anything in time. What the sages do not say is how much time is needed.

Ten Days Later

Several days have gone quickly by. Each one begins at six o'clock with an assembly on the fort battlements. We stand in the cold in our thin denims and respond with a yell of *'ici'* when our names are called and then we are dispatched in small groups on *corvée*. I have been working on a sawmill for the last few days, during which it hasn't stopped raining – freezing hands fumbling with logs, soaking wet denims, blue with cold – come on Africa!

11 March 1960

There are a lot of Germans here, with Spaniards and Italians not far behind in numbers. The Italians spend much of their time buying and selling odds and ends or exchanging foreign currencies – God knows why, there's little enough money around. They are born brokers but light on credibility. I have struck up a talking relationship with an English-speaking Dutchman called Hank. He's in bad shape having run off and left his wife after a family row and he's now regretting it. He has asked to be released but it is doubtful if they will let him go because it would open the floodgates to all the others who must have changed their minds by now.

There is also an Australian swagman here and it is good to have somebody who speaks more or less the same language. His name is Treers and three years in the merchant navy as a deckhand and several doses of clap are his chief claim to fame and the core of his conversation.

A Canadian called Gagnon arrived a couple of days after Treers and he also claims to have had a long and distinguished career in the canadian navy, but as an officer! Treers doesn't believe it – I can see why – and they are on a collision course. Gagnon is oily and unpleasant material. He brought with him two suitcases full of kit and ingratiated himself by distributing it among the parasites. The brokers could hardly believe their eyes.

We have been paid the equivalent of about three pounds in sterling. Not bad for a fortnight's work. The food situation is not good in that there is not enough of it unless one is first. Hardly a meal goes by without a fight. It is amazing to watch the food disappear when we sit down to eat. Eight people sit at one table and a basket of bread is placed in the middle. Immediately sixteen hands fall on it like a swarm of flies and the bread is gone in the flicker of an eyelid.

The atmosphere is generally better now. People greet one in the morning and say 'Hi' from time to time. I am called Johnny. Apparently all Englishmen are called Johnny, nobody knows why. I am picking up some French but spend most of my time talking to Treers. We talk about everybody else.

There exists in the French army an organization called the Deuxième Bureau, which is responsible for military intelligence of all sorts. This organization apparently works closely with Interpol with respect to Legion recruits. All recruits must pass the Deuxième and if one has anything of a past that might interest Interpol, it is at the discretion of this body whether or not one is handed over or hidden in the Legion ranks. The Legion is traditionally an asylum and will only release an individual if he is either too hot to hold or there is a risk that Interpol know that he is there and can prove it, in which case the Legion must hand him over.

I was interviewed by the Deuxième two days ago and machine-gunned with questions for about an hour. Questions varied from where I was born, why I was born, to details of my parents and schooling and other things, but above all, 'Why?' What was my reason for joining? And what is my reason? I don't really have a slick short answer. There are many reasons but it is very difficult to explain. I told them what I thought they would like to hear – military experience and all that stuff. It seemed to go down quite well.

A German sergeant who spoke English and acted as the interpreter between myself and the French officer echoed the sergeant in Paris and urged me to forget stories of camel-riding and Beau Geste and all that. I said I was forgetting pretty fast. He asked me if I wanted to reconsider the whole thing and I said 'No', and that was that.

We leave for Algeria tomorrow. Excitement is running high. Imaginations are working overtime. We have been given Legion haircuts – clean sweep, bald as eggs, known as *boule à zéro*. We look more like convicts than ever. I am looking forward to getting out of this rat hole.

12 March 1960
Reveille at five o'clock and we piled into trucks that took us down to the harbour. We left Marseille under a clear blue sky aboard the S.S. *Sidi-bel-Abbès*, a 5,000-ton troop-carrier cum cattle ship. The sleeping quarters are in the bowels of the ship and consist of a thousand deckchairs facing in every direction and packed as tightly as sardines in a tin. I stood on deck until the last pencil-line of land became invisible. I said goodbye to old Europe and turned to face Africa and God knows what.

The monotony of the journey today was alleviated by Treers and Gagnon finally coming to blows. Actually being on a ship has proved too much for our deck-hand and naval officer and they set to just after lunch. The fight was between-decks with all the chairs being flung about. Treers eventually closed with

Gagnon and was in the process of breaking his neck when I finally got him off – I don't suppose we'll hear much more about the Canadian navy from now on.

The wind is rising tonight and doubtless tomorrow will see some sickened landlubbers.

The Following Day

Awoke at first light in a heavy sea to be greeted by the most unbelievable scene of squalor imaginable. The sea was raging and most of the deckchairs had been overturned. Bodies were lying in every direction like drunken corpses, many were throwing up where they lay without bothering to move. Long queues led to the lavatories, which turned out to be so blocked with vomit they were no longer serviceable. The impossibility of getting within range of the lavatories led the impatient to go outside and crap on deck or over the side, frequently to windward! The whole ship was a floating garbage tank.

Among the passengers there were a few women and children: Arabs returning from disillusion in metropolitan France. When I asked why they were with us, I was told that they were travelling fourth and last class. That it was the last I had no doubt, the conditions of a fifth would have been staggering even by French standards.

The wavy day dragged on and the sea dispensed misery. A meal of sorts was served but there were very few takers and eventually we crawled into Oran. The Pilgrim Fathers could not have been happier than we to put our feet again on dry land.

We piled yet again into trucks and were driven to a camp where we were given a bowl of soup. The night was cold and the soup was appreciated. At midnight we were shovelled on to a rickety train with broken wooden seats and we rolled slowly southwards into the night towards Sidi-bel-Abbès, nerve-centre of the Foreign Legion.

14 March 1960

At three this morning, a grim hour anywhere, we shunted into Sidi-bel-Abbès. Tiredness was somehow no longer apparent. It had just become a part of us.

On the station we were greeted by our first active Legion

sergeant, who managed to get us into some form of order and marched us off into the night. The streets were dimly illuminated by yellow lamps, and as we shuffled along we almost looked like soldiers; ghostly figures shrouded in bulky greatcoats, plodding forward with heavy boots banging on the hard road, shattering the stillness of the pre-dawn hours, and all the while the guttural yells of the sergeant calling out the steps.

I remember very clearly my feelings this morning as we passed through the deserted streets of Sidi-bel-Abbès. Certainly there was something romantic about it all. Perhaps there was a faint chill of fear just below the surface, but it was smothered by curiosity. A vague reminiscence of my first day at boarding school; a definite feeling of being solo on this one; unhappiness nudging my elbow! But with all these mixed sensations there was a predominant feeling of being in the right place and doing the right thing. I was conscious of the fact that I was treading my own path, maybe for the first time. It was the sensation of free-wheeling downhill, aware of a gathering momentum, aware also that I had left the brakes behind in Paris, but somehow I knew that I was going to be O.K. – I would come through.

We arrived at a camp called CP3. Big iron gates swung open. We caught glimpses of guards with Sten guns wearing white kepis. Then we passed through a large courtyard and finally we were shoved into a barrack. The journey was over. Nothing happened and one by one we collapsed on the concrete floor and sleep flooded in.

It seemed only minutes later that the door was flung open and a yelling corporal started pushing us out. It was still dark outside and freezing cold. Coffee was being doled out of an enormous cauldron and it tasted delicious, like no other coffee has tasted, or ever will taste again. We were given a chunk of bread and a small square of cold raw bacon. Then we were formed up and searched. They took my address book and tore the maps out of the back of my little pocket diary. That scared me a bit. There was something sinister about it, as though they were cutting off the route back home.

Hot showers followed, the first in a fortnight and welcome. The warm water eased some of the tension.

The barracks here are in complete contrast to Fort Saint Nicolas. Everything is immaculate. The rooms are airy and the beds comfortable and well spaced out. The washrooms are spotless. We have been given new denims and boots. Morale is on the up and we are beginning to feel like human beings instead of vermin. Everybody is more relaxed and perky. It is as though we have woken up for the first time in a week. I'm picking up some more French and a bit of German and people are chatting a bit more. Faces are becoming familiar and some people are even smiling!

We have just had *appel*, evening roll-call. Everybody stands at attention beside his bed, there is a roll-call and a sergeant walks round and makes sure everything is in order and that's it. It's kipping time and don't I need it!

15 March 1960

Reveille at 0500. A cold wash, a shave and a similar breakfast to that of yesterday – but the coffee did not seem nearly as good! We piled into trucks (it's becoming a way of life) and were driven to a sandstone quarry where we spent the day swinging pickaxes and shovelling sand. The wind was freezing and played havoc with the sand and made it grisly work. A sergeant stood over us with a sub-machine-gun the whole time – difficult to tell whether he was there to defend us in case of enemy attack or to discourage us from any thoughts of running away.

We had a short break for lunch – tinned sardines and a chunk of heavy bread – and then we carried on until the early evening and eventually chucked it in and returned to camp.

The journey to and from CP3 gave me a glimpse of Sidi-bel-Abbès. The European population is almost entirely military. The Arabs make an interesting contrast. The women are completely shrouded in white, revealing only a pair of dark eyelashes and tattooed heels to the discerning eye. The men are dressed in rags: baggy trousers and carpet-like cloaks, often with enormous hoods attached. They squat on the pavements in little groups, whispering furtively (perhaps only when our trucks stop right in front of them), and they periodically spit out bits of black tobacco.

Small boys drive herds of sheep and goats down the main streets and military vehicles hoot, vainly trying to clear a path. The centre of the town is clean and modern shops adorn the roadside, built with an attractive yellow sandstone. There are many bars – evidence of a thirsty military population. We ourselves as raw recruits will not apparently be allowed into town for at least another two months, so the city's attractions must await future discovery.

Nine Days Later
Treers is fed up and he wants to get out.

We have been preparing for our departure to Mascara, a small town a hundred and fifty miles east, where we will do our basic training. There are two centres of '*instruction*', one at Saïda and the other at Mascara. Half of us are going to each place. Mascara enjoys a reputation for being a rough kind of neighbourhood. In fact, from the way people talk about *instruction*, I think we may be in for quite a bad time.

We have been issued with kit, everything from boots to tooth-brushes, and we have been relieved of our civilian clothes which have until now been kept in our lockers. In exchange for these clothes, irrespective of quantity or value, each man receives five packets of cigarettes. René Baumann who is from Curaçao fared worse than anyone as he happened to arrive with six suitcases full of clothes. He is an interesting guy and speaks six languages. We get on well.

During these last few days we have had more medicals and yet more interviews with the Deuxième Bureau, who asked the same sort of questions as were asked in Marseille, presumably to see if one was giving the same sort of answers. One chap got a hell of a hiding for apparently giving them a pack of lies which didn't correspond to the lies told them in Marseille. They don't like that.

We have had an I.Q. test. It was the usual thing with patterns and shapes and ducks coupled with some elementary mathe-matics and a bit of French history. There were also some questions designed specifically for each nationality and I had questions on English history.

The test is apparently the first of a series that we will have to take from time to time and the results have a direct bearing on our pay. Judging by the appearance of some of the scholars here today and the furrowed brows and scratching of heads, there is going to be a shortage of cash in a number of pockets.

Treers, after considerable interviews and lots of hard-luck

stories, has managed to persuade them to let him go. I feel glad
for him as he has been miserable and I don't think he would
have stayed the course although he is physically fit enough. At
the same time I am sorry to see him go because he is the guy I
talk to most. Gagnon I do not care for at all and I am relieved
to hear that he is going to Saïda.

Yesterday we were inspected by the man who will be our
commandant in Mascara, Captain Prat-Marca. A moustached
gentleman, very French – a handsome strong face with a straight
look that was good to see, clear eyes with humorous creases – I
liked him on sight. I liked his swagger-stick which he kept
slapping against his riding boots as he walked up and down the
ranks and I liked the jaunty angle of his kepi; but despite the
debonair appearance, there is about him a certain toughness,
which is indelible in those who are made of the right fibre.
I think we are in good hands.

So tomorrow we are off and the serious business of moulding
us into soldiers will begin. We will at last have arrived at the
beginning of it all. We have been paid again, the same amount
as before. Everybody has spent the evening guzzling beer in the
open mess, known as the *foyer*. The mood is festive. The
Germans are great singers and there was much singing with the
beer that was good to hear; old German marching songs which
Hitler would have been proud of; they generate tremendous
spirit! I'm feeling good and I think we are all in the right frame
of mind and ready for tomorrow.

25 March 1960
Twenty years ago today I was born. What an auspicious day to
be leaving my teens! I said goodbye to Daniel Treers and we left
Sidi-bel-Abbès in a long convoy of Simca trucks and drove to
Mascara. We followed a narrow road that wound its way
through wild countryside and up into barren hills and eventually down into the plain of Mascara itself, which stretches flat
as an airstrip to the horizon and nothing.

The town of Mascara is like a miniature bel-Abbès but
shabbier. I'm told all towns built by the French in North Africa
look the same. In the centre is la Place, with its trees and flowers
neatly arranged and benches scattered around for the evening
stroller to pause and watch the passers-by. The city hall, known

as the *mairie*, looks smart and serious near by and the *gendarmerie* is substantial and impressive at the entrance to the town, a symbol of something French and everything that French colonial power stands for. Scruffy bars and cafés run along the side of the street, the largest of which is the Café du Commerce where the Arabs sit and discuss their affairs, sip their coffee, chew their *chique* and pass the time of day.

We passed through the market where hundreds of Arabs milled around a similar number of stalls laden with fabrics and pots and pans of every conceivable shape and size and thousands of other goods and food and bits and pieces. As our trucks thundered and revved slowly through the crowded streets we saw squads of legionnaires, presumably recruits who have been here some time, marching along singing their hearts out in German and French. They march at an incredibly slow pace, almost a plod, and there is something sinister in it, and yet the singing atones for this completely – it is a really thrilling and inspiring sound with a richness of tone and tremendous harmony, as though a trained choir were in action – powerful stuff!

And then we were at the gates of the 5th Company of the Instruction Battalion of Mascara. Massive gates of wrought iron, flanked by immaculately turned out sentries with white kepis, stiff upper lips and Sten guns. The trucks pulled up in the middle of a huge mud patch of a parade-ground, down one side of which extended what appeared to be a never-ending horse trough which has since been identified as the communal washbasin. Corporals were everywhere, pushing us around and shouting incomprehensible French at everyone. Some order was established at last and names were read out and we were assigned to various sections and barracks.

The buildings are in tune with those at Saint Nicolas in Marseille; inside everything is of cold grey stone. In the barrack rooms we each have a metal bed with a straw mattress and a metal locker stands beside it. Our kit has to be folded item by item in the open locker: shirts, trousers, vests, socks and so on all stacked on top of each other so that the pile forms a perfect rectangle. A white scarf is folded down the front with a piece of cardboard behind it for stiffening purposes, so all that is visible is a neat square white panel. The beds comprise three separate parts, which had to be dismantled and cleaned. At evening roll-call, or *appel*, a sergeant will apparently inspect before lights out, and he will go over the beds and lockers with white-gloved hand in search of dust.

The overall atmosphere is one of frost and apprehension, as though bad trouble is imminent. I don't like it at all and it's playing havoc with my nervous system. We new arrivals feel terribly green. The French call new recruits *les bleux*.

The outgoing company which we will replace and which will now be sent as reinforcements to the various regiments is still here awaiting final exit. Their presence is symbolic of what we will look like in a few months' time – we hope. In contrast to us they are like a herd of young bullocks just kept from stampeding by an intangible discipline. Their morale is good and they create the impression of a force of enthusiasm and vibrance. They are continually on the move, running or assembling in small, neat, crisp-looking squads, or marching with their heads up and with their arms swinging like hell. They are in harmony in all their movements and this effect is heightened by the singing of these marvellous songs which one can hear constantly throughout the day. These men look fit and strong and quite unstoppable, like fast-moving tanks. We, *les bleux*, are spectators, non-participants, waiting for them to clear out so that we can get on stage. We have no camaraderie, no morale, no songs and we can do nothing. There is a sort of nervous tension in our ranks. It is difficult to relax and there is an edge in one's relationship with everybody else. We are perhaps all too preoccupied with number one at the moment, ensuring we do the right thing and that we keep a low profile. We need time.

At the evening meal, '*la soupe*', the old hands showed their form and one realized fully then how new we were and how far we had to go. We were all lined up outside the *réfectoire* and on the blast of a whistle the disciplined column filed in. There were long tables laden with food, along the side of which were small square metal stools, all in straight lines – perfect precision. Each man entered, removing his kepi as he did so, and stood to attention in front of his stool. Complete silence, absolute order, rigid discipline. The numbers were right, nobody was left wandering around looking for a place. The corporal entered last and called for a song, '*La tone*'. A single voice broke the silence with the first few bars, at the end of which he yelled

'*Trois*' and the old hands in silence counted four imaginary paces and then with a crash like a pistol-shot in a tunnel they yelled '*Quatre*' and blasted into '*La Légion Marche*'. In the enclosed *réfectoire* it was like being in a cathedral with sixteen choirs going for their lives – deafening and fantastic – tremendously strong and impressive. The song finished and the corporal yelled, '*Asseyez-vous. Bon appétit!*' and with a mighty roar of '*Merci, caporal*' we dived into the food, shovelling it into our faces with gusto as fast as we could, all mixed up together. The food was good: artichokes, egg mayonnaise, beefsteak, salad, cheese, all washed down with mugs of rough Mascara wine. There was a crescendo of conversation periodically checked by screams from the corporal of '*Un peu de silence*'. Everybody would start whispering and then the babble gathered momentum again and the cycle was completed by another frantic yell from the corporal.

There are a number of rules that are learned quickly in the *réfectoire*. The first is never to accept the offer of someone else's artichoke. This is fatal because while you are plucking away at the leaves the other fellow is scoffing your beefsteak and by the time you have waded through your own artichoke and his, the rest of the dishes have been licked clean.

The second rule is not to put your feet on the bar of the stool. Feet will remain at all times on the floor and the penalty for forgetting this is severe; the corporal comes up silently behind you and gives you a sharp rabbit punch on the back of the neck as you are about to swallow a mouthful of wine. It is a very nasty experience indeed and you only need one lesson to remember it a lifetime.

After the evening meal there is a period of about an hour when we can go to the *foyer* and have a few beers before we must begin cleaning our kit for *appel*. The *foyer* comprises a bar, a number of round metal tables and that's about it except for a sort of French billiard table and a broken pinball machine. The drinking gets quite serious and a lot of people with substantial capacities are in evidence.

The Germans are very pally with each other. In fact all the nationalities are cliquey. This is not unnatural in view of the language barriers. The Dutch, Germans, Spanish and Italians all seem to face the same difficulties when it comes to speaking

French. All our orders are given in French and the N.C.O.s speak French most of the time, but in the barracks or the *foyer* French is drowned completely in German, Italian and Spanish. There are supposedly fifty-two different nationalities in the Legion, but the Germans are certainly in the majority, followed in order by the Spanish, Italians, Hungarians, Dutch, Scandinavians, Greeks and the rest, and last of all the English.

There is a small British-speaking clique which comprises myself, René Baumann, de Graaf, who is a Dutchman and sleeps in the next bunk to mine, Dahms, who is German but has attached himself to us, and another Englishman called Robin White. We have our own table in the *foyer* and pool our limited resources to finance our beer.

White has finished his basic training and is leaving with the outgoing company. He is full of praise for the Legion and very keen on Prat-Marca, our C.O. He says basic training is pretty tough but one can survive if one approaches it with the right frame of mind – whatever that is! He's a quiet chap and rather difficult to fathom. I exchanged his information about the Legion with current affairs in England – hardly a fair swap. Apparently the next two weeks will be devoted to a mammoth spring clean which always precedes basic training proper. This involves repainting the insides of all the barracks, scrubbing floors, cleaning kit, rifles, and other equipment to be used for our instruction, until everything is immaculate. White made it sound like a lot of hard work.

In our barrack room there are twelve men including Dahms, de Graaf and myself. Most of the others are German. There's one big bastard called Wormser who does all the talking and calls all the shots. He's obviously the heavy amongst this lot and somebody to steer clear of. I don't think I like him at all. His right-hand man is a guy called Maltz who laughs loudly when Wormser makes a joke and runs to the *foyer* when Wormser wants beer and shits himself when Wormser coughs.

The evening *appel* was a quiet affair. We all stood by our beds waiting for the roof to cave in but nothing happened. The sergeant walked slowly up and down in sinister silence scowling but that was all. The corporal was at pains to explain that basic training proper had not yet started and when it did so *appel* would be a very different story!

28 March 1960

The spring clean has begun. We spent the entire day with a sprayer repainting the insides of the barracks. The lime in the paint is foul and gets into eyes and throats and is very painful. The cold weather has split my hands and fingers and the lime aggravates the soreness; and to think I came here for the sunshine!

29 March 1960

Continued the painting. The barracks themselves are three storeys high. After spraying all day we end with a big wash-up. The washing process necessitates the use of gallons of water brought by buckets up six flights of stairs and then brushed all the way down again. The only taps in the building are on the ground floor, and the only drains are on the ground floor, and there are no hose-pipes. The cleaning-up process takes about two hours, and is impeded by bullying corporals yelling at everybody, while the water gushes down the six flights of stairs like Niagara, with bucket-carrying slaves clambering up the stairs with their water loads adding to the confusion.

The weather is getting worse and is now bitterly cold. Eyes, skin and throat are now extremely painful from painting and life is in consequence very miserable. I have discovered a voracious appetite, which is unfortunately common to everybody, and our meals are proving insufficient. White told me that when *instruction* proper begins, appetites increase much more, money runs out and then one can see people in their true colours and correct proportions. Greed and selfishness come through with force and it is every man for himself.

The cigarette position is getting bad too, despite the fact that we are each issued with sixteen packets a month. As funds run out the heavy smokers spend much of their time searching the *quartier* for cigarette butts, and the more desperate sell their personal possessions including their watches for a song in order to raise cash to purchase the weed.

31 March 1960

A lot of men are suffering from gut trouble – good, more food for those of us who are not!

2 April 1960
Captain Prat-Marca, estimated by me to be the epitome of what a French officer should be – cold, aloof, a rigorous disciplinarian, but very fair – appeared on the painting scene today and showed concern for those of us who have been spraying the poisonous paint. It has become impossible to talk and my hands are agony if I use them for anything. Washing them is a nightmare, like putting them in fire.

Several Days Later
Basic training begins tomorrow. Our battalion is now up to strength and we number about a hundred. We are divided into four sections. The 1st Section, which I am in, is commanded by Lieutenant Otard (probably related to the brandy people, the officers here all seem to be loaded). He is rather wet-looking with a big sloppy red moustache. He is also overweight and gives the impression of being in awe of his N.C.O.s. Not a strong man, I fear.

His second in command is Sergeant Volmar. Very tough and very quiet. Doesn't speak much but when he does it's often with dry humour. He has eyes that smile much more than the rest of his face. I like him. There's something strong and good about him – for all his toughness he's the sort of man that would make a good father. I know he's married – I wonder if he's got any kids. Maybe there's something sad about him too.

Under him is Chief-Corporal Crepelli, who is Italian, with a face like a dried prune after thirteen years in the Legion. He is thin and sinewy like wire rope and his cheeks meet in the middle of his mouth. His uniform is always immaculate, he smokes incessantly and his eyes look like a couple of black pebbles which the average cobra would give its teeth for. His reputation as a killer is surpassed only by that of a Danish sergeant in the 2nd Section called Nielsen, who sports a great black beard and is known as the Sheriff. The Sheriff apparently keeps a collection of Arab ears in bottles of alcohol. These ears have been personally removed from the heads that went between them, which throws some light on the character of this Dane. Crepelli claims to have put over thirty people in hospital during basic training over the last two years and he is proud of this. He is in charge of our close-combat programme, to which I am not looking forward.

These then are the three men who will have principal control over us during the coming weeks. They are assisted by three corporals: Batista, a noisy Italian who shouts all the time, a German called Laurenz who shouts a little less, and another German called Weiss who shouts in the evening when he's drunk and is quiet during the day when he's nursing his hangover.

Over the last week or so the famous spring clean has been completed. The parade-ground has virtually been remade and the terrain where we do a lot of our field training has been weeded of every blade of grass. When we work in the open ground hacking away with our picks and shovels, clad in scruffy denims, with the corporals standing over us with their submachine-guns, the scene is that of a P.O.W. camp in Japan during the war or a penitentiary in an American movie. The work continued non-stop every day until after midnight, and we were up at five the next morning ready to go again.

During this time I had three pleasant days in the infirmary, which once seen could never be forgotten. The standards of sanitation were a new dimension in squalor; a dream world for bacteria. Each bed had just a dirty old bug-filled mattress and a blanket that had been there since time began. The food was inedible. I was dosed on bismuth tablets and gargled gentian violet all day. One thing about the infirmary, it is a definite deterrent to sickness.

On my return to the company I was summoned by the Deuxième Bureau where I was confronted by a lieutenant and two corporals, one of whom acted as an interpreter. I was given a letter from my mother and informed of her anxiety about my welfare, which was evident from the letter. It was over a month old and was a plea to consider carefully what I was doing before I went ahead. I had told my brother where I was going before I left for France and he had promised to let everybody know after I had gone.

I would have been in Marseille when the letter arrived but the authorities had obviously decided that it was better to let me get well settled in before delivering.

The officer said the British Embassy in Paris had been making a fuss and did I wish the Deuxième to admit or deny my presence in the Legion. Apparently, if you are under twenty-one and the right pressure is brought to bear and if it can be proved that you are in the Legion, they will sometimes let you go. I said I was quite satisfied where I was and that I would like to remain but that I would not like them to deny my presence as this would only make my poor mother more alarmed than ever. So I was asked to write a letter, which I did while they watched, in which I said that everything was O.K. and that I was having a ball. I said that I was here of my own free will and under no pressure to remain. The letter was sealed and taken by the lieutenant. That finally is a total commitment and if the door was not firmly locked before, it most certainly is now.

10 April 1960

Everything has suddenly become rather military. Instead of being treated like inmates of a penitentiary we are now being treated like recruits. I'm not sure which is the worse. Certainly nothing has improved since this morning, it's just different. The first parade is at 0700 sharp and there is a penetrating inspection. There is no spit and polish as in the British army but everything has to be clean. Boots do not shine but they must be black with dubbin. Our denims have to be washed and ironed every day and the N.C.O.s check the inside of our shirt collars to make sure that this has been done. We have two pairs of everything and it is apparently wiser to put on washed wet clothes, thereby showing an effort has been made, than to parade with a shirt that may have a grubby collar. Our teeth and ears are also inspected and generally one starts the day feeling quite fresh. This is a feeling which is very short-lived indeed.

After the inspection was over this morning and various extra duties had been handed out to those below the required standard, we followed Corporal Batista for a five-mile run into the hills, at the end of which most of us were ready to throw up. We were then divided into small groups and began normal schooling in army basics such as drill, weapon training, map reading and French. We have started to learn our first song. We are also learning to march. The slow marching pace is very much more difficult to accomplish than it looks and we are like a herd of goats when we get going; it's a complete shambles and the N.C.O.s get frantic.

But the day was a good one, full of activity, and even the N.C.O.s joined in the laughter as people made idiots of themselves and fell into all the classic pitfalls that go along with learning new things; not too difficult when doing basic training in a foreign army, in a foreign language, and where the comprehension rate is slow at its best.

When we returned to camp in the late afternoon we were put through a series of ghastly tests, such as running with sacks of sand on our backs, rope climbing, press-ups, abdominal exercises, knee-bends, hurdles, sprints and middle-distance gallops, and a crawling race under barbed wire. The results were all carefully recorded in a book and we will apparently have to go through the same thing again periodically to see if we are making any progress. It's quite competitive stuff and one can see individuals carefully monitoring their results and comparing them with other people's.

15 April 1960
The weather is warmer, morale is good, and we are binding together slowly into a unit. We are spurred on by a common dislike of the non-coms. There is nothing like a little hate for bringing people together! The N.C.O.s are not too scientific in their teaching methods and firmly believe that if they cannot penetrate the brain through the normal passage of the ear, then some success will be achieved by bashing a hole through the head of the wretched recruit. Crepelli is a particular exponent of this teaching method and runs a terror campaign in the weapon training sector. If you can't take a rifle to bits and reassemble it in seconds or if you don't know the name or weight of a part of the rifle, he will hit you with it. The effectiveness of this method of teaching remains to be seen, but it does undoubtedly stimulate effort.

We spend much of our time being punished for our shortcomings and these punishments usually take the form of crawling around on our stomachs, running up hills with sacks on our backs or standing to attention for long periods with a rifle held out in extended arms – tiring!

The principal aim of the N.C.O.s is to get our denims filthy as this will ensure that we are kept busy washing them during our fleeting moments of free time.

We are making some progress in spite of ourselves. My French is getting better with increased confidence and employment and we are becoming quite accomplished singers. Tremendous emphasis is laid on the singing. When we return to camp after a day in the hills we march proudly through the streets of Mascara, singing our guts out as we try to break the windows with our voluminous melodies. The slow marching plod and the sheer force of the body of men singing in deep ringing tones with improvised harmony is like nothing I have ever seen or heard before.

The local people stand staring, mesmerized, as they have probably done for years and will continue to do, for it never goes out of fashion to watch the Legion marching, and it is a sight and a sound that grips you and holds you while it passes. The excitement on the faces of the watching crowd produces a chill down the spine and a justifiable feeling of pride. It is at moments like this that our heritage is felt, as a thousand tales of the Legion cross the faces of the onlookers, and I am indeed proud to be in these ranks. Even the corporals strutting beside us like swaggering peacocks are full of goodwill, with their chests puffed out eyeing the citizens, as if to say, 'All our own work – trained and produced by us', and they wallow in the awe of their audience.

But we are far from perfect, it is early days and sometimes the singing is chaotic. The N.C.O. in charge will then call us to a halt even if it's in the middle of town and he will have us crawling through the streets on our stomachs, ignominious wretches, kicked like dogs and yelled at as though we were vermin. The atmosphere is killed stone dead in a moment and the expression of the crowd changes first to amazement and then to humour as they move away smirking and thanking their lucky stars it is we, not they. And we suddenly forget visions of the glorious Legion as pride is pricked and reality returns. With our faces in the dust and the boots of the man in front an inch from our noses, we crawl and concentrate our minds on hatred of the stupid noncoms. Perfection and imperfection are black and white to them, each inducing a corresponding reaction, probably involuntary, of applause or abuse and the instinctive utterances that go with it.

18 April 1960

Yesterday was Easter. We were given special food and plenty of it. At lunchtime the officers and their wives came round the *réfectoire* with eggs and hot cross buns and cigarettes. It was a charming gesture and done without formality. They obviously wanted us to enjoy our day and they succeeded. Our commanding officer, Prat-Marca, normally so cold and aloof, was running round like a mother hen dishing eggs out in every direction. It was a good day and reminded me of old friends but without sadness.

There is a new duty N.C.O. for the week, none other than the dreaded Sheriff, and I made contact with him this afternoon. It is a regulation that legionnaires salute officers and N.C.O.s when they walk past them or before they request permission to speak to them. I passed Nielsen this afternoon and as he appeared to be in deep conversation, I did not salute. This was a mistake. Suddenly his hand shot out and grabbed me by the lapels so that I had great difficulty in moving. He just held me there with my feet barely touching the ground while he carried on his conversation. He then turned to me and, peering through the black glasses which he always wears, he asked me why I had not saluted. I said I thought he was engaged in conversation and couldn't see me, to which he replied that he sees everything and he let me go. Not a man I would like to cross at all – ever.

And then this evening at *appel* he went berserk. At *appel* one has to be in bed asleep with one's eyes shut convincingly, or standing to attention at the side of one's bed in uniform. To be in bed is risky as it indicates over-confidence and it encourages sadistic sergeants, of which there is no shortage, to turn one's bed over. Despite the energy that went into cleaning kit, polishing floors and windows, and dusting beds, lockers and lampshades, before *appel* this evening, because we knew the Sheriff was on duty, many came to grief. Beds were overturned and dismantled, lockers were emptied and the contents hurled through the window into the night with not the slightest consideration for personal property. Many received punches and kicks, Engel worst of all.

Engel is a really tough human being by any standards. Tonight he was suspected of being drunk, the most cardinal sin of all, and the Sheriff beat the living daylights out of him. Poor Engel is a wreck. His face looks rough at the best of times, but when the Sheriff had finished with him it was beyond recognition.

There is no reason for this kind of brutality and it is quite incomprehensible to me that the officers never remark on the beatings some of the men have obviously had when they appear on parade in the morning. I suppose they regard it as part of basic training and yet the powers of a mere corporal are such that the opportunities for victimization and bullying are so totally obvious I would have thought that they would have been on the look-out for it.

Having said that, however, I do notice one thing about Crepelli and the Sheriff: although they are not slow in pulling punches they are fairly straight as long as you do your stuff properly. Crepelli applauds good performance just as vigorously as he attacks bad performance, particularly when bad performance is inexcusable. He was for instance terribly excited and enthusiastic when he discovered that I could shin up a rope twice as fast as anybody else and without using my feet!

The English appear to be held in high regard here, which is welcome. I think we are thought of as something quite strange. There are very few Englishmen in the Legion and I believe the general feeling is that we are all cracked and maybe slightly dangerous and therefore best left alone. They remember the war!

I read Volmar correctly – he's a good man. I think he disapproves of some of Crepelli's teaching methods, but he would never show it intentionally. Of the other men here it is still too early to say. We don't really mix. Everybody is independent to a great extent. Nobody is keen to stand out in front or over-expose himself and nobody is prepared or wants to lean too heavily on anyone else in case the support collapses. In this atmosphere a dependence on oneself is the surest way of remaining on the path.

We all join in the singing and the drinking in the *foyer* in the evening, but there is still an overall feeling of uncertainty about the other people. There is also the feeling of competition, particularly amongst the Germans. They don't like to be beaten in the runs or on the march. Maybe it's their pride.

The average age here is about twenty-two. Most of the men are young thugs and some clearly have criminal records, but the

Legion is a great leveller and everybody is on his own. There is little time to play or idle around and hence there is relatively little time for cliques and gangs to form and grow, although the various nationalities do still tend to stick together. There is no evidence of an outstanding bully or really big bastard, except Wormser, who seems to instil fear in his fellow Germans. I don't like him at all but he keeps his distance from me so I am not particularly concerned.

We spend an hour a day now doing close combat with Crepelli, who is a judo expert. The preliminary lessons are devoted to learning to fall and roll from any position in any terrain. We are now well versed in the fatal spots of the body on which a blow can kill. It is daily routine for us to bang the sides of our hands on concrete for half an hour to toughen up the chopper. Potentially we are lethal.

Money is running out and we are always hungry. The morning slice of bread which is all we get is totally inadequate for the amount of energy it is supposed to generate. Cigarettes are in short supply and it is a sobering sight to see young healthy fellows so desperate that they spend half their free time searching the compound for fag-ends. White was right.

23 April 1960
I went into town today for the first time to deliver a message to Volmar's house. He has a very beautiful wife. She seemed to know who I was and she filled me up with tea and cakes. She was fantastic. I felt very young, like a schoolboy being invited to have tea with his housemaster's wife. I also felt tremendously free walking through the streets of Mascara. My whole day was made by this simple outing.

25 April 1960
We were on the shooting range today for the first time. This is not unnaturally a big feature in our training programme and Volmar says we have many more hours of shooting to do before we are ready. The French have three 7.5-millimetre rifles in use, each referred to by the year it was manufactured and the factory where it was made; like the way they name wine.

The factories are located at Saint-Étienne, Tulle and Châtellerault. The rifles made in 1936 and '49 are bolt-action repeaters and the '49 has a device on the barrel to enable grenades to be fired from it. The latest rifle is the '56, which is semi-automatic, light in weight, and ideal for the type of fighting we will soon be doing. It's a killer at two hundred yards.

In addition to these rifles we will also use a sub-machine-gun called a *pistolet mitraillete* '49 which is similar to the Sten, and a light machine-gun which was produced in '52 and is a very handy piece of equipment indeed. It fires from bands or magazines and is very accurate when handled well but it weighs twenty-six pounds and is a bore to carry. We are well armed.

Our standard armoury also includes some quite fancy grenades. We learn every single detail of all these weapons; names, lengths of the components, weights and so on, and we can take them to bits and reassemble them blindfolded.

We have been given some general information on the spread of the Legion. At the present time it comprises a force of about thirty thousand men scattered over a wide area. There are four infantry regiments in the northern part of Algeria, and three others in Madagascar, Djibouti and Tahiti. There are four additional infantry regiments tucked away in Sahara and two parachute regiments and two cavalry regiments. That's about it, except that one Legion regiment is worth ten of anybody else's!

26 April 1960
The Sheriff finally had a go at my kit this evening because he decided the underside of my boots had not been polished properly. He's got quite a long throw when it comes to chucking stuff out of windows – the bastard!

28 April 1960
The days continue very full. We are all tired at the end by the time we have finished our extra duties and the various punishments that are heaped on us for every little misdemeanour. *Appel* is a strain after that. But we are fit and it is a fast, active, open-air existence, with very little time to sit and brood. And we are learning too. One can see clearly the difference between what we are now and what we were only two weeks ago. There is an energetic crispness in the way we form up on parade and

the way we do our drill. The marching has precision about it and rhythm and when we sing we mean it. There is a pride in what we do and there is a feeling of tremendous drive all the time.

We were introduced to the *parcours de combattants* (combat course) today. It's a killer. The obstacles include climbing rope-ladders, jumping over walls, crawling under wire, climbing ropes and jumping into deep trenches and scrambling out again. It is a continuous process of ups and downs and taken at a run in the stifling heat of the afternoon it leaves one totally and utterly exhausted. For a really shattering and excruciating, agonizing, blood-draining and choking experience, the *parcours de combattants* is the perfect sport.

Camerone Day is approaching. This is the big day in the Legion calendar and commemorates their greatest battle fought in Mexico on 30 April 1863. In this battle sixty legionnaires held off a force of two thousand Mexicans, half of whom were mounted cavalry, in a fight to the death. (See Appendix for further details.) The Legion goes mad on Camerone Day. Officers and N.C.O.s do all the *corvée*, including serving the food. There will be side-shows and a parade of floats through the town. There will even be a bullfight. It is apparently a carnival of carnivals and frantic preparations are under way for all the many events.

30 April 1960

It was a day of great celebration – extra food, and very good food, and masses to drink. A grand performance was given in the town stadium of bullfighting, cycle racing, snake charming, and a mock Battle of Camerone which would have done credit to any Hollywood film set.

This evening has produced mass intoxication, sometimes with far from amusing results. The Germans get very uptight when they feel an imaginary code has been broken – de Graaf was sick all over the barrack room and they decided this was not on and they gave him a very hard time – he was showered and beaten up, then they scrubbed him with hard-bristled brooms and subjected him to the most unpleasant and meaningless exhibition of brutality – all for having vomited in the barracks – something which most of them will do before long themselves. Poor de Graaf. I felt very sorry for him and though I registered disapproval I didn't do much about it – what does that make me?

The Next Day

Merciful Sunday. A day of sobering up and for those who were slow in doing so, the N.C.O.s got stuck in and quickly brought them back to the realities of life with a bang – or two. I have *piquet* duty tonight, which is all I need. This entails getting up every three hours and patrolling through the streets for an hour or so. Once over the hump of being yanked from sleep I quite enjoy wandering through the deserted streets in the early morning. It gives me time to think, but it makes for dreadful Mondays.

A Week Later

The weather has become unbearably hot and we are beginning to understand the strength of the Algerian sun. Water is a word with a whole new meaning. Our days continue as before but I think some of the steam has gone out of us with the coming of the sun. We do the *parcours de combattants* every morning at first light and we follow it up with close combat, drill, shooting, and then punishments such as a couple of hours' extra drill, or three times round the *parcours*.

It is now two o'clock in the morning and we have just returned to camp. We have been out in the hills trying to get the hang of moving intelligently at night with the aid of a compass and the stars.

I enjoy marching at night, it's peaceful after our hectic days. I like listening to the feet softly padding on the grass of the hills or ringing on the hard road. The sky is a planetarium of a million stars and the throbbing whistle of the crickets, which never ceases, massages the mind into the past – pleasant thoughts of England, good times gone and imagined good times to come. Faces I know well and have not seen in an age appear in the mind's eye, smile and fade away – imagined voices of welcome herald the future return home. I am thousands of miles away and my feet look after themselves – and then suddenly shattering reality – we are marching through the streets of Mascara. Two hundred voices singing in the night, the slow haunting songs of the Legion march. It is long past midnight. Curtains are drawn back from darkened windows and faces appear. Faces sometimes of children, held by parental hand, looking down in awe at soldiers marching through the night. The Legion passes – what romantic visions are conjured up in infant minds? And even we in the ranks feel an emotional breeze pass among us. It is great to march through the streets at night with the Legion. But reality is the morning – reality is the sweat of another day.

10 May 1960

There is an Englishman in one of the other companies here in Mascara. He deserted two days ago and has now been caught. To desert is generally considered acceptable, but to be caught is an appalling disgrace and there is apparently no sympathy spared at all on the offender, no matter how brutal the punishment he receives. The Englishman is a cab driver from Yorkshire. He has had his hair all shaved off and is now inside doing time – hard time by the sound of things. The sergeant in charge of the prison is a Romanian named Peltzer. There are a lot of stories about him – all bad. Apparently two deserters were once found dead having been cut up by Arabs and stuffed into a fox hole. Peltzer had the bodies brought back to the barracks and laid in the middle of the parade-ground. Then he made all the recruits turn out on parade to show them what happened to deserters and he yelled insults at the dead bodies and kicked the bloated carcasses as he did so. God help the cab driver!

11 May 1960

We did a ten-mile route march this morning with helmets on our heads and sacks and rifles on our backs. From now on we will do one every week and it will be five miles longer each time. The hills are high and the valleys are deep, the sun is hot and the pace is fast and it is very shagging work indeed.

Letter from my old chum Ian McCallum. What a good man. It's so good to receive news from home, to sit down and read a letter in a friend's hand. A letter slices through distance. Without them, I really wonder if I would make it. I wonder if any of us would. Letters produce amazing changes in people. A man's face will suddenly light up at the sight of an envelope with familiar scrawl – he grabs it and hurriedly seeks a quiet corner, anxious to be alone with paper and private thoughts like a small boy with a chocolate cake. The letter is initially jealously guarded until absorbed and then after a time shared with those without – snatches of script are read out to a friend and a snapshot of wife and children or girlfriend grudgingly produced and then finally proudly presented. What a splendid thing is the postal system!

14 May 1960

Well, I finally went into town this evening with Weber. Weber is a little Swiss guy; tough as hell and takes himself rather seriously. This was the night we had all been waiting for and with our pockets stuffed with loot it was going to be a ball. It turned out to be a disaster because we were only given passes until nine o'clock, which meant that we had to be back for *appel* and there is no surer death warrant than to be drunk at *appel*.

And tonight who should be on duty of all people but the dreaded Sheriff. It was murder! Thank God I wasn't too smashed. But one or two of the lads were paralytic and when they returned from their happy carousing they were suddenly alarmed to find themselves swaying in front of Nielsen's black beard. He slaughtered them.

Engel in particular got the worst of it yet again. The Sheriff's got a thing about Engel. Engel was rash enough to take a swing at Corporal Weiss in his drunken stupor. This was fatal, and when the Sheriff heard about it, he went for him, and literally knocked him cross-eyed. I've never seen that before and it was frightening. It gave me a sick feeling in the gut to watch somebody nearly beaten to death in front of my eyes with everybody, including me, too damned scared to do a thing about it.

Mascara is not worth it. It's a very dull little place at night; all the colour has gone and all the people too. All that is left are hundreds of legionnaires and an equal number of squalid bars. There is nothing to do except drift from bar to bar, and either get drunk or just bored. The chances of meeting what one's mother would describe as a nice French girl are about twenty million to one against. The odds against getting shacked up with a nice whore are the reverse – so that's something to look forward to anyway.

I heard a record tonight on a juke-box sung by Jim Reeves, and it reminded me of something – I don't quite know what – happier times maybe. I played it over and over again and drank my beer and felt sad.

15 May 1960
I received a letter today addressed simply to 'Simon Murray, Légion Étrangère, Algeria'. It was from Jennifer and her friend Christie, written while having cool drinks in the Lansdowne club. Jennifer's letter cajoles me for running away and generally conveys the message that nobody has any sympathy and I deserve what I get. Nice stuff! Christie's letter cheers me on for joining the adult world and leaving that of the mixed-up teenagers – splendid girl!

23 May 1960
A Spaniard decided he'd had enough and shot himself last night while on guard duty – our first suicide. I wouldn't have thought things were that bad.

Another incident occurred with a rifle in the barracks this afternoon which left an indelible impression on those who witnessed it. We were cleaning weapons for an inspection and Dahms put a 9-millimetre sub-machine-gun bullet in the breach of his 7.5-millimetre rifle and pointed it at de Graaf in fun. Unfortunately, the gun went off and de Graaf collapsed in a heap.

The whole room just froze for a full thirty seconds. Then de Graaf moved and turned out to be unhurt. The bullet hadn't come out of the gun but was jammed up the barrel. It took us a few moments to convince de Graaf that he was still alive; after all, if someone puts a bullet in a gun, points it at you from ten feet away and pulls the trigger, you assume if it goes off that you are dead.

When we had recovered from the first shock, we began frantic efforts to dislodge the bullet from the barrel before Crepelli came to pass the inspection which was only minutes away. Dahms was in a state of such nervousness that he could hardly hold the rifle at all. Efforts to bang the bullet out with a ramrod failed and unfortunately the sound of the shot had carried to Crepelli and we heard his footsteps approaching along the passage. He of course found the rifle and bullet and quickly extracted a confession from the now gibbering Dahms.

Then as we watched in stunned shock, he suddenly hit Dahms with the rifle butt across the side of the head as cold-bloodedly as a man chopping wood with an axe. And as Dahms lay half senseless on the floor, Crepelli kicked his body mercilessly, all the while cursing him with a stream of volatile Italian blasphemy. Nobody moved a muscle; we just stood frozen like gaping gargoyles hardly daring to breathe lest the wrath of Crepelli be turned on one of us. It ended as abruptly as it had started and Crepelli stormed from the room yelling threats of instant death to anyone unwise enough to point a loaded gun in the barracks again. Nobody will. We slowly came alive again and resumed breathing. We washed Dahms down and surprisingly enough, apart from a livid bruise, the damage was far less than we had feared, but our memories were scarred for ever.

Crepelli passed the rifle inspection ten minutes later. Never had he seen rifles as clean as ours.

24 May 1960

The sun is getting hotter. We have a siesta now after lunch as it is too hot to move; it is also too hot to sleep, so one just sits or lies motionless, while the flies buzz.

We were out in the hills again today and the sun crucified us. At midday it is unbearable. Everything is still as the sun takes command – even the tall dry grass wilts under the oppressing heat – everything bows to the sun. It is too hot even to sigh, we just lie and slowly melt – only the mind can move. I saw a mule pulling a cart on the middle horizon this afternoon as I lay under a tree during the siesta. I could hear the slow plodding hooves and the creaking of the wooden wheels from a distance of nearly a mile as it rolled very slowly through the shimmering heat. I could hear it because everything else was perfectly and utterly still and silent. Only the occasional chuckle of the birds in the trees where they sat waiting for the evening cool interrupted the quiet of the afternoon. I think my mind traversed the twenty years of my life as I lay under that tree and I remembered all the people who have made it. We marched back to camp in the cool of the evening and we broke into song as we reached Mascara. We sang well.

30 May 1960
We spent the entire day with the light machine-gun. It is important not to shine when firing the L.M.G. even though punishment is the penalty for shooting badly. The L.M.G. is heavy and if you perform well with it you become the *tireur* which, although it carries honour and prestige, means that you will have to carry it on the march. This is a trap into which one must not fall.

We also had our first swim today. Otto Schmidt, who hates water and cannot swim, was forced off the high diving-board with disastrous results. He was dangling from the top board by his fingertips while the mob, led by Wormser and aided by Maltz, stamped on his fingers; but his fear was stronger than his sense of pain and his fingers would not release him and he hung there swinging from side to side. Eventually they broke his grip and down he tumbled as his body was swinging inwards towards the concrete perimeter of the pool. He landed across the side and smashed three of his ribs. Poor Otto. Actually I have no great sympathy, he's a thug. He and Maltz were the ringleaders in the beating up of de Graaf after Camerone.

4 June 1960
I went into Mascara this evening and visited the military brothel, known as the *bordel militaire controllé* or just B.M.C. It was not a particularly inspiring establishment and having seen some of the talent, enthusiasm was rapidly extinguished. I must say I think the French attitude to military brothels is enlightened. Every regiment in the Legion has its own brothel which goes with it on operations into the interior. The thinking behind military brothels is based on the correct assumption that soldiers will go to brothels anyway, and it is therefore preferable that they go to brothels controlled by the army where the women are inspected daily and there is obviously a much better chance of limiting the spread of disease.

Each girl is numbered and the time of the event is recorded together with the name of the client and if someone does get clap there is a reasonable chance of locating the source. The punishment for catching a dose outside the military brothel is eight days' prison. Should someone catch it in the B.M.C., and this can easily be checked from the records, then there is no punishment, only injections. However, a lot of guys feel that the talent in the open-market bordellos is better than that supplied by the military and they therefore go hunting in the Arab quarter of town. After they have done their screwing they cover their tracks by an immediate visit to the military brothel, where they are checked in, and in the event that they have caught something they pin it on the girl in the B.M.C. She in the meantime will have passed it on to half a dozen others and if it's just after pay day she might well have passed it to half the regiment. The system is not therefore completely foolproof.

The *bordel* has a bar and there is always plenty of atmosphere. There is no obligation to get involved just because one goes in, and the bar enables one to have a few drinks and inspect the merchandise at leisure without necessarily making a commitment. The bar does however in time contribute to the lowering of one's standards, and this can lead to a plunge which might not have been taken in a more sober environment. Costs range from about one pound (sterling) for a quickie to five pounds for the night. I shall have to start saving my money.

6 June 1960
Some good news – Wormser deserted last night. The general feeling is one of good riddance. Maltz without his front man is looking vulnerable – there are one or two of the boys, including de Graaf, who have got a score to settle with friend Maltz.

A Fortnight Later
The days go by. We are tougher now and think nothing of a thirty-mile walk through the hills. On our treks the column stretches across the hills for miles and from the top of the mountains the men in front look like a trail of ants marching down into the valleys and up and over the other side, reappearing periodically across a whole range of hills; tiny specks of human beings going on and on for ever.

We have learned to shoot effectively in daylight or at night-time. We know our weapons and we know how to use them. It is not through want of practice. Many hours have been spent squeezing triggers on the range and many millions of shots have been fired. It is daily routine to go to the range, fire shots at two hundred yards, and if the results are bad we crawl to the targets, patch up the holes, crawl back and do the whole thing over again.

The N.C.O.s continue to keep the pressure on. Endless inspections, endless cleaning of kit, oiling floors and cleaning lavatories followed by endless punishment and extra duties. But we are beginning to look like the company that preceded us, and which impressed us so much when we arrived. We are more of a team as a section but we are still independent. Many people in the company are still strangers.

De Graaf caught up with Maltz today. I don't know what started it but suddenly they were shouting at each other and then they were at each other's throats. Nobody intervened. De Graaf is small and well built, but he had right on his side and got the better of Maltz with a kick in the crutch that brought him to his knees and a punch in the mouth that finished him. Some of the others were unhappy about it all but nobody moved. I bought de Graaf a couple of beers in the *foyer* and treated him like a champion. Poor old de Graaf, he is very homesick and confided in me his plans to desert, but I don't think he'll try. He says his parents have written to Madame de Gaulle and appealed for his release – not a chance.

Crepelli has been somewhat relaxed recently. He was quite chatty the other day and told us something of his family background. His mother runs a brothel in southern Italy. He says the business is profitable and he intends to go and take over some day. Now that is really an inheritance.

Lieutenant Otard is trying to persuade me to volunteer for one of the parachute regiments. But these are the fall guys in more ways than one and I think I'll leave the heroics to someone else. Otard does not like my attitude and I find quite a lot of punishments coming my way.

24 June 1960

We are on alert. Three French farms were burnt to the ground two days ago and each section is taking it in turns to go out and patrol the hills. We return periodically for some sleep but invariably we are off again before our heads have hit the pillow.

This morning as we were about to set off on yet another jaunt at three o'clock, Otard called me into the *bureau de semaine* and produced a form for me to sign, volunteering myself as a parachutist. I refused initially, but after he implied that I was scared – which I am – I finally said I would go and signed the paper. This is all unsatisfactory as I am not keen on heights at all. There is no justice in the world – or is it just here?

A Week Later
The first phase of basic training is over. We have completed a final exam which tests us in everything we are supposed to have learned during the last few weeks. Everybody passed – we have to otherwise it reflects badly on the N.C.O.s.

We are going to the seaside for a few days to clear our minds.

3 July 1960
We are camped by a tiny fishing village on the Mediterranean coast called Sassel. The village is a select holiday resort for wealthy French colonialists – known as *les colons*. It was attacked by fellagha two years ago and seventy-odd people were killed. Now the Legion rest camp overlooks the village and it is regarded by the local French community as a nice safe place for a long weekend.

Our tents stretch to infinity along the dunes above the beach and present an amazing spectacle. The heat is unpleasant, everybody has chronic diarrhoea, known as *la chiasse*, and the flies are agonizing but all in all it's not bad when compared to Mascara. The atmosphere is relaxed and the N.C.O.s are showing signs of behaviour that indicates they might actually be human beings after all.

I have been into the village a couple of times in the evening. It makes one feel almost like a civilian again; the full effect of that feeling cannot be understood until one has experienced a few months in the Legion.

I have become quite pally with a Hungarian named d'Église. He is a good lad; more phlegmatic than his compatriots who tend to be competitive, hot-tempered little sods, but he is quite able to take care of himself when aroused.

I spent hours this afternoon soaking up sunshine sitting on the rocks staring out to sea. It reminded me of my trip to South America on the *Saint Arvans*, just after I had left school and was infatuated by the idea of going to sea. I was the galley boy and I used to sit on deck peeling potatoes and watch the endless movement of the ocean.

I remember watching the sea during the lunch break in Marseille one day and I remember specifically trying to imagine what life would be like in six months' time and here is that time become the present. I thought I had a good imagination – that's what my history master used to tell me – we were both wrong.

It is now the evening and the sun has set as it does so very quickly, like a great orange balloon floating down to the horizon. And then suddenly it's gone and darkness rushes in – voices begin to carry and disturb the silence; distant singing from the tents touches the ear and is lost in the sound of the lapping waves, carried by the breeze that is suddenly noticeable when the sun dies. I enjoy the evenings; one can be still and peaceful with one's thoughts and look at the endless blackness of the sea, or one can whoop it up with the boys in the *foyer* singing songs and quaffing draughts of ale.

I am becoming a moderate player of chess with instruction from d'Église who is a master. He carries a small board with him wherever he goes and settles down to play in the sand every time there is the slightest break in the day.

4 July 1960

I finally tangled with Otto Schmidt this afternoon. He pushed past me in the water queue. I had been waiting half an hour in the stinking heat and there were signs that the water was going to run out. All it needed was for Otto to barge in front to set the detonator off. It was like that night so long ago on the train from Paris to Marseille. I turned Otto round, thumped him in the chest, gave him a hard shove with my foot behind him and he went flat on his back. Unfortunately I didn't hit him hard enough and he was up in a flash charging like a rhino. He hit me amidships and we went sprawling over, arms and legs swinging. I managed to get a grip on his bull neck (like clinging to a barrel of oil) and somehow hold. I was squeezing with every ounce of strength I had, while Otto rolled and bounced and elbowed me in the gut. It was a classic cobra and mongoose situation and I knew that if I let the bastard go I was a dead man; so I held on and gradually his enormous strength started to give out.

A crowd had gathered and as Otto's struggles got weaker somebody moved forward and dragged me off. I had a very nasty moment because Otto lay still and his face was purple. However, a bucket of our precious water over his head brought him round. De Graaf watched the whole scene and it is obviously the best thing that has happened as far as he is concerned since he joined the Legion. We have been celebrating this event this evening in the *foyer* and we drank to the damnation of the likes of Otto Schmidt and Maltz. I think we will have less trouble from that quarter from now on. The only bad piece of news is that I gashed my leg in the fight and cuts always go septic here thanks to the flies, so I can look forward to a poisoned leg before long.

Ten Days Later
Sassel has lost some of its attraction, if it ever had any. The hot sun has become too hot, the flies are driving us nuts, and the sand is in everything, our clothes and our food. The nights are cold and damp. My leg is septic from the gash I got in the fight with Otto. The medic pours iodine over it every day with no effect at all.

On the entertainment side, two of our lads pinched a speed-boat in the village one night and made off in the direction of Morocco, which is about eighty miles away. Enterprising stuff! Unfortunately they ran out of gas and swam to shore, were spotted by a helicopter and finally picked up by a patrol. They will apparently be sent to the penal battalions in Colomb-Béchar way down in the Sahara. What a finish to a holiday.

A day in the Colomb-Béchar prison begins at 0430 and there is an inspection of the barracks at 0600. This is normally followed by hard labour swinging a pick and shovel or a heavy hammer bashing stones under the boiling Sahara sun. Endless inspections punctuate the day; there are no recreation facilities, there is no *foyer* and there is no cinema. There is, in fact, nothing to alleviate the terrible boredom and the monotony of the existence. The brutality is indescribable and the punishments coldly severe. Month after month without freedom, no visits into town, not even time to sit and have a quiet beer once in a while – just nothing, except the sweat of labour in the endless heat and *le cafard*. *Le cafard* is described as the sensation of millions of tiny beetles crawling around inside one's head and it is a feeling that must be held in check because it is a signal that one is in a condition that immediately precedes madness. *Le cafard* is a parasite that feeds on the mind, corrodes the spirit and ultimately reduces the physical being to a wreck.

We are returning to Mascara tomorrow. I don't feel very rested.

18 July 1960

We leave for parachute training tomorrow. There are nine of us. I have persuaded de Graaf, against his better judgement I'm sure, to volunteer as well. Volmar invited me to his house for dinner this evening and said I could bring anyone else as well, so of course I asked de Graaf; but because of all the preparations for departure we were unable to get clear of the barracks before ten. It was a tragedy because Volmar's fabulous wife had prepared a feast, and when we did not arrive, they had presumed that we were not coming. When we finally did get to the house they had eaten and cleared away. I felt desperate as they were so disappointed and it was such a tremendously human gesture to have made, utterly foreign to the Legion. It will be remembered, though it was a small incident, as one of the great sadnesses of my life – I shall remember for ever because we missed it and it was terribly important to me and I think it was for them too. We drank a few Scotches and salvaged something of a party.

The Sheriff joined us later and he and Volmar told us some splendid stories of the Legion. They have both been in eleven years, it is in their blood and in every line of their oak faces. The Sheriff is really quite human when he's not killing people.

Eventually we said our farewells. I was very sad indeed to say goodbye to Volmar. I don't suppose I'll see him again – the Legion is spread wide and thin, and he is retiring in three years. He has been a Murray supporter all the way through and I have felt his encouragement as a source of strength. He would be a good man to have around if the chips were down and I shall miss him and his great sense of humour. It was our last night in Mascara and when we left Volmar's house we decided to drink the place dry – we won't be coming back!

19 July 1960

We paraded early – just the famous nine. Prat-Marca passed the inspection and gave us each a firm handshake and a final word of advice and then we were driving out through the gates of the 5th Battalion for the last time. All the lads came out and cheered us off. Faces and waving arms. Friendly faces for the most part, bobbing around in the crowd each marking its little cross on the mind to be buried in the memory and resurrected from time to time; to be triggered back to life by some incident or perhaps to be forgotten for ever. Weber, Batista, d'Église, Laurenz, Verner, René Baumann, and even that shit Maltz was there and Otto Schmidt – two guys I will remember but not by choice. And then the faces were gone and we were roaring through the streets of Mascara. A last look back at the town and then into open country. Phase one was over and we drove towards Sully.

PART TWO

Sully

We arrived in the late afternoon. Sully is an absolute shithouse and it is where we will live for the next six weeks or so while we do our para training. It is a farm situated about ten miles from Sidi-bel-Abbès. The dormitories are enormous converted barns, the *lavabo* is a horse trough in the open yard outside the barracks, and the *réfectoire* is in a loft above disused wine vats. There are no lavatories as such, but a trench three hundred yards from the barracks represents the facilities; we share them with the flies.

We don't have plates to eat off as in Mascara, so we have to use our tin *gamelles*, which substantially reduce appetite – like drinking Dom Pérignon out of a dirty coffee cup. All in all this is a hole and I don't like the look of it one little bit.

We met the camp commandant this evening, one Captain Glasser. He looks tough and sound and a typical no-bloody-nonsense French officer.

20 July 1960
There are two sections here at Sully, each comprising about twenty men. We as the latest arrivals are Section 2 and the others in Section 1 are about a month ahead of us in their parachute training. Our section commander is a Lieutenant Letang.

He doesn't seem too sure of himself and his two sergeants do most of the talking on his behalf. The first of these is a huge

giant called Krueger with a face as impassive as a concrete slab.
He speaks in a very quiet voice with a heavily pronounced Slav
accent. He is unquestionably as dangerous as hell. He was a
paratrooper in the German army and took part in the defence
of Monte Cassino. That's enough to make anybody bitter. The
second sergeant is Wissmann. He's Dutch – very bouncy and
rather impressed with himself. He speaks very good English.

In addition to the two sergeants, we have two corporals:
Malloni, an Italian, and a German called Kahn. They seem
reasonably peaceful.

We started our day by being issued with a whole lot of new
kit. This included a good pair of boots. It is marvellous to be
free of the terrible *brodequins* that we have worn to date.

We then had the usual series of tests that seem to recur
regularly in our lives. The order of the day was rope climbing,
press-ups, abdominal exercises, a five-mile jog in full kit, a
series of sprints including a hundred-yard dash with a colleague
on one's back, a fifteen-hundred-metre run, and several other
forms of torture. The boys were obviously checking us over,
hammering the plaster to test for weak spots.

My knee is getting worse and is now an unattractive open
ulcer. The medic here obviously went to the same training school
as the man at Mascara and is prescribing bucket-loads of
iodine, which apart from stinging like hell has no effect at all.

A Dutchman called Heinz has deserted from the first section.
Wissmann has assured us that he will not get far. The nearest
frontier is Morocco and there he will run into a barrage of
electric fences and a nightmare of barbed wire and mines. These
run the full length of the frontier down into Sahara on both the
Moroccan and the Tunisian frontiers and were constructed by
the French to keep out the thousands of fellagha on both sides
of Algeria who were driven out in the middle fifties when this
war started in earnest.

A Few Days Later
Wissmann took us for close combat this morning. We do it here
on concrete and the whole atmosphere is much more serious and
tougher than at Mascara. This is all unexpected as we had anticipated the opposite and were of the opinion that we had
broken the back of basic training at Mascara. We could not

have been more wrong and I have the horrible impression that we are only just starting. I think Wissmann is slightly mad and when he gets angry he is disturbing to watch. When we were doing close combat this morning he watched very carefully to make sure nobody was going easy on anybody else and twice he called people out whom he suspected of not putting enough feeling into it when they were throwing people over their shoulders. He then showed them how it should be done and it was a vicious demonstration. He's the kind of guy who gets pleasure out of inflicting pain. That's a sign of bad things to come.

Four Days Later
These are bad days. Hot tiring days full of boring routine instruction that we have done before and on top of that we are pushed around by Wissmann and the rather thick and stupid corporals, Malloni and Kahn. The food here is unbelievable; almost inedible after Mascara. At Mascara we were on a healthy diet even if we didn't get enough to eat. Here the diet is distinctly unhealthy and there is insufficient fresh water. It has to be brought each day in a cistern from bel-Abbès. By lunchtime it's already warm and undrinkable.

Krueger broke Martinez's leg today while demonstrating a judo throw. Martinez is Spanish and he has a lot of pride. He made not a sound when it happened and somehow managed to half stagger back to his place in the line, while Krueger jeered at him and called him various names. Martinez tried a sort of weak grin and even that must have hurt like hell. After it was over we helped him to the medic, who confirmed immediately that the leg was broken. He is now in the infirmary well plastered up; and Krueger doesn't give a damn. De Graaf has also run into problems in the medical world; he claimed he had a bad foot and was sent to bel-Abbès to the quack. The doctor said there was nothing wrong and he has been given eight days' prison (standard for shamming) for his pains. That's one remedy I suppose.

29 July 1960
Lefevre and Aboine deserted this afternoon during the siesta and at about seven o'clock this evening news came through that

they had been caught by a regular army cavalry regiment. I was on guard duty at the time and was ordered into the jeep which was sent to collect them. The collection committee comprised the company adjutant, Chief Sergeant Westhof, Wissmann and myself. On our arrival at the regular army camp, the two prisoners were dragged forward and Westhof staggered everybody including myself by pulling out his pistol and dropping both of them to the ground by a blow to the head with the butt of his gun. Lefevre's head started to bleed like hell. They were then bundled into the jeep.

The mixture of horror and astonishment on the faces of the French soldiers was something to see – my own face must have looked a bit dazed too. We returned to Sully and the two prisoners were paraded in front of Captain Glasser in his office. I was on guard outside the room. He beat the living daylight out of them and since then they have had a terrible time.

For openers they were given three hours of *la pelote*. This takes the form of the prisoner being equipped with a sack of stones on his back (the sack has wire shoulder straps), and a steel helmet on his head without the interior, and then he runs. A sergeant (in this case Wissmann) stands over him with a whistle and a rope's end and according to the number of blasts on the whistle, one, two, or three, the prisoner punctuates his running by doing a forward roll, crawling on his stomach or marching at knees bend. When there is a slow in the pace, then the rope's end comes into play. So it was this evening with Wissmann holding the rope and the whistle and every time they slowed or collapsed – as they did many times – he beat them with his thong. When they were exhausted with not an ounce of strength left in their bodies they were made to crawl through an open sewer, and finally as the last indignation, they had to crawl on their bellies around the barrack room, gasping and grunting, while we stood to attention, each man beside his bunk. They crawled past our feet, covered in slime and filth, and they no longer resembled human beings. This was the punishment for deserters and it was to be a lesson to all of us. There was not a man among us who had not considered desertion, and there was not a man among us now who for all his feelings of revulsion and hatred against this meaningless barbarism was not also secretly afraid at what he saw – afraid at such brutality; that it could be administered by a sadist like Wissmann, with no control and no appeal to any authority except that of the Legion – and in the Legion there is no appeal, and the authority is in those in whom it is vested, and it starts at the rank of corporal.

31 July 1960

Lefevre and Aboine are doing four hours' *pelote* each day: two in the morning and two during the siesta in the hottest part of the day. Aboine who is a Negro seems to be standing up quite well in spite of the fact that he apparently has an advanced state of syphilis for which he is filled with penicillin every day. Lefevre on the other hand looks like a dying man. His eyes are sunken sapphires in black swollen sockets and he is completely devoid of any human spirit – just a moving wreck. I hope he pulls through. He looks like a man with no will to live.

3 August 1960

We started our parachute training in earnest this morning with a flight in a Nord Noratlas aeroplane which is the jumpers' carrier wagon. It's a pretty antiquated machine with a sausage-like carcass equipped with a few benches which fold up against the side of the aircraft when the action starts and a couple of wires which run the length of the bulkhead for the static lines, and that's about it. Although we were not jumping ourselves there was quite a lot of excitement watching the others go. It was terrifying in fact and when I think that we will be jumping out next time we go up, it's enough to bring me out in a rash.

We have been running around over the hills a lot recently – tactical training in movement of troops over mountainous terrain – and this together with a ten-mile run to bel-Abbès and back every morning has hardened the sinews so that we are probably as fit as we will ever be. The *parcours de combattants* is much more strenuous here than the one at Mascara, but we can leap over the walls, jump the trenches and climb the ropes like apes swinging in the trees. There's no fat on anyone.

We were introduced to the stop-chute today. This is an apparatus for jump training and landing. It consists of a platform about twenty-five feet above the ground on which the jumper stands suspended in a harness. On the command 'go' the jumper launches himself off the platform (a nerve-shaking

experience) and just before he hits the ground the harness pulls
him up short, God willing, and he is left dangling, swinging to
and fro until he is suddenly released and lands with a thump on
the ground like a sack of apples. The object of the exercise is to
simulate landing and we are supposed to roll. We have been
rolling around *ad nauseam* over the last weeks simulating this
landing but alas the training appears to have been wasted.
Wissmann was not pleased at all with our efforts. Planchet in
particular upset Wissmann by refusing to jump. Wissmann half
kicked him to death, which worried none of us in the slightest;
Planchet is a horrible grimy little shit. He is a Frenchman with
a dark swarthy complexion and on first impression he looks like
a thug; a closer inspection however reveals a pair of snake's eyes
with a very obvious streak of yellow running through them. He
personifies deceitfulness and cunning and has guts made of lime
juice. He's puke-making.

Faugloire, who is another Frenchman in our ranks and a
pretty unattractive one at that, claimed this evening that he had
had some money stolen from him – our first theft. He has
reported it to Krueger, who has gone raving mad. We have had
a complete inspection of every item of kit we possess, including
any personal possessions, and from now until further notice all
our meals will be eaten standing, all movements from place to
place will be at the double and any of us seen walking at any
time will automatically be punished. In addition each evening
after *la soupe* will be devoted to arms drill, followed by a kit
inspection. In a nutshell, life is going to be murder. All this
because of Faugloire. If the truth were known, he probably
lost the money playing cards or blew it in town in a drunken
stupor.

The atmosphere in the barracks has suddenly changed to one
of suspicion. Everybody is suspect in this sort of environment.
Suspect number one in my book is Planchet, who sleeps in the
bed next to Faugloire.

The indignation that is aroused when there is a *voleur* in the
camp is a paradox. Less than 10 per cent of the men here have
not done time for robbery or at least been scheduled to have
done so, which is the reason that they are here. Yet at the top of
the list of Legion codes of ethics is 'Thou shalt not steal'. The
penalties for this crime are varied and depend to a large extent

on the prevailing atmosphere at the time the thief is caught. By issuing his punishments Krueger has gone a long way to ensuring that the atmosphere will be at its worst when the thief is discovered. If he survives the initial onslaught, he may be spread-eagled on to a table with bayonets rammed through his hands pinning him down. This is apparently the traditional treatment for hands that get stuck in the till. I have not seen this but have had lurid descriptions given to me by those who have. It sounds gruesome but I should think it as much a deterrent as the Arabs' system of cutting your hand off for the same crime.

Late news is that Heinz, the Dutchman who ran away three weeks ago, has been caught and is now cooling off in a cell in bel-Abbès. Wissmann is delighted and looking forward to Heinz's return to Sully.

A Week Later

Life goes on. We are spending more and more time in the hills and are now very familiar with the terrain. Reading a map is like reading a book. We play sophisticated games of hide-and-seek. Krueger goes off into the bush with a squad representing Arabs and the rest of us track them down. He is well versed in the ways of the fellagha and some of his ambushes into which we fall bring home to us very clearly how inexperienced we are.

We spend hours listening to talks on the ways of the fellagha, learning to appreciate how they live and move, how to spot signs of their presence in the area, and above all how to recognize their booby traps. When we move at night the front man in the column often holds a long blade of grass in front of himself to detect the thin wire that may be stretched unseen across the path. That wire could be connected to a grenade strapped to a tree beside the path with the pin half out. The slightest pull is all that is needed to set it off, and if the fuse within the grenade has been tampered with, the blast of death is instantaneous with not the slightest fizz of warning.

The fellagha are full of tricks and surprises. The flag found in the hedgerow is picked up by the unsuspecting, a mine is triggered and a head or limb is blown off; the innocent-looking can of beans that has been dropped by the roadside contains a detonator and half a pound of plastic, and every door is the entrance to a potential explosion.

There is no let up by the fellagha and if we relax for a second it may be our last. This is the message and those that take it in will see out the next four years. Those that do not haven't a chance.

It is the season of the grapes and they are in abundance. They make for excellent refreshments on our journeys through the countryside. The only trouble is that they are one hell of a laxative.

Krueger has been out of action for a day or two with tooth-ache and it appears temporarily at least to have put the subject of Faugloire's money out of his mind. This is good news and we have ceased the evening drill. I suppose we will now never know who took the money or whether or not there was any money in the first place.

Nice letter from Jennifer this evening. No lectures this time! She and Christie appear to be having a great holiday all over Europe – much better than my holiday in Algeria.

9 August 1960

Estoban, a Spanish fellow in our section, deserted last night while on guard duty and made the fatal mistake of taking his sub-machine-gun with him. To desert unarmed is one thing, but to desert with a weapon is suicide. We were aroused at crack of dawn and with two lethal-looking dogs at the head we set off in pursuit. Wissmann gave orders that he was to be shot on sight. I asked him what action we should take if he tried to surrender and Wissmann said that for Estoban's own sake he would be much better off dead. This was sobering stuff at five o'clock in the morning.

I do not know Estoban well. He came from Saïda. He is very quiet but not in any way furtive. He is always cheerful when he greets one in the morning and I would rate him as a nice man. Apparently he has a very sick mother in Spain who is dying and he has gone off to see her according to his fellow Spaniards. He may not make it.

All through the long hot day we ran over the hills after the dogs, up mountains, down into valleys, through woods and over streams, and by the end of the day the dogs were dead beat and so were we. Many of us who had secretly been wishing Estoban well at the beginning were in a very different frame of mind by the end. But we saw not a sign of him, not a trace. He is safe for tonight -- as long as the Arabs don't catch him.

The first section left for five days' operations this evening and I have just returned as part of the escort required to bring home the empty trucks. There is something special being in an open truck at night, roaring along the lonely roads – I love it. The feeling of mystery is prevalent when men are moving quietly in the night. There is a combination of something sinister and yet romantic about it all. Nothing happened but I will remember evenings like tonight for all my days, because they epitomize the whole feeling of adventure that somehow keeps me going. Sometimes it disappears momentarily and I am left wondering what the hell – but it returns and with it my energy, my curiosity and my desire to press on.

So of this evening as we journeyed through the darkness I will remember the black silhouettes of the silent men sketched against the dim glow of the night sky – the million stars and the trees rushing past as black shadows; the faint tail-light of the truck in front, the vague outline of the one behind – no lights, no talking, no cigarettes, except for the occasional surreptitious drag in cupped hands – the sudden glow and a face – gone in a flicker, followed by the pungent smell of exhaled smoke caught for a second in the nostrils and whisked away on the wind; and all the while the steady whine of rubber on the hard road.

And suddenly we leave civilization as the lorries turn off the macadam and take the stony track that climbs into the mountains of nowhere. Revving engines and grinding gearboxes as the trucks grapple their way round dangerous corners; visions of bottomless valleys just below us as we hug the hillside and wind our way ever upwards. In the distance a million miles away there is a pinprick of light like a solitary star in the night. It is an Arab dwelling nestling down for the night – cosy thoughts – I wonder where Estoban is. The trucks come to a stop – everybody out; silent muffled voices giving orders; the stifled curses as heavy rucksacks are hoisted on to backs; the accidental bang of a weapon against a neighbour; more curses, impatient whispered commands for silence and then they shuffle off into the darkness. Footsteps fading fast and finally complete silence. We wait in the lorries still as the night – give them half an hour, time for a quiet smoke – no lights – and then the crisp whispered order – back to camp. The engines rev, we turn around and head for home, once more roaring through the darkness – the stars have gone, it's cold and suddenly it starts to rain – those poor sods out there – and we race on.

Thoughts turn to the barracks and the waiting bed suddenly so very snug and comfortable. These are the moments that I will remember.

A Week Later

Yesterday was Sunday. I was planning a visit to town with Harry Stobbe, but unfortunately my pass was torn up because I put the wrong date on it. What kind of bastards are we dealing with? They think it spells discipline, but in my book it spells horse shit.

Poor Estoban was picked up two days ago; luckily for him it was the regulars who caught him and not the Legion. He's sitting in a cell in bel-Abbès at the moment awaiting his fate. Wissmann says he will get six months to a year in the penal battalions in the Sahara following his court martial. Poor devil. He was a nice quiet harmless chap who kept himself to himself; we hardly knew he existed until he took off. He must have been as lonely as hell.

Ten Days On

The days trickle by slowly, terribly slowly. They are always the same: shooting, weapon training, marching up and down the hills, close combat, guard duty, inspections, punishments, more shooting and more punishments. They have invented a new one for us; it's called 'tenue campagne'. The form is that at *appel* we parade with every item of kit that we own packed in three enormous sacks. The man being punished is rigged up in full battledress, with greatcoat and helmet. In other words, he is all set to go on a campaign. The sergeant of the guard then marches him to the guardhouse with his sacks, empties all the kit out on the floor and inspects it. Everything has to be spotless. He then instructs the man to take his kit back to the barracks and appear in a particular uniform in the guardhouse in three minutes.

This goes on for some time. Each time the wretched guy gets to the guardhouse he is informed that he has failed to make it by so many seconds and another uniform is selected and he is told to appear again in so many minutes. Everybody mucks in and helps to get the fellow dressed and all the different uniforms are laid out ready for him when he comes running back from the guardhouse. He rushes in shouting the required uniform and he is grabbed and the clothes ripped off him and the new uniform buttoned on to him. But we have over twenty different forms of dress. There are, for instance, four types of guard uniform: summer, winter, night and day. Each one is totally different. Then there is sports kit, battledress, denims, camouflage, parade and so on with a summer and winter variation.

It is very seldom that the sergeant of the guard is satisfied until he has been through the whole wardrobe three or four times and it is usually well after midnight before he gets bored. It's fine for him as he is on duty anyway and will probably stay in bed half the following day, but for us it's hell; we are creased at the end of the day and need every minute of sleep we can get. The last thing we need is to be buggered around by some stupid sergeant until the early hours of the morning.

We are depressed as hell. It is a far cry from Mascara. There is no life in the section at all. The food continues to be appalling with the inevitable effect on morale. There is no camaraderie. We are twenty-four isolated individuals. De Graaf is miserable company these days. We are fed up with being pushed around by these second-rate N.C.O.s, particularly the corporals who have no fire in their bellies, no enthusiasm, no sense of humour, and are quite incapable of generating any kind of spirit in the section. There is no direction and no sense of purpose. We are just drifting. There is no focal point on which to concentrate; there are no objectives at which to aim. It's as stagnant as a blocked drain. The sergeants are as bored as we are, but they have the advantage of their mess and the refuge of their private rooms, access to the night life of Sidi-bel-Abbès whenever they feel like it, and the Caesarian pleasure of kicking us around and watching us suffer during the day.

The sweltering heat doesn't help matters either – one is sweating permanently, night and day, sleeping or awake – there is no relief at all. On top of this there is a constant shortage of water and it is now rationed; we must use our ration for washing, shaving and drinking. By mid-morning it's already warm and useless as a thirst-quencher, which is just one more unnecessary irritation caused by bad administration. My leg from the famous fight with Otto Schmidt is still oozing pus after all this time and I despair that it will ever heal in this climate while we continue to be fed on slime. We all pray to get to the regiment and out of this quagmire before we go completely mad.

24 August 1960

Some relief. I managed to get a pass out to bel-Abbès with Harry Stobbe and Henry Schaeffer. Schaeffer is a young German. Very fit, probably the fittest in the section. He is totally competitive and although I quite like him I don't altogether trust him. He can run faster than I can, but I beat him when it comes to rope climbing and high-jumping and I know that it irritates him. We were being marked for perform-ance one day when doing various sports and I heard him asking the sergeant how many points I had collected. He sees me as a rival. I shoot better than he does too. We are accumulating points all the time and Schaeffer is keen to come out top. But I don't think there are any great rewards involved for the man with the highest points at the end.

Anyway we went into town and our first move was straight to the bordellos. I remember my old friend Francis Widdrington once quoting his commanding officer in the Welsh Guards as saying, 'Your prick is your most precious possession and some people put theirs where I wouldn't put the ferrule of my um-brella.' This was one of those places. We left Schaeffer there (he was clearly never in the Welsh Guards) and went out and had a fabulous meal in the Foot Bar and washed away the bad taste of Sully with a few gallons of excellent red.

We then adjourned to the Garden Bar where there is a ravishing barmaid called Patricia. She's got a figure on her like Lollabrigida and she is largely responsible for the popularity of the establishment and its rating as the best bar in town. She is of course much in demand and my efforts to attract her atten-tion have so far been unrewarded except for a few smiles, which in themselves do not have enough depth to lead me to believe that they represent a promise of greater things to come. How-ever, perseverance may yet bring more substantial rewards.

Harry Stobbe drank himself to death at the bar until he threw up. I have never seen anybody drinking and throwing up at the same time until I saw Stobbe do it this evening. That's quite an achievement.

26 August 1960

A day on the shooting range. One of the early lessons one learns when using an automatic sub-machine-gun is that when one has ceased firing, it is advisable, indeed it is mandatory, to remove the magazine and pull the breach back a couple of times just in case a bullet has been left up the spout. This procedure is learned on the very first day on the range and drummed into one so that it is never forgotten. Today Legionnaire Belombe forgot.

Belombe is a Frenchman. He's very tough and he's a likeable guy too; by far the best of the Frenchies! He is more phlegmatic than an Englishman could ever hope to be, he drinks like a fish, is totally unshakeable and can never be surprised by anything, not even by what happened today. He is slow in all his movements, he is very calm and he is concrete from the neck up.

When he had finished firing this afternoon he casually pulled back the breach with his finger on the trigger without removing the magazine and sent a *rafale* of bullets into the air which nearly wiped out half the section. Miraculously nobody was hit.

When we returned to camp, Belombe was put to the *pelote*, in combat uniform. After two hours he changed into No. 1 dress uniform and continued jogging and rolling with the old familiar whistle bleeping away. He changed uniforms every two hours from then on and carried on running and rolling with the stones on his back until midnight. The sergeants alternated with the whistle taking it in turns while the other went to get a beer. It's thirsty work watching somebody crawl around on his gut for hours on end! At midnight Belombe began an eight-hour guard stretch, at the end of which he begins a fifteen-day prison sentence. But as I say, he's tough, this Belombe, and he can take anything that they can hand out. They know this and it irritates the hell out of them – but he is unbreakable.

29 August 1960

A new sergeant has arrived called Blanco. (He would have been a laugh in the British army with a name like that!) He's

Spanish and the Spanish are delighted as they anticipate a soft deal. The Spaniards are very loyal to each other in this respect; quite different from the Germans who are great believers in rank.

Letang is a bad officer. He's totally wet and completely over-shadowed by his N.C.O.s. He has no discernible qualities of leadership, in fact he has no discernible qualities at all. I don't like him and I think he knows it. I don't think he likes me either if it comes to that.

We have spent the last couple of days familiarizing ourselves with explosives and mines. Mines are lethal things and the guys who defuse them deserve all the medals they get. There are hundreds of abandoned Arab *mechtas* around the hills, and these little farmhouses make excellent targets for practical demonstrations of explosives. We have had great fun blowing them all up.

In fact all the desecrated little dwellings look sad in these lonely hills. Life completely has gone out of the mountains where once there were small homesteads, goats, and quiet people. The piles of rubble mark the path of the French in 1957, when they adopted a policy of scorched earth, which was the systematic destruction throughout Algeria of all the out-lying farms that could in any way be used as points of refuge by the fellagha. The inhabitants of the farms were moved into collective compounds and more or less kept as prisoners, although the action was classified as a policy of centralization, adopted for their own good to protect them from the rebels. It is questionable whether or not this move assisted the French cause; for whilst undoubtedly it made the problem of food supply and shelter that much more difficult for the fellagha, it simultaneously nevertheless alienated many Arabs who had previously been well disposed towards the French.

This type of guerrilla war is won or lost by the relationship one has with the local population: once their support is lost, then so is the war and from then on it just becomes a matter of time. How much time is another thing!

The French have not been very subtle in their treatment of Arabs in the towns either. The Battle of Algiers in 1957 must have lost them many friends. There are terrible stories of French interrogation of Arab prisoners at this time. The effectiveness of torturing people to make them betray their cause cannot be disputed. But with all the good results – the 'fingering' of many fellagha, the betrayal and subsequent capture of many of the rebel leaders – was a steady build-up of hatred against the French – a hatred that comes from living in fear and terror. And this antagonism drew the Arabs, so often before divided among themselves, into a common cause; it made them feel the necessity of combining for survival and it made them finally aware of their own strength. The French became the foreign intruder and the concept of nationalism was born in the Arabs, which was never there before. By their short-sightedness the French have forced nationalism on the Arabs and despite de Gaulle's avowed intention to keep Algeria as part of metropolitan France, it is doubtful that he will succeed. The war drags on and bleeds the French treasury. We mercenaries fight the lost cause – a cause that will be buried in the French political arena, not here. The heap of dead bodies gets higher each day and the white crosses mark the pathway to the inevitable end; for the end is inevitable – the result will be as in so many British colonial struggles – it is a question of time. I wonder how many more crosses must be struck before the end comes – the end for the French, when a new nation will be born, conceived entirely through French misunderstanding.

4 September 1960

The summer sun has disappeared quite suddenly and it is dark when we rise in the morning now and cold too. They don't turn on the generator until the evening, so in the cold darkness the day has a depressing beginning. A sudden shout of '*Debout là-dedans!*' shatters deep sleep and twangs the nerve ends, and the clanking of the ladle against the coffee urn scrapes the mind awake. The sound of metal is as cold as the ring of steel gates in a prison cell. A dark form appears beside one's bed and ladles steaming coffee into the tin mug which one is unconsciously holding out. A long pull generates heat inside and cold hands clutching the mug begin to come alive. We sit for a few precious moments waiting for our eyes to penetrate the light of another day and then the screams of the corporal quicken the blood flow as we shamble outside, form up and canter off into the dawn for a five-mile run to Sidi-bel-Abbès.

We have been introduced to Sergeant Lustig, late of the German army, in which he apparently served with distinction as a paratrooper. He has a reputation built up on a mass of stories of courage and ruthlessness and he has a total disregard for everything and everyone. He is said to have delayed pulling the cord once when free-falling until he was a couple of hundred feet above the ground, with all the spectators standing to attention in the traditional manner, presuming his death imminent.

He is typically Germanic in appearance: handsome, if that's your taste, blond, blue eyes, looks about thirty-five, is nearer forty-five, and is as tough as granite. In some ways he is not unlike Krueger and he applauds good performance just as vigorously as he condemns any sign of weakness. He gave us proof of this on the stop-chute today with those who failed to jump off with sufficient enthusiasm or those who put their hands down when landing instead of rolling in the prescribed manner.

Hesitation to Lustig is cowardice and is instantly punishable. The punishment is to stand the man to attention with his hands behind his back and then thump him with every ounce of strength, deep in the solar plexus. Nobody survives. The body folds into a crumpled form, sags to the ground and is left writhing and gasping in agony with the lungs screaming for air, like a pole-axed ox. Lustig enjoys inflicting this kind of pain.

Having witnessed this a couple of times, I jumped off the top like a shell out of a cannon and landed like a golf ball. He liked this and the English are in favour for the moment. I am nevertheless doing abdominal exercises in preparation for the inevitable as my luck has never been particularly spectacular from a durability standpoint.

Letang has decided that we are slack and has instigated a tightening-up programme. All pass-outs have been cancelled until further notice and a series of inspections has ensured that any free time we have is fully occupied in preparation for them. The general consensus of opinion is, 'Fuck Letang', which I endorse. What little morale was left has now been completely eliminated.

Blanco showed his true colours today and confirmed what I have long been aware of, that there is no love lost between the Spanish and the Germans. I think this runs quite deep. We had just finished one of our never-ending inspections and Blanco was balling out Legionnaire Ryevski for some misdemeanour or other. As he walked away, Ryevski mumbled something in German to his neighbour. This was an error, for however innocent the remark, Blanco assumed the worst and turned on him. Five times he dragged Ryevski to his feet, as each time he collapsed under a hail of punches and a barrage of kicks and all the while Blanco screamed a torrent of insults at him and the world in general. He finally stormed out of the room leaving the bedraggled carcass of Ryevski slumped on the deck. The room as one man released its breath which had been held in check during the tornado and then Ryevski staggered us all by getting to his feet with a great big grin all over his face. They're tough, these fellows, and can take a knock or two.

We will soon be leaving for Blida near Algiers where we will do our first six jumps and obtain our wings. We can't wait to get out of here. However, before we get to Blida it is necessary to qualify by completing a series of tests, the first of which is a rugged march to see if we are fit enough and this begins tomorrow.

Two Days Later
The march was a killer. We covered fifty-four miles over the hills at a steady pace of three miles an hour. We left late in the afternoon in order to take advantage of the cool evening and tramped several miles before midnight. Then after a few hours' sleep we began again at four the following morning. The column was soon strung out like an untidy necklace with half the beads missing. We were carrying a lot of kit in the way of rifles, grenades, munitions, rations, sleeping-bags, first-aid kit, shovels and beer and by noon we were in a pretty sorry state. The corporals, who were wearing soft boots and carrying nothing, cajoled us with yells and threats as we staggered along. Legionnaire Klaus at one stage fell flat on his face, but he was revived with a few kicks and carried on. Klaus is O.K. – loud mouth and very full of himself in the barracks but not so full of himself when the going gets tough – but he's harmless enough.

We eventually arrived back at Sully half out of our minds. Most of us had blood all over our feet and so they will soon become septic and will ooze pus for weeks. This is the bloody nuisance of it all. Klaus's feet are particularly bad. He thinks he will never walk properly again in his life. He takes himself seriously but I think he'll live for a little longer yet. Those who are foolish enough to wear socks on the march suffer badly at this point, as when the socks come off skin and pus come as well in a putrid sticky mess. Bare feet go better in leather in the long run. There are many theories about footwear – one interesting idea is that if you fill your boots with urine and then march in them, they will fit you perfectly for life. I haven't tried this out but it might be worth following up.

9 September 1960

Old Kracker ran into trouble on guard duty last night. He is a big oafish German and he's a nice friendly guy; always in good humour, does his share of the work and probably a bit more, gets tight now and then and is pleasant with it – in general a simple soul, built like an ox and as strong as one but quite unaggressive – big teddy-bear stuff. The world is full of them and they are right up in front with the good guys.

He fell asleep on guard duty and Wissmann found him. He took Kracker's rifle and smashed the sleeping man across the side of the face with the butt – known as a *coup de crosse*. Christ, what a wakening!

Kracker, after a brief visit to the infirmary, is now in prison with a face like a football, and he has stopped smiling. Poor old lad. There's a Kracker in every section of every army and in every form in every school; they are nice people. Wissmann is a terrible bastard. What kind of animal would do that?

In the meantime we continue with our various tests. Some very sad news: one of the things we have to complete is a run in full kit with rucksacks and rifles over a distance of about six miles. It has to be done in under the hour, which is not too difficult if one keeps up a steady jog. De Graaf failed to make it because he says his feet are still infected from the march. But others have bad feet too and they all came home. Poor old de Graaf has lost any enthusiasm he had completely. I ran with him for a long part of the way but all the fight had gone out of him. Sully has drained the spirit from him.

Last thing this evening I managed to persuade him to have

another go and I practically had to drag him in front of Lustig to get him permission to run again tomorrow. Lustig was very good about it, very sympathetic, but said the decision was not his and he would refer the matter to Letang. It will be sad if he does not come to Blida after all the shit he has had to wade through to get there. I will be very sorry to leave him behind as we have come a long way together and he is the only real chum I have here and certainly the only one I can trust.

The Next Day
De Graaf is not coming. He still believes that his parents' letter to Madame de Gaulle will result in his release – poor bastard, it's a pipe dream. Others who will also not continue their journey to Blida include Aboine, Blood, for whom I do not care an iota, that little French creep Lasalle, and the dreadful Planchet. De Graaf is in bad company.

Out of the original twenty-six who arrived we are down to sixteen. Desertions, broken limbs, jaundice, prison and finally the tests have swallowed the rest.

12 September 1960
Letang has gone – good riddance. A new lieutenant called Rigolot has arrived straight from Saint Cyr. I liked him on sight; he's a good man.

A Week Later
We were up with the dawn and drove to Sidi-bel-Abbès where we caught the slow cattle train to Oran on the first leg of our journey across northern Algeria to Blida. The relief at leaving Sully was marred by the sad farewell to de Graaf – probably won't see him again but I'll remember him always – we went through Legion basic training together – that is unforgettable.

The train journey is a long one and we stopped at every tiny village along the route. At each station thousands of Arab children would rush to the windows like locusts offering their wares in extended little hands: melons, dates, couscous, lemonade in plastic bags, and bad oranges.

There was one incident along the way which I will never forget, for it was the hardest punch I ever saw. We were four or five of us standing by the railway track during the two-hour

wait before the train left bel-Abbès. Marinoli was there and
Harry Stobbe too. Stobbe is about six feet three inches of solid
muscle from head to toe. He probably weighs about fourteen
stone. Marinoli is smaller but also heavily built. Mario, as he is
called, has had an open ulcer on his ear for two months or
more – like every other cut or graze, it just will not heal in this
climate. These open sores continually oozing pus are soul-
destroying and drive us mad; and so it was with Mario today.

After weeks and weeks his ear was beginning to heal and a
scab had formed over it. And then as we were chatting away,
Stobbe, who was three parts drunk having been celebrating our
departure since dawn, gave Mario a playful slap across the side
of the head and opened up the ulcer all over again. If one could
understand what Mario had been through with this continually
dripping ear over the last two months and the misery caused by
it, and if one could appreciate the relief at the first signs that
the infernal thing was beginning to heal, and if one could also
imagine the white anger that would be aroused by a drunken
slob pulling the scab off just when it was on the mend, then and
then only could you understand Mario's reaction to this playful
gesture.

His right hand came up like a piston rod and travelled a bare
eight inches. He didn't draw back and strike, he just brought it
straight up and hit Stobbe on the side of the jaw, lifting him
completely off his feet, all fourteen stone of him, and depositing
him flat on his back on the other side of the track. Behind that
punch was the energy of a madman and the force of an express
train. None of us who saw it could believe our eyes. It was
unquestionably the hardest punch any of us had ever seen or
were likely to see again, unless Stobbe was foolish enough to get
to his feet! He didn't, but he sat up after a while, in a sort of
stupor with his eyes unable to focus on anything. Mario's
temper abated slowly and after a few minutes he collected himself and then we made a move to pick Harry up. We all of us
made a mental note to steer very clear of Mario's ear and a
further note never to pick a quarrel with him on any account.

25 September 1960
Blida is a dream world. It is a huge military camp run as the
regular-army parachute-training centre. We are guests! It is

unbelievably luxurious after what we have been used to. The food is fantastic and there is an unlimited amount of it, something which we have never had in the Legion. Delicious beefsteaks appear at every other meal with fresh salads, and breakfast produces endless amounts of scrambled eggs and toast.

There are two cinemas, four or five dining halls and three large *foyers* which sell everything from Herme's scarves to five-course banquets. It makes one realize how far down the Legion is on the French army logistics list for everything except weapons.

On the first day at the camp I met a splendid medic who was staggered at the state of my leg, which is still showing no signs of improvement after all this time. He has spent a lot of time in London and we chatted about old England which he appears to miss as much as I do. Oh to be in England – parties, friends, *The Times*, and tube trains; cinemas in Leicester Square, weekends in the country; all far-away stuff – another existence. England was a hundred years ago.

The training is good. We learn more here in a day than we did in a month at Sully. The N.C.O.s, known as *moniteurs*, are great guys, full of humour, without all the endless forced toughness that Legion N.C.O.s wear as part of their uniforms. We are in a mixed company (known as a *promotion*) with regulars who outnumber us five to one. On the first day we had to do another round of prequalifying tests; twenty-four of the regulars failed to pass, so our *promotion* is rather smaller than scheduled. The *promotion* is divided into sections, called sticks, and we spend the time of day practising landing, jumping off the stop-chute or whizzing across the compound suspended from a pulley, simulating landing in a high wind. Periodic breaks are called for *casse-croûte* and beer. The atmosphere is friendly and cheerful and morale is at sky level. The *moniteur* in charge of our stick is a Sergeant Lejeune. None better, he's a terrific guy, and full of sound advice like, 'If your 'chute doesn't open when you jump, remember to keep your left hand held high.'

'Why?' asks innocence.

'In order not to damage your watch, which could be useful to the guys on the ground.'

We know how to fold our own parachutes to a precision (in the Legion we fold our own so there can be no complaints if they don't open). We have now had about as much theory as we can absorb as far as parachutes are concerned including steering them in different directions, accelerating and slowing them down, and what to do when they don't open. There's little left to do except get up there and have a go.

I had a letter from Jennifer yesterday. She is gallivanting around Italy. My God these girls live good lives! Also received a fourteen-page screed from Alister Hall in Hong Kong. He must be ill! He sounds disappointed with it and disillusioned with the Lancers and army life in general. The superficiality of it all, particularly Hong Kong, has prompted the age-old questions of 'What is it all about and where the hell am I going?' The response to these questions is often demoralizing because too frequently it is, 'Christ knows – and he ain't saying!' Anyway, Alister has only two more years to do against my five and frankly I think he's got the better slot.

Last thing today we went airborne with some of the boys who were free-falling. They look fantastic, but standing at the door of the aeroplane looking down and knowing that the next time it will mean jumping out is a very sobering experience indeed.

28 September 1960

We rose early this morning, but I had been lying quietly awake for some time before the bugle. This was D-Day at last, and the old adrenalin was wasting no time in getting the pumps warmed up.

We were all subdued somewhat and took our time getting dressed before sauntering over to the *réfectoire* for coffee. Not too much chat! We drove quietly to the airport and were issued with our 'chutes. We put them on, tested and adjusted all the many straps and then took them off again, placed them in rows and stood by, smoking and talking while we waited for the arrival of the planes and the order. Eventually it came with a shout, *'Equipez-vous!'* A shot of adrenalin ran the full length of my body and I was running forward into the line.

The packs were hoisted on to our backs and we began fastening the straps. We had been through this procedure a thousand times and could do it in our sleep but this time it was for real. Fingers were not functioning at all well, and one was feeling

. distinctly short of breath – or was it only me? I was frantically chewing gum and hoping to hell that I looked relaxed but I was practically shitting myself. Everybody else looked as though they were having a ball. Eventually we were finished and the *moniteurs* walked down the line checking that everything was in order. Surprise, surprise! Almost everyone had made a mess of it. Straps were hanging down, buckles were unfastened, one 'chute was already half out of the pack and so on – a disaster!

The *moniteurs* repaired the damage and we shuffled off towards the aircraft. On board we were thirty-six, sitting along the sides of the plane with four men on the floor because there was not enough room on the *banquettes*. The engines roared and off we went. The excitement was intense. A pants-wetting fear was held in check by a mountainous curiosity.

Old Lejeune gave me a grin, I gave him a lopsided one back, and he broke up laughing, the bastard. Somebody started singing and we all joined in – another disaster! The senior adjutant in charge of training was on board strutting up and down with a huge smile on his face enjoying our misery. He had spent hours teaching us how to jump out of an aeroplane correctly and he was now about to see if his lessons had paid off.

We taxied slowly into position for takeoff – a last frantic rev of the engines and we were off.

Minutes ticked by and out of the oval window I could see the ground a thousand feet below. The plane stopped climbing and began cruising horizontally. (The old heart was pumping like a two-stroke and nobody had ever chewed gum as vigorously as I did then.)

The red light suddenly went on on the bulkhead and Lejeune waved us to our feet with a yell of, '*Debout! Accrochez!*' We got up and hooked our 'chutes on to the overhead wires that ran the length of the aircraft. The *moniteurs* passed quickly down the two columns of men, running their hands down our packs to make sure that we were properly connected to the wires. We were like sardines. My legs felt like water.

'*Bon voyage!*' from Lejeune as he checked my gear. I gave him my watered-down-gravy grin which I keep for these occasions. The roar of the engines was suddenly subdued in the shadow of an agonizingly shrill buzzer. My gut did a backflip. The red light changed to green and the first man was at the door in position to jump. The *moniteur* shouted 'Go!', slapped him on the back and out he went. The column shuffled forward and the next man was in position. I could hardly breathe. My mouth was as dry as a salt lake and I never knew I could be so scared. Jesus, what a coward! But if you're shit scared, you're shit scared and there isn't much that can be done about it.

The column moved forward relentlessly and I was practically at the door. I could see Maraskal at the door in position. Lejeune shouted 'Go!' but the bastard didn't move. Lejeune shouted again and slapped him hard on the back. But Maraskal was just frozen there. Lejeune shouted frantically at him above the roar of the engine and hoofed him in the arse, and suddenly he was gone. And then it was me at the door, standing with a hand on each side, one foot forward, looking into the sky but seeing the ground so far below.

I was in position, my mind desperately trying to remember the instructions on how to jump out of the aircraft. The adjutant was tucked down by the door watching us go out and making notes. There was a tremendous roar of the engines in the ears and time stood perfectly still. And then in the far distance Lejeune's voice was shouting – difficult to hear – maybe there was a mistake and it was all off. The touch of a hand on the back of my pack.

And then I wanted to go. I leapt as far and as hard as I possibly could using all my strength. Falling, falling, into a bottomless pit; down and down. My eyes were so tightly shut they were almost inside out. And then a sharp crack as the 'chute opened and I was floating on the air, suspended and unmoving. An amazing sensation. Perfect stillness, perfect silence. A fantastic and absolutely magnificent feeling. Right out of this world. I could see the plane behind and above me and two other jumpers emerged and fell with their 'chutes trailing behind them. The 'chutes opened at the end of the static line and they were floating gently like a couple of seagulls on the wing. Below, the ground was covered with white blobs where people had already landed. It was like being suspended from a balloon and we just floated for a while. But then the ground was suddenly approaching fast. This is ankle-breaking time. Legs together, knees slightly bent, elbows tucked well in, hands on the shoulder straps under the chin and head down. Hold the position and wait for the crunch. It came and with a sack-of-potatoes-like crash I was on the deck and feeling terriffic. A piece of cake!

They say the first jump is the best. This is the one never to be forgotten. It takes the longest time and all the new sensations are miraculous. It was certainly a sensation and I can't wait for the next jump tomorrow.

On the ground we tucked into buns and oodles of beer. Everybody was full of their particular jump and experience. We were all in great form and absolutely delighted with ourselves. The adjutant appeared on the scene and dragged me out in front of everyone by the ear and declared, '*Voici mon champion du promotion. Il a fait un saut sensationnel.*'

I was embarrassed but rather chuffed nevertheless. He said that he had never seen anyone make a first jump like that in all his years at Blida. Most people apparently fall out but it appears that I went out like a champagne cork. He was delighted with the whole thing and I think I was too. Just goes to show what panic can do to the adrenalin, and what adrenalin can do to the springs in one's feet.

The result of the jump was two broken legs, one fractured vertebra and a few sprained ankles. Ten people refused to jump at the door at the last second, the moment of truth. One of them was a legionnaire. For these people it is a terrible experience that they will carry with them for the rest of their lives. For in that moment that they failed to overcome their fear they became cowards, not just to everybody else but to themselves. That is the tragedy. The non-jumpers have to return with the plane to collect the next stick and this must be real agony. They must face the terrible shame on the ground of clambering out in front of their fellows awaiting their turn to embark. They must look into those rows of eyes reflecting scorn, contempt and surprise, to the shock on the faces of their friends as they climb out to failure. The legionnaire must feel that he has let down the entire Legion. It is not difficult to imagine the terror he must have gone through to choose to return and face his comrades, branded as a coward, rather than to jump. Poor bastard!

When we returned to camp, a Legion sergeant whom I did not know lectured us on cowardice and told us to take this poor sod who had brought disgrace on the Legion into the barracks and beat the hell out of him. To prove what? That we legionnaires are tough and will not tolerate fear? To prove it to whom! To ourselves? Perhaps, but we know better. We know that every man is afraid sooner or later. There is no disgrace in fear. Some overcome it and some don't, but the actual decision that governs an action in front of fear is probably made in the fraction of a single moment, and for the rest of our lives we may have to live with that moment when we chose to funk something. So it is with this man. Nobody touched him, thank God, but he is condemned.

A Few Days Later

It's all over. Tomorrow we return to Sully. Blida has been memorable and fantastic. It has been fun too and I will remember it because it will stand out so starkly against the grimness of what our lives had been up to this point. We completed our six jumps, each with a variation on the one preceding it, and finally received our '*brevets*'.

There was one Roman candle during our stay. I was on the ground looking up watching the jumps. After the first jump we no longer go one at a time but everybody charges straight out and, going through both exits, we can clear the entire plane of thirty-six in nine seconds. That's moving! On this particular occasion I looked up from the ground to see the parachutes opening like bubbles being blown from a bubble pipe, but one instead of floating like the others just kept falling like a stone. Everybody on the ground suddenly stopped talking and stood absolutely still watching this tiny black speck of human life hurtle to the ground and death. There was a *moniteur* standing beside me and he suddenly opened his lungs and yelled '*Ventral!*' with all his might in a long agonizing desperate cry. But the falling body could not hear. And then, just as gravity was about to deal a death blow and it was surely too late, there was a speck of white and then the burst of a full white canopy. He had pulled the reserve, the ventral had opened. He floated the last few yards to earth and we breathed again and carried on drinking our beer and eating our *casse-croûte*.

Today was our last day. We had a big parade this afternoon and were awarded our wings. The adjutant called me out to the front of the parade followed by another legionnaire and four regulars and declared that in the opinion of himself and his fellow N.C.O.s we six had been adjudged to be the best in the *promotion* and he presented us each with a memento. I was given a cigarette case. What a marvellous gesture! Old Lejeune signed it for me afterwards. He is a splendid man and I will never forget him.

PART THREE

The Regiment

2 November 1960
Camp Pehaut, just outside the coastal town of Philippeville, is the base camp of the 2ème Régiment Etrangère de Parachutistes. It is situated on a hill overlooking the sea, approached by a steep winding road ending with the impressive entrance to the *quartier*. The *quartier* is all sand, with a number of yellow-stone barracks, with orange-tiled roofs, scattered around at random. The barracks themselves are clean, containing nothing on the impersonal stone floor except double metal bunks, on each of which is a straw-filled palliasse and a straw-filled grey-cloth pillow. There is a washroom at one end of each room where apparently there is sometimes running water and sometimes not. In addition there is a Nissen hut which houses the *foyer* where on auspicious occasions film shows are conducted.

The regiment is absent at present on operations some three hundred miles south in the Aurès Mountains. The *quartier* is occupied by the base company, which is apparently full of the most worthless members of the regiment. The appearance of those present here would seem to confirm this.

We will stay here for three days or so while we are kitted out and then catch the first liaison convoy with the regiment.

The last three weeks at Sully have been hell. I was right about Rigolot, he turned out well. But the N.C.O.s didn't change. They never eased up on us for one second when we got back

from Blida. I am glad it's over. Most of the lads from Sully
went to the 1st Para Regiment. There doesn't seem to be any
particular significance in this, and it rather depends on which
of the two regiments has seen the worst of the action recently.
This determines the number of vacancies. Six of us have come
to Camp Pehaut. Stobbe, Marinoli, Schaeffer, Peloni and
Lefevre. Our numbers are constantly in decline.

3 November 1960

It is universally accepted that new recruits in any army are
allocated more than their fair share of the work ration. Here
there is no exception to this rule, only a slight differential from
the normal in that we have been allocated *all* the work. Thus the
days have taken on a similar format to those early days in Paris
and Marseille when one was never without a potato knife in
one hand and a broom or shovel in the other. Life for members
of the base company is obviously very cushy. Excellent food
– steaks and plenty of wine to wash them down – access to town
in the evenings, bathing in the afternoon, and generally a pretty
relaxed existence.

In the *foyer* this evening I was able to learn something of the
general method of operations against the fell. The normal practice is for the regiment to be out on ops for periods of about
four months and then to return to Philippeville for about fifteen
days for rest and refitting of equipment.

When the regiment leaves the base camp at Philippeville,
everything goes along with it – the *foyer*, the *bordel*, field
kitchens, etc. An advanced base camp is formed in a given
sector of operations and from this the companies go out on
sorties for three to five days at a time. Each man carries rations
and ammunition for about six days and half a small tent, which
can be joined to another to form a two-man unit. The advanced
base camp itself is uprooted and moved every three weeks or so,
depending of course on the activity of the fellagha. It seems as
though we will be spending very little time in Philippeville.

Four Days Later

We left Camp Pehaut at dawn in a convoy of six lorries and
drove south all day. Soon the lush colours of the Mediterranean
coastline were left behind and the scenery changed to drab

brown as we approached the barren Aurès Mountains. We passed through Batna and took the main route south-west towards Rhouffi, and in the evening as darkness was falling we arrived at the operational base camp. This presented the most incredible sight.

A thousand tiny tents were spread in every direction as far as the eye could see; and yet a closer look showed that there was in fact distinct order in the way the tents were placed. All were in straight lines but there were so many that this was not at first apparent. Scattered among the small tents were a number of large *guitounes*, obviously officers' tents and facility tents such as the hospital, *foyer* and so on. The field kitchens could be seen on one side, with enormous cauldrons giving off steam and a promise of warm food to come.

Everywhere is thick dry dust – not sand but powdered mud as fine as talc. One's feet sink in it. Eyes peer out of featureless powdered faces. It covers eyebrows and hair and clog up nostrils. It is bitterly cold here. The whores in the *bordel* must be pretty tough to stand this.

Myself and Harry Stobbe have been posted to the 3rd Company and on arrival we were marched into the C.O.'s tent. He sat at a small table on which was a lighted candle, dimly illuminating the dark interior. It was rather sinister and totally without warmth as far as welcomes go. Our C.O., Captain Willemin, was cold and brief in his address; a far cry from Glasser. Beside Willemin was a lieutenant, introduced to us as L'Hospitallier, commander of the 3rd Section to which we have been assigned. He looks lean and tough like nylon rope.

The regiment is moving base camp tomorrow and some of us will remain behind to clear and move the tents. The rest of the company will leave for two days in the hills and join us at the new site. Stobbe and I have joined our tents – there's hardly room to move. The camp settles down to sleep – murmurs turn to whispers and so to silence. This is a long long way from anywhere! No plant grows here or shrub of any kind – it's as cosy as the Arctic.

8 November 1960

The company left this morning and we took down the larger tents and, having loaded all the gear on to the G.M.C.s, we drove west over the mountains to El Kantara. This will be our new base. El Kantara is a small *douar* made up of a few mud huts. We have pitched the tents on a flat plain with a gorge on one side at the bottom of which there is a refreshing-looking stream which a thousand palm trees follow to distant hills.

It is now evening. The tents are all up and we are sitting around a fire heating our canned beans and ravioli. Quiet talk. The jackals break the silence of the night with their screaming which stops as suddenly as it starts. There is a Belgian with us who is leaving tomorrow having completed his five years. I suddenly feel terribly envious – and here I am just starting! I had a couple of beers with Peloni tonight sitting overlooking the gorge and we talked about many things. He asked me if I had a girl in the U.K. and did I think she would wait – very romantic. I said I thought she might and he told me I was crazy. That figures!

9 November 1960
We continued preparing the camp under a warm sun – nice leisurely pastime – much too good to last. Peloni and Marinoli are being sent back to Philippeville to do a driving course. This is a great skive because it means no marching – the hardest work they will ever do is drive a lorry. This leaves Schaeffer, Stobbe, myself and Lefevre as the only ones from Sully days. To think we started out in Mascara a bunch of a hundred and now we are four. The Legion must be spread over a lot of ground.

The regiment has returned. Everybody looks whacked.

The stream makes an excellent washroom for clothes, shaving – everything. Looking down on all the naked bodies among the rocks and in the water reminds me of Kingsley's *The Water Babies*. One can see the stream winding its way for miles among the palm trees – fabulous place for a camping holiday.

I was summoned in the afternoon to the N.C.O.s' tent where I met Chief Sergeant Katzenberger, late of the S.S. Corps, who is second in command of the section, and two sergeants, also German, Karos and Dornach. Katzenberger looks very mean indeed and certainly not a man to cross. There is nevertheless a sign of humour which may or may not surface – time will tell. He said he'd known five Englishmen in his time in the Legion (twelve years) and all five had deserted and he would therefore be watching me closely. Karos appears to be quite passive but

Dornach looks like the chief slicer in a slaughterhouse – fat and probably a bully. It is early to be characterizing individuals in the section, for what they seem to be now, relaxed and refreshed, may be totally dissimilar to their natures when the circumstances are different.

There is Corporal Hirschfeld – German – he is the *chef* of my *équipe*, which has in addition Theobald, Demar and Auriemma, a very relaxed Italian, besides myself. Hirschfeld is a veteran of eight years; many decorations are evidence of an experienced *combattant*. He is about thirty-two and appears quite friendly.

Theobald, German, has the appearance of a Greek and the character of an Italian; very happy when he's happy, drinks a lot and talks more – I liked him instantly.

Demar, German, very tough indeed and very remote. A cool customer by any standards, entirely dependent on himself. He told me that the marching was lethal and that to begin with I would have difficulty keeping up. This is apparently normal with all new arrivals, however fit they may presume to be, and is accepted up to a point – but only up to a point. This I am not looking forward to.

Then there is Auriemma, the happy-go-lucky Italian; dead lazy, very relaxed and casual, probably a small-time crook in a small provincial Italian town. A story told of Auriemma which seems to sum him up is that once when asked his occupation in civilian life, he replied, '*Je donne un coup de main à mon père*' (I give my father a helping hand). And when asked what his father did, he shrugged and said, '*Eh – rien*' (He's unemployed).

11 November 1960
Sunday. The field kitchens are in action and produced excellent chicken for lunch. I began to get to know a bit more about the men in the section, most of whom have at least three years' service. The atmosphere is friendly and there is a ready response to questions and a cautious welcome. There is a willingness to share, little things, and everybody is chatty to a point – not very communicative about themselves, but on every other subject.

Most endorse Demar's view about the marching and recall episodes in their careers when either they or someone else in the section has been marched to a standstill. This seems to carry tremendous significance with everybody, this marching. It makes or breaks; there are no half measures and you're not one of the boys until you have proved yourself in the field. I am myself reasonably fit and I cannot see how it can be so bad. However, life is full of surprises.

It is evening and there are two poker schools in progress in our tent. The players form dark silhouettes that flicker under the glow of candles, one of which sticks up by each camp-bed in the tent. I now know the names of all the section and will record for memory's sake those which spring to mind. There is Podel. He is a lance-sergeant or chief corporal, *caporal-chef*; German, very quiet and slightly furtive-looking. He has a number of decorations which may or may not mean he's worth more than he looks.

There are two other corporals – Pitchidelli and Weiss. Pitchidelli is Italian and a noisy one but appears to be efficient and is probably good value if my judgement is right. He has a reputation for being fair. Weiss is Belgian, also incredibly noisy; half intelligent and the sort of man with whom it would be easy to lose one's temper. Chauvin 'Charlie' is the radio – quite a character. He looks about fifty and is actually thirty. He drinks more than the rest of the section put together. In addition to the radio, which weighs 22 pounds, he carries in his sack enough beer to quench the thirst of forty men and two *bidons* full of wine as well. He has never been known to fall on a march and his legs, which look like matchsticks, are apparently made of steel.

Then there is Skarsinski, known as 'Starry', from Poland, who is the medic – he is straightforward and appears cheerful. He is very thick with Panzas, a dark swarthy Spaniard, who looks the type that can smile while slitting an infant's throat.

Koch is a young German, full of beans, full of himself and fairly full of bullshit, but I quite like him. Prinz and Fisel are the batmen to L'Hospitallier and Katzenberger respectively; both are German and both are rather wet. There is also Rottloffe, known as 'Elch', meaning elk, because he looks like one, and Plaumann. They are from East Germany. They are fairly serious, as one would expect them to be. In addition, there is Steffen, a young German who is not dissimilar in character to Koch, and Grueber, another German, who appears quite pleasant but who is in fact I think slightly round the bend. He is the only one who speaks a bit of English, with an accent that is almost incomprehensible. He has got some very odd theories indeed on the last war. And finally there is a young Frenchman, Caulier, who is new like Stobbe and me. He did his instruction at Saïda.

That is the section and the closest company I shall have for many moons. Time will paint their portraits more fully and add colour to this brief sketch.

12 November 1960

The regiment has eight companies and fields about a thousand men, eight hundred of whom are operational. Of the eight companies there are four combat units, one transport, one 'shock', the *compagnie d'appui*, and finally the base company in Philippeville. Today four companies have been out on ops; we have been in reserve, with helicopters ready to transport us to the scene of the action should there be any. There has been none and the day draws to a close with a few beers in the *foyer*.

13 November 1960

We are on standby again. This gives one an opportunity to attend to personal matters, writing letters or playing poker. Poker is officially banned but most N.C.O.s and officers turn a blind eye. It is banned because it is believed, and history has corroborated the fact, that a man who loses at the table will go to great lengths to recoup his losses, including stealing; and in the Legion theft is more serious than murder.

Last thing tonight Katzenberger came to the tent with the two sergeants to issue the orders for tomorrow. *Réveil* is set for 0430. We will drive eastwards for operations in the Aurès Mountains. Each man has been issued with three days' rations.

14 November 1960

It's dark and very cold in the early hours. For the old hands it was the beginning of a normal day as we kitted up in the dimly lit tents. Shadows flickered in the candle flame as bodies moved around collecting equipment, rations, radios, etc. Each man sleeps with his rifle or sub-machine-gun above his bed, with ammunition pouches and ammo bands draped over it. For the new arrivals there was a definite excitement in the air. Everybody got on with his job. Only the corporals shouted, 'Do this! go and fetch that!' or rebuked somebody complaining that he had to carry the extra radio or ammo yesterday and, '*Nom de Dieu*, why doesn't somebody else carry it today?'

Finally we were assembled by sections outside the tents in the darkness. Senior N.C.O.s presented sections to section leaders, section leaders presented sections to the company adjutant, in this case Adjutant-chef Kautz, Kautz presented the company to Captain Willemin, Captain Willemin handed the sections back to section leaders, who handed them back to senior N.C.O.s. We in the ranks stood to attention or at ease as the chain of command was passed up and down the hierarchy.

This is the army. There is a reason for all this, and it has been done since the armies of Alexander, but no one has ever discovered what the reason is. From the assembly we got into the lorries for a three-hour drive south through Biskra and then north-east along Highway 31, branching off to the east at Tifellel and on to the rough tracks that climb into the mountains. By daybreak we were on the march, upwards. The pace was phenomenal, just short of a run.

We climbed for about three hours to a height of 3,500 feet. At the top of the mountain range we could relax as the operation went into effect.

From where we sat along the hilltop, spread out in a long line like happy hunters in their butts waiting for the grouse to fly over, we could see the whole of the enormous wooded valley below. Two dive bombers were in the process of bombing the hell out of it, and way to our rear the artillery guns started up with muffled thumps. Suddenly, there was a crash in the valley as a shell hit and billowing smoke and dust geysered up to mark the spot. On the other side of the valley could be seen in the distance a host of helicopters, depositing the 1st Company – *bouclage* – the other side of the net.

Eventually we received an order to move, and the search began. This is the dangerous part of the game because the bombs and shells do not often succeed in moving these wily birds unless it's a direct hit, and if there is no way out they will make a stand.

As we walk down the valley sides they can follow us in their rifle sights, or more likely over their shotgun barrels. You pray that if you are one of the chosen then you or one of your colleagues will see them before they decide to pull the trigger. Our advantage is that we are many and they are few; that their weapons, like ours, are for close combat and not for long range – so they have to wait; and there are many trees and bushes and matted undergrowth which suddenly hide a target that is moving just as you may be about to shoot. Nevertheless, they have the edge as their guns are cocked and need only the squeeze of a trigger; ours are not, for it is too dangerous to descend through undergrowth with a cocked sub-machine gun; a trip and a fall can send a spray of twenty bullets into your colleagues.

The 1st Company sat tight on the top of their hill; they were really in the 'butts' today and we were the beaters. There were no birds caught and in the evening when the work was done we pitched our tents. It is very cold indeed at night in these mountains.

15 November 1960
Réveil 0400. A two-hour drive deeper into the mountains. We marched till midday to 6,000 feet. It was exhausting work – really exhausting. Thank God for the snow on the mountain peaks which was cool and refreshing. At the top we had half an hour to brew a little coffee and eat some tinned cheese before the descent. We turned every stone, but not a sign of life, not even a snake. In the late evening we returned to El Kantara, arriving at about two in the morning, very ready for bed.

17 November 1960
Up at 0300 this morning and, following the familiar pattern, we drove through the cold darkness back to the mountains. Another valley to be searched. We marched for many miles draining the moisture from our bodies – sweat was pouring from our foreheads like dripping rainwater. The pace was fantastic and breathing became so tight that suffocation seemed imminent. It was like being a squeezed lemon.

We saw a number of wild boar in the hills; they are enormous and will suddenly charge out of a bush across the path but they seldom attack. They look like miniature buffaloes, heads lowered, hulking shoulders moving at great speed.

Night has fallen and we are camped on a plateau. Each man has built a small stone wall around his sleeping place as protection in case of a sudden attack. I have guard duty from 0200 until 0300 and *réveil* is set for 0400. This means I will get no sleep after two o'clock. Once awakened, there is no more sleep because of the cold.

18 November 1960

Another day has come and gone. We have pitched our small tents in a valley and have cooked our evening meal of tinned beans and soup. The men are clustered in small groups around the fires. The fascination of flickering flames in the quiet of the evening grips the eyes and will not release them. I watch the silent faces staring at the fires, each man appreciating the privacy of his own thoughts: thoughts of past joy, thoughts of past misery; thoughts mostly of people. It is the end of another day; the best part of every day, to lie by a warm fire in the peacefulness of a still night, lost in these mountains, lost in thought.

During the day from the mountain peaks it is possible to see for miles and miles the never-ending hills stretching to the blue horizon. It is a most awesome spectacle of fantastic beauty, impaired slightly by the sheer barren loneliness of the place. There is no sign of man, no trees, no birds, just dust and shrub and bare rock; at night so cold, by day reflecting a sizzling heat and holding the secrets of a million caves where the enemy hide and wait their chances when we relax or drop our guard. Today we caught five Arabs. The 4th Section stumbled on one of their caves and those inside decided to make a stand – but a grenade in the cave changed their minds and three of them surrendered; the other two died with the blast.

19 November 1960

Operations continue. We have been on the move for five days now. I nearly dropped this afternoon. This marching is something else. Theobald offered to carry my *sac* and that was just enough to keep me going. What a good chap he is – tough as hell and small and scruffy like a Shetland pony.

As we progress on our way we frequently come across Arab *mechtas*. It is generally accepted that we can help ourselves to the livestock on these farms and the officers turn a blind eye. Thus, having passed a farm one will notice movement in the sack of the man in front of one and hear clucking from within. These titbits make excellent extras to our staple diet of tinned sardines. Very boring for the farmers!

After a long *fouillage* down through a rugged valley and then a five-mile gallop, we finally caught sight of the friendly waiting lorries. The sight of them sent a flood of relief through me, like cold water to a parched throat. I arrived completely exhausted, convinced that another hundred yards would have been totally out of the question.

We returned to base camp to a proper cooked meal, our first in five days. And a wash in the stream. Wonderful to be out of our clothes at last after five days of constant wear day and night, walking and sleeping – it's like taking off a layer of greasy skin.

The post has arrived and I have a letter from Jennifer. It is unbelievable that a piece of paper can transport so much so far. A letter here is like suddenly seeing a London bus – a sudden burst of civilization in this dead forgotten corner of the earth; and a parcel too of Cadbury's chocolate. I never realized that a bar of chocolate could have such an effect on me – a strange mixture of sheer delight and the sudden excruciating pain of longing to be home – the feeling of suddenly being with all one's friends again, brought to life in flesh and blood through the lines of Jennifer's letter, and the shattering loneliness that accompanies it with the realization of distance and time between the truth and moment of dreaming. I wonder if she will ever understand the effect her letters have – and I wonder if Peloni was right and that the passage of time will corrode the thin line that links the spirits and spans the distance between us. I will dream tonight and be disappointed in the morning.

20 November 1960

Four companies are out. We are the working company in camp, and also the *section du jour* within the company. It is therefore my lot to be sent to the kitchen for *corvée*. The field kitchens are extremely efficient and well managed. Here a banquet for a thousand men can be produced when required. It is the nerve-centre of regimental morale; without at least one proper meal a week life would be tiresome – if two are on, then so much the better. The chef is an Italian muscle-man, almost as broad as he is tall. He can decapitate a bullock with one swipe of his beefy arm – not a man to meet on a dark night. He is affectionately called Pedro and when you speak to him you smile in order that there should be absolutely no possible chance of misunderstanding through the language barrier.

The 4th Company 'found' a number of cows yesterday and Pedro axed them one at a time. There were cows' heads all over the place. I felt very sorry for the waiting animals who watched the whole performance in gloomy silence, knowing their turn was coming and offering not the slightest resistance as their inevitable fate slowly overtook them.

I have met a splendid Turk from the 2nd Company, who calls himself Joe. He speaks excellent English and has lived in London. He has been in the Legion four years and is making great plans for civilian life which is only about ten months away. We adjourned to the *foyer* this evening and swapped yarns over some excellent Kronenbourg beer.

21 November 1960
We are moving base camp to Medina, which is about eighty miles east of El Kantara, buried in the mountains of Chélia. Here the Djebel rises to 7,000 feet and it is difficult marching country. An advance body set off in the trucks early in the morning to pitch tents at Medina and the rest of us started out on foot three hours after midnight on operations. We marched in torrential rain for five hours and found ourselves strung out along the top of a mountain chain as the first light crept over the horizon, ready to go into action.

Dense fog clung to the hilltops and with visibility reduced to a yard, it was futile to consider a *fouillage*. We sat and waited all day long, freezing in the cold, damp, clammy mist, waiting for the order to move. It never came and in the early evening we pitched tents.

The rain has not stopped for one second and everything and everybody are soaked to saturation. The ground is covered in thick wet mud and the cold is almost unbearable. We lit small discreet fires earlier and warmed tin mugs of water for our dehydrated soup. The soup reminded us that we had blood in our bodies as it burned its way to the pit of the stomach and generated a tiny spark of inner warmth. It's going to be a wet and cold night – so what's new?

Midnight has gone and I have just completed two hours' guard, standing in the open under the torrential rain that never ceases. I am covered from head to foot in mud. Demar is asleep next to me in our tiny ridiculous tent. My sleeping-bag is water-logged and I have no option but to climb into it as I am, with boots and everything covered in this fucking mud, and grope for sleep which will not come.

23 November 1960
The morning dawn came drizzling through grey as lead. Floundering in the mud we stuffed our drenched sleeping-bags into soaking *sacs* and hoisted them on to our backs and began the long slog back to the lorries and then back to Medina.

Medina is situated in a vast open plain surrounded by the mountains of Chélia. It is as cold as the Arctic here and each section has been issued with a stove which offers some relief. We spent the day consolidating installations, digging drains around the tents, and ditches for refuse and latrines, and sawing wood for the fires.

Eggs are on sale at a small *mechta* near by and thanks to the stoves we can eat them *ad nauseam* which helps combat the cold. This is a God-forsaken spot. The wind roars across the plain like a cold steel javelin and scrapes the bones with a howling wail as it passes clean through you irrespective of any amount of clothing. *Quelle misère!*

25 November 1960
Pay-day. Poker games in full swing. Flourishing business in the *foyer* as almost every man in the company fortifies himself with two cases of beer. Kautz, the adjutant, eyes us coldly as we return to the company with the cases under our arms. He is apparently teetotal and comes down like a ton of bricks on anyone inclined to excess – hallmark of a convert.

There is also excellent trade in the *bordel* and the egg business is picking up. It is a happy day with plenty of food and beer to be had by all, while the money lasts.

It's ten o'clock in the evening. Snatches of 'Lights out' sound faintly on the bugle against the frolics of the wind and candles are extinguished in the tents with the usual exceptions as play quietly goes on. Theobald is heavily involved in a game and to date has lost four months' pay, with Demar close behind on three months. Charlie Chauvin has consumed two cases of beer and is still afloat – just! It is getting colder and snow is imminent.

26 November 1960

It is mid-afternoon and we are sitting at intervals on the top of a mountain overlooking a valley, in which there are a few isolated *mechtas*. These farms are often used by the fellagha as sources of food supply, sometimes with the agreement of the farmer but more often without. We sit in silence and watch for any irregular movement on the farms which could indicate the presence of the fell. It is a peaceful occupation. Everybody has brought along an adequate supply of food and beer to supplement the normal rations. Demar is already asleep twenty yards to my right; Auriemma is reading a novel nearby in the middle of a bush. It is a pleasant way to idle away the time of day.

What a wonderful country this is. Watching the smoke spiralling up from the little farms in the valley and the cows lying in the yards, it is hard to realize that there is a war on, it all looks so peaceful – and we, armed to the teeth, sit waiting for the fellagha to come, which would be the signal for an all-out attack on the farms. It would be a massacre. But it was not for today and towards evening we returned to camp.

Gradually I am getting to know the people here. A number of the Germans appear to have broken marriages behind them and alimony charges that they were not prepared to meet; also punishment for juvenile delinquency appears much harsher in Germany than in England. The Legion is an alternative to three years' prison for quite minor offences, which had they been committed in England, particularly by someone under twenty-one, would have been dealt with far more leniently – maybe the offences weren't quite so minor.

27 November 1960

We covered many miles today on a trek that would have flattened a mule. We climbed to 6,000 feet. As *section du jour*, we
took the lead marching in extended formation upwards at the
head of the company. Marching in extended line, particularly at
the pace of Hirschfeld, is of course twenty times worse than
marching in column. One has to gallop to keep the line straight.
The terrible ache in the legs and back is surpassed only by the
frantic strain to get breath into the lungs. The taste of blood at
the back of the throat is slightly terrifying as one literally drags
the air down into the lungs. I don't know how I made the top at
all, but somehow staggering and stumbling, with Hirschfeld
bellowing at me to keep in line, I kept on my feet. Dead from
exhaustion and on the last verge of resistance, we eventually
arrived at the top. I would have welcomed a bullet.

It is now evening, freezing cold as always. I feel a bit cut off
from the rest of the section – not so much because of the language or background difference, I speak French and German
quite adequately so there is no language problem now, but
because they will not accept one completely until one has proved
oneself in marching. Caulier the Frenchman has much more
difficulty than I do. However, he is not a *voltigeur* marching
with a Sten at the front but carries a rifle and marches behind,
where he is far less noticeable. Marching will come with practice
and habit.

Weiss has an enormous hole in his inside thigh the size and
depth of a golf ball. It looks revolting and is obviously poisoned.
Skarsinski, the medic, pours brandy in it and says it will be
fine. Weiss says nothing and drinks more beer. So does the
medic.

The inseparable pair Panzas and Skarsinski have finally
separated. The spells of idleness, the drink, the cold, and other
things tend to get on one's nerves. They started arguing in the
tent tonight and Starry called Panzas outside to settle. The
Spaniard never moved, nor did anyone else in the tent, for this
is the traditional way of ending disputes and it is considered
absolutely no business of anybody else, N.C.O.s and file alike.
The Spaniard was subjected to every name in the dictionary by
Starry and called a coward a thousand times over, but to my

utter amazement he never moved, not even with every man in the section silently condemning him. Every man understands fear, but they never quite forgive cowardice. By not moving, Panzas died in spirit and in the eyes of those who witnessed the event – poor bastard!

30 November 1960

Another ghastly march from crack of dawn to sundown, with a one-hour break. The rain continues incessantly. We patrolled through the hills, forever climbing. Again the frantic breathing, the surging panic that one is about to collapse from sheer lack of oxygen, and the terrible ache in the back from the *sac*. At one stage my legs just buckled under me.

Hirschfeld, who had been yelling at me to go faster for the last hour, at this point lost his temper and came over and started kicking me in the back and hauled me to my feet. Somehow I kept moving.

Karos explained later that he had seen it all before, and that whilst Hirschfeld was to me the biggest shit on two legs he was in fact doing me good in the long run. A thoroughbred horse will run until its heart bursts and it dies on the spot. A man will go to thirty per cent of his capacity and then he drops – but he is not dead by a long way. At this stage the mind must take over or force or fear take over the mind to extract another thirty per cent at least that is available. I reckon I give seventy and Hirschfeld extracts another twenty leaving a very small balance of ten. It is interesting to note that five people in the 2nd Section who are old hands collapsed on the march today. And for all this we saw nothing, not the slightest smell of an Arab.

1 December 1960

At last the fellagha! We started out this morning on what was to be a routine patrol through the mountains and began climbing the main Chélia peak, which is 7,000 feet, shortly after lunch.

The 2nd Company, which was to our right on an adjacent hill, suddenly came under fire and we were immediately ordered to the top of our peak at a run, so that we would be overlooking the other hilltop on which the enemy was entrenched. Within minutes reinforcements arrived and the sky began to hum with helicopters. The deafening never-ending chatter of machine-gun fire and hand grenades quickly stirred the scene up into a full-scale scramble.

At one stage an attempt was made to drop the 1st Company by helicopter on to the hill held by the Arabs, but as the first wasp came in and made ready for a quick touchdown to drop the men, a burst of machine-gun fire practically cut it in half. The helicopter managed somehow to get off again but not before one man had jumped. As the helicopter took off, he found himself alone facing the enemy and a hail of bullets. He was carrying five grenades and by some miracle, throwing them in every direction and at the same time madly running for cover, he made it.

Meanwhile from our vantage point overlooking the enemy hill we were able to do some damage with the L.M.G.s and our mortar, and to a lesser degree the rifles. The sub-machine-guns were useless. It was practically impossible to see the Arab trenches so well were they dug in and camouflaged.

The 2nd Company lost over twenty men in the first barrage of Arab fire, of which five were killed outright and the rest wounded. A sergeant in the 2nd Company met a gruesome death when he was hit by an explosive cartridge which in fact hit one of the hand grenades hanging from his webbing. The subsequent explosion practically blew him in half. Lefevre, our friend from Sully, was shot through the head and killed. The bullet went through the emblem on his beret. He has done nine months' service. And Joe, who was laughing and drinking with me but what seems a few minutes ago, was also killed. His plans for civilian life died with him.

All the long hot afternoon we slogged it out with the Arabs. So well dug in were they that without the helicopters it is doubtful whether we would have moved them before nightfall, for our mortars seemed to have little effect. Intensive machine-gun fire from fast-moving Alouette helicopters finally wore down the resistance. At about four o'clock the 1st and 4th Companies were ordered to '*Montez à l'assaut!*' and in one line began to move up the hill.

We could see them weaving their way upwards, darting from rock to rock, never still for a moment except for the fractional pause for breath behind cover and quickly on again. We in the

3rd continued to rain cover fire on to the other hill and continued to receive it back – they don't give up, these Arabs. The 2nd Company had withdrawn to lick its wounds and grab some food, having been on the hill all afternoon.

And finally in the late afternoon it was over. The legionnaires could be seen on the hilltop, darting from bush to bush and bunker to bunker, firing bursts from their sub-machine-guns and dropping grenades into the trenches. Fifty-three Arabs lay dead. There were no prisoners today. Geneva's hands do not soothe insults at this distance, and the feeling is mutual.

The Legion counted nine dead and thirty wounded. The arms captured from the Arabs included some twenty sub-machine-guns, half a dozen light machine-guns, Brens and German '42s, and several rifles. Quite a bag! But the day was not yet over.

The 3rd Company had been involved in little of the direct action and it was now our turn to move. Behind the hill on which we were situated was a valley, so steep-sided that it was almost a gorge. Helicopters flying overhead had reported signs of fellagha in this valley and we were ordered to search it. The 13th Demi Brigade, also in the sector, moved a company across the bottom end of the valley to seal the exit and we began the descent.

The valley itself was about a mile and a half long. Its sides were incredibly steep, and thick shrub and undergrowth covered its floor while tall fir trees totally eclipsed visibility from the top. We set out in extended formation, ourselves as *section du jour* taking the centre-line through the most difficult terrain, flanked by the 4th and 1st Sections either side.

Progress was slow because of the undergrowth and there was an air of keen alertness. With visibility restricted to but a few yards, there was not going to be much warning for what was coming. And we all knew it was coming, because with the 13th blocking the exit there was no way out.

Halfway down I stumbled across the entrance to a small cave with straw outside it, which was quite obviously used as a cache. The question was whether or not the birds were still inside. L'Hospitallier came to inspect and half the section gathered round the entrance. L'Hospitallier radioed to the overhead helicopter who confirmed that this was where the Arabs had been seen, and he gave Dornach orders to send a volunteer into the cave – no move – and as he gazed around those lean faces they all gave him the same look, meaning, 'Do it yourself, slob.'

A cave is a certain death-trap for the first man in and inevitably for those inside too eventually. Inside a cave one can see absolutely nothing, but for those already in the blackness a figure entering with the light behind is no less than a sitting duck.

Dornach suddenly called my name out and passed me a torch. So I was to be the sucker. Theobald and Auriemma mumbled disapproval, but made no move.

In a moment the torch was strapped to the end of a stick which I held in my left hand, keeping the light well away from me, and with my sub-machine-gun cocked in my right hand, I darted into the passageway, moving in short bursts from left to right, stopping but for a fraction of a second. Each moment I expected to hear the sound of machine-gun fire – but nothing – and then suddenly frantic calls from L'Hospitallier, '*Sortez! Sortez!*' and out I came as fast as a champagne cork. The spotter above had signalled the presence of three Arabs a hundred yards ahead directly in our line.

We began to move off again, now with extreme caution. When you know that a hundred yards in front of you, sitting in a bush or tree perhaps, there is a man whom you cannot see, waiting with a shotgun or sub-machine-gun, waiting to blast the hell out of you, you approach very carefully indeed, and with a distinct feeling of discomfort in the pit of the stomach. As the distance is reduced, so the advantages of the waiting man become less. Visibility, before in his favour, is now even. Slowly the gap narrows, and one is suddenly surprised to be walking very slowly on tiptoe.

To my left was Martinek and beyond him Auriemma, and to my right about five yards away was Theo. I could see none of them but I could clearly hear their movements as they struggled through the bushes. In front of me was a small clearing, not more than fifteen yards across, and as I edged towards it, I thought I saw the bushes move beyond me.

There was a sudden scream of '*Attention!*' from Martinek and a sharp staccato burst of machine-gun fire – bullets really whistle when they pass close by. In the same second I was flat on the ground, literally squirting bullets into the bushes in front where I had seen the movement, using my gun like a hose to water roses. Theo, Martinek and Auriemma were all firing madly too, and suddenly from Theo a yell – '*Grenade!*' Firing stopped with a stunning bang – all heads down and arms across the eyes – a sizzling silence while breath was held, and then the almighty blast shattered the eardrums as it careered round the valley in a bounding echo.

It was an offensive grenade thrown by Theo. No shrapnel, just a blast to put the enemy heads into the earth, and as the blast was still ringing in our ears, we were all once more pouring rounds into the bushes. The sound of machine-guns chasing the echo of the grenade blast was like the dying cackle of wicked demons.

Screams of '*En avant! En avant!*' from the rear urged us forward – and it was over. In the bushes were three young Arabs, so full of bullets they looked like the pockmarks of some rash on their faces.

They were well equipped: two Enfield rifles and a British Sten gun, binoculars, compasses, and good boots. In their *musettes* they each had shaving kit, a toothbrush and a blanket; and on their persons a few scraps of paper. We took their arms and equipment and Auriemma took the boots from one of them, which fitted him well, and we proceeded on down the valley, eventually meeting up with the 13th, who had lit fires in the early evening, around which we stood awaiting orders to pitch camp.

In the French army they employ loyal Arab regulars, who serve under French officers. Four days ago one such battalion of Arab regulars stationed in a garrison fort in the mountains rose up one night and shot and killed their officers and indeed some of their own kind who refused to join them and, having sacked the fort, they went over to the fellagha. The French army have photographs and details of all these men and for very obvious reasons are unlikely to rest until all of them are taken. For this reason, every time an Arab is caught or killed in this sector, an officer from the Deuxième Bureau comes to inspect the prisoner or cadaver to establish whether he or it is one of those from the fort. And so today, having arrived at the valley bottom and surely the day's end, we were met by an officer of the Deuxième. The *équipe du jour* was ordered to furnish two volunteers to go back to the three dead Arabs and to remove their heads and bring them to the officer of the Deuxième for inspection and photographs.

Dornach, with commendable persistence, called myself and Auriemma, and off we set once more, up the valley in search of the cadavers. Light was falling fast and they were by no means easy to find at all and it was an hour before we arrived at the fatal spot. Dornach, with frantic gestures and urgent whispers, told us to keep absolutely quiet and our eyes well skinned for signs of trouble. In this he was right, for should any Arabs have been passed over and now find us cutting off the heads of their compatriots, it is doubtful whether our demise would have been pleasant.

Dornach got to work on the heads with a small sharp pen-knife, cutting across the necks. I was numb inside and felt nothing as I watched Dornach hack away, with bloodied hands, like something out of *Macbeth*. He didn't turn a hair, and could well have been skinning a rabbit for the concern it gave him. It took him half an hour to cut off two heads and by this time the company, fearing trouble, had sent men back to look for us. We could hear them calling our names in the distance, and Dornach with bloodied finger to his lips gestured us to silence. The calling came gradually closer; and then suddenly from quite near my name was called and I shouted in reply – with one bound Dornach dropped his knife and grabbed his Sten gun which he pointed directly at me. He looked completely desperate and with muttered curses said one more sound from me would be my last. I believed him and loathed him as I did so. Eventually he finished his work, and for my troubles he gave me the two heads to carry in my *musette*. The third head we left, because it was no longer recognizable behind the mask of bullet holes. Down the valley we went again, the heads dripping blood in my *musette*, over my sleeping-bag, over my tinned rations, and seeping out at the bottom of the sack and running down my back.

Heads are heavy and it took us three-quarters of an hour to get to the bottom. By this time it was dark and when we arrived men drifted over from the fires where they were preparing food to see the heads now on display in the headlights of a jeep.

Photographs were taken and I was asked to dispose of the heads, which I did, carrying them by the blood-soaked hair, one in each hand, and throwing them into the bushes.

There then followed an incident that I will recall to my dying day with a shudder, but which at the time caused an uproar of laughter. Some Spaniards in the 2nd Section had prepared a small cauldron of soup by adding water to the dehydrated-soup packets in our rations. The *équipe* had eaten and there appeared to be a considerable amount left in the pot, so they called over a German and invited him to fill his tin mug. Just as he was about to put the cup full of soup to his lips one of the Spaniards, with a mighty guffaw, reached his hand into the cauldron and pulled out by the hair one of the Arab heads, which he had retrieved from the bushes. On looking up at the noise, one could see the scene and follow the story at a glance – the Spaniard stood there with the ghastly head dripping soup, dangling by the hair from his outstretched hand, while the German stood aghast, white as a sheet, frozen for a second, and then promptly turned and threw up. This gave rise to another guffaw from the Spaniard and his chums. There is no accounting for people's sense of humour, though I must confess at the time I laughed like hell; so did we all – that is, except the fellow who had received the soup. He never actually touched a drop, it was the nearness of the thing that made him ill, as it does when you narrowly miss a bad accident in a motor car.

This then was the longest day. When we had finished our meal, we boarded the trucks and drove back to Medina. Here we spent the next two hours taking down all the tents, aided by the lights of the *camions*, and stacking all the gear aboard the vehicles. Towards midnight we set off on the long drive, right through the night, back to Philippeville – home! Thoughts turned to Christmas – and the night was cold.

PART FOUR

Les Colons

17 December 1960

We have been back in Philippeville for a couple of weeks now. The days are a mixture of boring chores when we have to do the work in the company, endless routine inspections, and going into town to amuse ourselves. On Sundays, there is *'quartier libre'* all day. During the week one is allowed out in the evening with a pass, but there is a snag attached.

The snag is in the form of Regimental Sergeant-Major Berggruen, by whom one is inspected before leaving the camp. He is a man of parts (mostly private) and personality, all of which are unattractive. He is French by birth but his enthusiastic service in the forces of Hitler's Storm Troops during the war has cleft any loyalty to his country of birth very much in twain. His reputation for sadistic brutality indicates that he was able to pick up a few pointers from the troops with whom he served and he loses no opportunity to put the fruits of his learning into practice, particularly when he is dealing with scum such as myself and anybody else below the rank of corporal. The inspection is tough and the reward for being improperly dressed (the Italians always try to get away with coloured socks) or having a slight mark on one's kepi is to have one's pass torn up and in all probability one will receive a thump in the stomach into the bargain.

This becomes quite a deterrent after a while and the evening

turn-out for '*permission en ville*' gets smaller each day. Philippeville is just not worth all the trouble. Its main attractions are
the bars and *bordels*. There is a rather charming little *salon du
thé*, with an equally charming waitress, which I discovered on
my first day into town. Unfortunately, many others have
discovered her too and I had hardly been in the place for five
minutes before it started to fill up with legionnaires, all calling
for cream cakes in gigantic quantities to prove their affection.
Nobody seemed to be getting anywhere near the cream they
were really after, nor I, but she had delicious smiles for all of us.
Her name is Chantal.

The normal routine on the outings into town is to drift
around the bars knocking back Pernod, chatting to other
legionnaires or regulars of the French army until one gets bored
of talking about the war, and then there is the choice of a
cinema or a *bordel*, and that's about the size of it. There is no
way of getting back to camp until the truck leaves the town
centre at 1 a.m. and the last hour after midnight has struck is
always depressing. One wonders why one came into town at all.
The brothels are closing, the bars still open have one or two
stalwarts drinking or sleeping at the tables, and but for this it
becomes a ghost town. I usually end up buying a *casse-croûte*
and wander through the deserted streets eating it. The occasional
hail from out of the darkness of the other side of the street
sparks recognition in the form of a dishevelled, drunken colleague who wants someone to share a last drink with him – I
decline and continue my aimless wandering. Eventually the
lorries and back to camp, all singing and laughing after one hell
of an evening.

It is impossible to make contact with the civilians because
they all seem to have disappeared by the time we arrive in town
and even when they are there on Sundays they don't seem to
see us. They do, of course, and that is why they keep their
distance. I got into conversation with the owner of a small
bistro one evening as I consumed the inevitable plate of steak,
frites, and a litre of *rouge*, and we talked about the future here.
He was optimistic, said his family had been in Philippeville for
three generations, and he didn't see why they should not remain
for another three. This is quite a sizeable town by provincial
standards and, as he says, the French built it over a period of a

hundred years so why the hell shouldn't they have the right to live in it. I think he's got a point but there are many who do not agree.

De Gaulle has been in Algeria recently and he has been broadcasting speeches which many here regard as treasonous as he outlines his reasons why the Muslims of Algeria should be given the opportunity of deciding their own future. He is desperately seeking a solution to this war, not for the sake of peace itself but because this endless fight is draining French coffers and, unless the outflow is stemmed, France will soon become an economic wreck. In 1958 when he returned to power in France, de Gaulle's words to the French colonials in Algeria were '*Je vous ai compris – Algérie française*'. It now seems as though he is changing his tune and is looking for a different solution which will give the country independence and yet somehow keep it tied to France.

But the Arabs are set on total independence, and the French *colons* are equally determined to retain all that they have here. The *colons* are extremists in every sense of the word; they do not understand compromise and they will go to extremes to keep what they believe to be theirs by birthright.

There have been riots during the last few days which have resulted in some two hundred people being killed. Because of this, we are now *en alerte*. At the beginning of January there is to be a referendum which will be held in France as well as Algeria. The referendum is understood to be de Gaulle asking for a free hand to negotiate with the F.L.N. for the establishment of the Algeria of tomorrow, which will be the first real step to independence, but perhaps on his own terms.

A few days ago a small group of Europeans attacked some Muslims in the Algiers suburb of Belcourt. The Muslims retaliated by running amok stabbing Europeans and setting fire to some of their shops. This started a chain reaction amongst the Muslims all over Algeria.

The French security troops have a delicate task in all this. There have been cases of troops firing on French European demonstrators and in fact two Europeans have been killed by French troops. The French troops could very easily squash the Muslims but they know, and so now do the Muslims (aye, there's the rub), that de Gaulle will not sanction the use of the methods that flattened the Casbah in the blood-bath of 1957. If the Legion is called in, this will be tantamount to such an approval and then God help the Muslims! So we wait like Napoleon's dogs in *Animal Farm*; and I think I differ from my fellow soldiers, for I hope we will remain chained, whereas they strain at their leashes like panting Dobermanns, desperate to be let loose amongst a Muslim crowd which they can tear apart with the fangs of their sub-machine-guns.

De Gaulle has not yet clearly shown his hand but there is a growing mistrust in him by the *colons* and with it a mounting opposition which will explode into something terrible if they believe he is about to sell them out.

De Gaulle's war may therefore eventually not be with the Arabs but with the French settlers here. What will be interesting to see is the French army's stand in all this. Will they support what they have been fighting for these last few years, or will they obey the command from home and bring the Europeans to heel?

19 December 1960

Things seem to have quietened down and we will be leaving for Medina in a couple of days. I am sorry that we are not spending Christmas in Philippeville. Despite its shortcomings, at least it is part of civilization and it is warm. Medina is neither. Medina must surely be the arsehole of the world.

PART FIVE

The Djebel

21 December 1960
We left Philippeville at three in the morning in heavy rain and a driving wind and both followed us south all day; down Route 3 through Constantine and on to Batna and then east along the desolate road to Medina. It looked as I remembered it, as bleak and cold as Dartmoor.

23 December 1960
The rain has not ceased since we got here and the endless passage of vehicles and tramping feet have turned the entire area into a quagmire. Our time has been spent searching for wood and collecting rocks and stones from old *mechtas* which we have sledge-hammered into gravel to form paths in the mud. It is now snowing hard, thank God, and there is some hope that the ground will be firm tomorrow. Nothing is worse than the mud – except perhaps the cold.

We have started preparations for Christmas. The Germans take their *Weihnachten* very seriously and tremendous effort and enterprise go into decorating the inside of all the tents. Each section builds its own little crèche and takes great pride in doing so. The celebrations take place tomorrow night and Christmas Day is apparently a day of recuperation. This will be my first of five Christmases – Christ, there is still a long way to go!

It is midnight. I have just finished two hours of guard duty. Outside it is freezing hard. The cold is like a surgeon's knife without anaesthetic. The bodies in the tent are silent in shallow sleep. This must be the loneliest place in the world.

Christmas Eve 1960
It is Christmas Eve and everything is set for a great feast. All the camp-beds have been stacked in the corner (thereby ensuring that no one will get any sleep tonight) and the long trestle-tables run the full length of each tent. These are adorned with multi-coloured Arab rugs and there is enough alcohol on the tables both in variety and quantity to drown a regiment. The crib looks well and the whole place is illuminated by a million candles. The atmosphere is certainly very Christmasy, or at least festive. Each man in our section of twenty-four has contributed two cases of beer to the drink pool and the N.C.O.s have each added another five. The company contributes an abundant supply of wine, cognac, Ricard and the like, and on top of this we will be on the end of the best eight-course meal that Pedro and his merry band of chefs can produce.

At seven o'clock the colonel will pass through each section of the regiment to wish everybody a *Bon Noël*, in return for which he will receive a rendering of '*Stille Nacht*' or some other suitable chant and then we will be into what promises to be the bun-fight of a lifetime.

Christmas Day 1960
It is not easy to describe last night. There was a moment after we had assembled in the main tent and received a Christmas present from Captain Willemin in the form of a track suit and a pullover when we sat down to supper. We sat at a magnificent table, laden with delicious food fit for kings. There were cold meats of every sort, roasted chickens, hams and legs of lamb, cakes with mountains of cream, fruits and cheeses like dripping Brie, salads, celery, liqueurs, chocolates and brandy, red wines, white wines, rosé and champagne, all in quantities that would feed five thousand times our number. Pedro had done an unbelievable job.

But that moment seems long since past. It was the beginning of a great evening but it became a nightmare. It seemed to be the aim of one and all to drink themselves into a stupor as fast as possible and very soon the whole place had degenerated into a sink of pigswill. This was not merriment, it was a disastrous chronic abuse of a festive occasion that could have been something quite magnificent. To have set the scene with which the evening started in these barren mountains was a tremendous achievement. So much effort had gone into it that it was a great sadness to see it ripped and torn to shreds. Drunkenness produces different characteristics in different personalities, from solemn slumber to screaming rage, and last night we had it all.

The food was hardly touched but the liquor was consumed in total. God knows where it all went. Soon there were bodies swaying everywhere and those that were not swaying were either unconscious on the floor or heaving their guts out into the snow outside. The noise was that of a crowd of Arsenal football fans gone mad; and then the fights started. Hirschfeld went berserk at some early hour of the morning and ran screaming after Grueber swearing his death. He would undoubtedly have killed him too if he had caught him, he's as strong as a horse. It took ten men to hold him down and even then he managed to break loose and go charging out into the night where Grueber had vanished.

At midnight a man in the 2nd Company ran amok into the night firing his sub-machine-gun into the heavens to welcome the coming of Christmas Day. He simultaneously ended the life of one of his fellows who caught a stray bullet in the side of the neck.

Fires were burning outside the tents and rockets were going off all the time. To me it was more like a Guy Fawkes night than Christmas. There was not the slightest air of moderation in anything, there was no control; it was like the release of pressure from a burst water-pipe of pent-up emotions.

The night staggered on through into the morning and in the early hours outside one could see figures moving around in the light of the fires. Some were single, moving slowly with an almost sinister air, tightly wrapped in heavy greatcoats and their thoughts against the freezing cold; others were in groups, singing and staggering like revellers returning from a night on the town. Somehow sad but maybe not sad. This was not the time to be morbid.

I drank all night non-stop but I remained cold sober. I was unable completely to partake. I was on the fringe of it all and glad to be so. I think I was slightly numbed by the whole thing; numbed by the cold, numbed by the stark harshness of this Christmas spirit so forced and so absolutely compulsory, as though an order had been issued that all would be drunk tonight. There was just no merriment in it. I gradually filled up to the top with raw spirit and I eventually subsided along with the other dead on to a packing case in the corner of the tent where I fell into a frozen slumber.

This morning was really the wakening of the dead. It was a scene of utter misery, with the hangover payments being made in full. The suffering was universal and nobody was spared. There were many braves, like Theo and Auriemma, who carried the festivities into Christmas Day without any let-up and showed no signs of intentions to slow up the liquor intake before New Year's Day. Tempers became very frayed at the edges as the day wore on and the cold knifed into our bones with a continuous ache that demands attention and will not allow the body to come to rest for a moment. It was a free day and we drifted through it, eating, pretending to drink and enjoy it, unable to sleep, longing for the morrow and the return to sanity and normality.

This then was my first Legion Christmas – not the merriest, but not through want of trying. Four of my friends sent me Christmas cards. Jesus, how far away everybody is from here!

Boxing Day 1960

Normal operations. It snowed heavily throughout the day and we trekked in the mountains until nightfall. Chauvin slipped and broke his arm and is now relaxing in hospital in Batna, lucky man. When we got back to camp we found the entire tent full of snow, one of the tent flaps had broken. Katzenberger came into the tent about an hour ago with our orders for tomorrow. There is still considerable unrest amongst the Muslims and more riots are anticipated at the time of the referendum on 8 January. Tomorrow we are leaving for Algiers. Our new role in life is to be guardians of the peace between the Europeans and the Arabs. This could be interesting!

27 December 1960
Early this morning under a dark and angry sky and heavily
falling snow, we packed light gear into the trucks and drove
north. We left the main *guitounes* behind with a group from
each company forming a rearguard.

We spent the day in the open trucks with a vicious wind
driving into our faces without relief. Snow covered everything
in the lorries and we were frozen absolutely solid. The only
movement we made during the day was to dismount from the
trucks to put chains on the wheels or to take them off again
when the going got better, which it did occasionally for short
periods. Never have I felt the cold as I did today, in spite of the
fact that I was wearing a long woollen vest, pullovers, a track
suit, combat uniform, and a lightweight greatcoat. In the early
evening we broke the journey and pitched our small tents. We
nourished ourselves on cold sardines and prepared for a filthy
night. I have developed a painful sinus which is causing the
right side of my face to throb incessantly, so I am not anticipating one of the great kips of my life tonight.

29 December 1960
Never in the history of time was there a wakening like that
which aroused us yesterday morning. Napoleon's retreat from
Moscow was like a summer stroll in Hyde Park compared to
the way we met this day.

At five in the morning, while the night was still as black as
pitch, rain started to pour from the heavens in bucket-loads so
that within fifteen minutes we were flooded. It rained for an
hour before the cold turned it into an avalanche of hail and then
finally into snow. Within no time at all we were in the thick of
a ferocious blizzard and five inches of snow covered the ground.
All this was happening in total blackness. There was not even
the glimmer of a sense of order at all. Total chaos reigned. Our
tents had collapsed and people lurched around trampling over
each other and over the gear. Everything was lost as we
floundered up to our knees in terrible mud. Our hands and
bodies were frozen to the bone so that they refused to function
and we endeavoured somehow to load our kit into the trucks.
People tripped over guy-ropes in the darkness and clothes and

blankets disappeared into the mud for ever, along with food and ammunition. The mud was everywhere, over everything, in our eyes and nostrils, in our ears and in our God-damned mouths. Tempers were lost along with everything else and the misery of it all was indescribable. And all the time the cold burned into our skin and numbed the brain so that at times total despair overcame one.

One would find oneself standing absolutely still beginning to seize up completely, and it was only someone crashing into you in the darkness or a voice bellowing in your ear that prevented you from just folding up into a ball and going back to sleep in the snow and the mud.

Eventually, mercifully, the first glow of daylight came seeping over the horizon and we were able to see. What an unholy sight it was! We got the trucks loaded and pushed them through the squelching mud on to the road again and by eight o'clock we were once more rolling north. It was the same as the preceding day, sitting huddled in the lorries freezing to death, changing the chains on the wheels every hour. My aching face and sinus was pushing my eye through the back of my head and the pain kept me suspended one millimetre from the brink of madness.

We pitched camp again in the evening – God knows where, I was too tired to notice. Our tents were useless and our sleeping-bags were sodden rags of liquid mud, so most of us just lay on the ground and draped our tents over ourselves and waited for the morrow and pneumonia.

All the next day we continued our journey north and then turned westward before we reached Algiers. Disappointment that we were not going to the great city that I had heard so much about but to which I had never been. We followed the coast road west and then turned south and in the mid-afternoon we arrived at Sidi-bel-Abbès, where it all began so long ago.

The whole town turned out to greet us. A guard of honour was on parade and the Legion band drummed out its great music as our trucks slowly wound their way through the crowded streets. A lot of familiar faces flashed by. There were shouts of greetings above the cheering as old friends recognized each other. Outstretched hands from the crowd found those extended from the trucks and clasped for a second in friendship but the lorries kept moving so everything was somehow just a blur and the faces that one recognized were a flashback in the mind. But with that flash of recognition came real pleasure as one suddenly saw a familiar face from *instruction* days. They threw beer and wine into our trucks and the continuous cheering and the blaring music made it all a carnival scene.

All too soon it was over and we were through our home town, the last strains of music had died away and the waving hands had faded into the distance. It was somehow very good and it left me with a warm feeling. It was brief but good – snatching a piece of the past – reliving a day in the sunshine – the feeling that one has friends fortifies the spirit like nothing else can. And then we were back on the road; this time north-west to Morocco. We came to rest outside the town of Tlemcen and camped in Nissen huts long since abandoned; but what a blessing to sleep under a roof. We were able to eat something warm at last and experience our first moments out of the wind in what seemed an age.

30 December 1960

At last the journey has ended and we are in a small military camp just outside Marnia. The companies are all spread out over a distance of about ten miles and we in the 3rd have fallen on our feet in this camp. It belongs to the regular marines who are absent in Algiers. The *quartier* is small and compact, amazingly comfortable by Legion standards, and we are delighted with it.

The Moroccan frontier is about three miles away and clearly we are here in case the hordes of fellagha sitting on the other side think the coming referendum heralds a return home to Algeria. This would be a mistake on their part and any premature activity by them along these lines would be rebuffed by our machine-guns.

New Year's Eve 1960

It is the end of the year, a year that I will not forget. A year I am happy to see the back of; my first year in the Legion; last February seems a long long time ago. It is the eve of the new year and we have nothing to drink, not a single beer – very different from Trafalgar Square and Piccadilly Circus.

1961

1 January 1961
Just before one o'clock this morning, Katzenberger came into
the barracks and roused us all out of bed. By a miracle, he had
managed to get hold of a case of beer (he must have gone to a
nearby regular army camp and begged or stolen it). What a
good man. He was determined to see that his section would not
leave 1960 on a thirsty note. He went round the section and
shook each of us by the hand and gave us each a couple of beers.
There was something very splendid and fine about it and I was
very touched by the whole thing.

I borrowed a transistor radio from Starry and picked up
London. They are one hour behind and I was just in time to hear
the New Year greeting from the B.B.C. – 'A happy New Year
to you all' came over the air in that wonderful familiar voice
that I had not heard in months and the nostalgic chimes of Big
Ben bonged in my ear as I stood by my bunk with the tiny radio
pressed against my head. And in between each stroke of the old
clock the voice that was all my friends at home continued its
message of goodwill, 'To those abroad away from their families,
to those in hospital . . .' and so on. It made me feel homesick
and very solemn, and while all the lads around me went berserk
with their two beers, I was in another world.

4 January 1961
The food is excellent, the beds are comfortable, there is running
water, we can have a shower at will, and there is even a cinema.
It's a Butlin's holiday camp compared to what we have been
accustomed to for so long. The weather is much warmer here

and today seems like the first in a long time that I have woken without a pile of snow on my bed.

Theobald, Decalewe and Corporal Wilke were caught playing poker at two o'clock this morning. They have paid for their crime with eight days' prison which will include two days of *la pelote* and of course they have been given *boule à zéro* haircuts to cool their minds.

We went on a short patrol along the frontier this morning. It's an amazing sight. The French have built a network of barrages of barbed wire and mines which run from the northern coast the full length of Algeria deep into Sahara in the south. On the other side of Algeria a similar barbed-wire barrier runs along the frontier with Tunisia. It is the old principle of the Maginot line and like the Maginot line, it is not impregnable. The Arabs frequently manage to break through by using bangalores. A bangalore is a long tube stuffed with explosives which is fed under the wire. When it explodes, it sets off any mines that happen to be in its way and it channels a path through the barbed wire. The boys then rush through and quickly disperse into the hills before any counter action can be taken. The name of the game is to anticipate where they will make their break and to let them do it and then ambush them as they come through.

On the other side of the barrage is no-man's-land which extends between the two frontiers over a width of about one mile. In this area both we and the Arabs patrol and set ambushes. It is subject among other things to periodic bombardment by artillery and mortar from both sides and is considered as a place in which it is unwise to hang about for longer than is strictly necessary.

Two enormous food parcels have arrived from Fortnum and Mason. Christmas cake, tinned fruit, cigarettes, and a dozen other things. It's like receiving a tuck parcel at prep school – fantastic, and it brings everybody so near. Algeria suddenly becomes civilized. We had a party in the section with all the goodies – lots of laughs. The lads in the section think I am some kind of eccentric millionaire and they cannot understand what I am doing here. I'm not sure that I can either. And then yet another parcel from Ian McCallum. What a good man – a hundred Turkish cigarettes and *Wit and Wisdom of Oscar*

Wilde. I wrote letters to them all and could not have enjoyed writing more. Fortnum and Mason in Marnia – the mind boggles!

8 January 1961

Today must mark the turning-point in the history of Algeria. This was the day on which the first real step towards peace was taken; a peace which must be synonymous with Algeria's independence. The result of the referendum was an overwhelming '*Oui*', which will give de Gaulle the power he needs to prepare the way for talks with the F.L.N. The Europeans seem to have accepted the result calmly enough, which is surprising and slightly sinister.

We were given the afternoon off and descended *en masse* on the little one-horse town of Marnia. It is some time since I have heard from J. and in a rash moment I blew six months' salary on a watch for her. I have left it with the man in the shop to send, which I now regret as it will probably never reach her.

Eight Days Later

Nobody seems to be quite sure what the next move will be. It is understood that talks will soon begin between the French and the F.L.N. Right now nobody is certain whether we should get back to the fighting, hand over our weapons and go home, or what. It is interesting to speculate on the next move and who will make it, the Arabs or the French. Perhaps it will be *les colons*.

During the last few days we have continued operations on the Moroccan frontier and we have seen no sign of the opposition.

We had a section of the S.A.S. troops working with us one day and very fine troops they are. These are Arab soldiers in the French regular army. They were incredibly thorough in the way they approached the bush when searching and they left not an inch of ground uncovered – good soldiers. God help them if the French let Algeria go and they wish to stay. They will probably have to go and live in France and do the chores for the French. I don't envy them – the French are not that great at showing gratitude – 1945!

26 January 1961

On 20 January we left our cosy little camp and drove east again to Sidi-bel-Abbès. It was sad to leave the regular-army camp that had been our base for these last two weeks. It has been good to come back to in the evening after a hard day's marching in the mountains. There is something very different about a brick building and a pathetic soggy tent, particularly when the rain is hosing down. Bricks and mortar represent permanence and stability; living in our tents and moving every three weeks is by contrast a restless, nomadic existence and is therefore tiring.

In bel-Abbès we installed ourselves in the barracks of Camp CP3, where I arrived one early morning in the dim and distant past. It all seems so long ago and under such different circumstances – then a rather frightened raw recruit, now an old hand, an *ancien* as they say here. In the Legion one becomes a veteran after the first two days!

We were given the good news that we were going to stay in bel-Abbès for a day or two and that first evening we fell on the town like a bunch of jackals. Great festivities. Suddenly we are very popular with the locals and there is a rush to buy us drinks. This is certainly something new. We are the symbol of their continued right to be in Algeria, or at least the insurance of it, they think. We do not think – we are not paid to think. I went to the Garden Bar, our old haunt from Sully days, and spent much of the evening talking to Patricia. There is a bond between us and I like the way the situation is developing but time is not on my side. If only I had two more days. She was all smiles and in terrific form but there is no bed there – yet.

Harry Stobbe and I travelled our old circuit. We went down all the old passageways and into all the old bars. Not much change on that front. On our last day we had a parade through the streets of bel-Abbès. As usual the whole town turned out to watch us. The pavements were packed with cheering faces and waving arms and the Legion band excelled itself. All very good for the ego.

I bumped into Lieutenant Rigolot just before we left. It was good to see him again. We could become good friends in other circumstances. Here the rules dictate that officers and men keep their distance. We talked of Sully days – he told me of the deaths of Krueger, the wild Hungarian, Klaus, and Dahms. These with Lefevre make four out of our little section at Sully after only three months. Can it be only three months since we were there? This is not a good average considering that I have another forty-eight months to go. Poor old Dahms. I liked him – I'll always remember him from the day Crepelli beat him up for nearly killing de Graaf when we were cleaning rifles at Mascara. And Klaus's sore feet will trouble him no more.

We left Sidi-bel-Abbès in the late afternoon of the same day. A detachment of officers saw us off at the gateway to the town as our column of trucks solemnly rumbled past and the Legion band played us out. Rigolot was one of the officers and our eyes met – salutes – mutual respect. And Patricia arrived, looking fantastic in an open red car, crying out my name, 'Johnny', above the clamour of the music and waving frantically. She drove behind my truck out of town. I was at the back and we looked at each other, a lifetime apart, seeing, feeling, but not even the touch of a finger – a fork in the road and she was gone. Time, the master, had won as always. Rigolot and Patricia were both people with whom I needed more time. God knows when I'll see them again. Patricia and I were two ships passing in the night. Nothing happened – the excitement is what might have happened.

We drove east through Mascara (more memories but no stops) and then on to Tiarret where we camped that night. And in the morning we turned south and headed towards Batna and the Aurès Mountains. The weather got steadily worse the further south we went and the temperature nosedived. We had a miserable cold night just outside Batna and then at dawn the following morning we were given orders for a 180-degree turn and raced north again to Philippeville. The weather was foul all the way. It chills the soul to watch Arab children walking through the mud with shoeless feet when we pass their little villages.

We arrived at Camp Pehaut in the evening. Home sweet home – *la merde*.

Three Days Later
We left Philippeville at dawn yesterday and drove westwards in
the direction of Collo. By 7 a.m. we were out of the trucks
and combing the hills. This is mountainous country. The physical relief is totally different from the dryness of the Aurès
Mountains in the south. Here it is almost tropical by comparison and the thick matted undergrowth is evidence of the rainfall
which never ceases. We flogged through the undergrowth all
day and covered about twenty miles, hacking away with our
coupe-coupe. Slow progress – sweat and fast-flowing mountain
streams kept us permanently soaked from head to foot. We live
and breathe 100 per cent humidity. Maybe it is the balance that
keeps us going, being dehydrated by sweating and at the same
time replenished by the perpetual immersion in moisture.

In the evening, soaked to saturation, faces and arms scratched
to hell and clothes in shreds as Nature's mark of disapproval at
our disturbance of the undergrowth, we learned that the lorries
had been unable to make the rendezvous because the rain had
washed away the road. Exhausted to a man, we marched another fifteen miles back to camp – what a life.

And this morning we were on parade again at five o'clock,
having had little sleep as the endless rain had sorely tested our
tents and found them wanting. We had been obliged under the
circumstances to spend half the night digging drains around the
tents to prevent flooding. As we stood on parade this morning
in the dark, the rain just hosed on us and the bloody N.C.O.s
kept us waiting fifteen minutes while they finished their coffee.
Inexcusable.

10 February 1961
Demar was right about the marching. Every day we rise at dawn
and then begin our wanderings. There is never any rest, there is
no respite from the routine of the effort, of the bent backs and
the sweat. And even at night we are restless, prowling the hills
constantly prodding the invisible enemy waiting for him to
make the slightest mistake.

One evening we left camp just after midnight and had a
nightmare journey across twenty miles of this rugged country.
The ceaseless rain and the wind had brought down many trees

over which we stumbled in the darkness. We crossed rushing rivers and scrambled on hands and knees up slippery banks. Visibility was nil and the sound of heavy breathing from the man in front was the lantern through the night. Many fell and were made to continue by force and even threats of being left behind. Caulier collapsed after the first five miles which we covered in just over an hour.

We arrived somewhere in the early dawn and took up positions as the guns. Our friends in the 2nd Company worked the daylight shift and sought to drive the birds our way. None came by and in the late afternoon, with daylight fortunately still in the skies, we wandered home the way we had come, with empty nets, empty stomachs and empty souls, wondering just what the hell this was all about.

On another day we mounted an operation on a grand scale, involving about 30,000 troops. By using helicopters effectively we can put hundreds of men in a tight circle on the mountain tops covering an enormous area. Rabbits caught inside this circle are in for a bad time and a series of pincer movements must eventually flush them out unless they are clever enough to slip through the net at night. They often are! These large-scale operations usually follow reports from reconnaissance aircraft of movements of fellagha troops at a particular point, and the speed at which the operation is put together determines its success.

On this particular day the *alerte* went up mid-morning and within minutes the sky was black with the shadows of the enormous banana-shaped helicopters hovering over us. We were whisked to the hilltops and when we landed the place was abuzz with choppers spewing men out all over the mountain side. Tremendous excitement as we all rushed about in little groups, taking cover here there and everywhere as the action was about to start. We searched the valleys, we turned every stone and shook every bush and tree, but there was not a sign of them. Where the fuck are they, these guys? A three-hour forced march brought us back to camp with aching limbs and broken backs where sacks had strained against the shoulder muscles and the spine had been the fulcrum of a ton of munition, food, water-bottles, grenades, shovels, radios, and a host of other useless garbage. And all for what?

And on return to camp, a letter from J. She's engaged. Long silence shattered by realization of total loss – and yet somehow I knew it was coming. The pain of a limb being removed – I know now how it feels – the weight of tremendous pressure on the breast increased a hundred times. How far away I am in time and distance from all that is normal. I wonder if it's changing me.

A Week Later

When we awoke this morning Demar was gone – completely disappeared without trace. All his kit was still beside his bed. Somebody saw him leave the tent at about 5.30 a.m., presumably going out for a pee, but he didn't return. The latrines are about a hundred yards from the camp and the general opinion is that he could have been snatched by an Arab patrol. Desertion seems unlikely, particularly as he left his cigarettes behind – serious smokers don't like to be without their weeds. Also, he was in good form yesterday, which is something unusual for Demar. But he's a loner and it would take a great mind-reader to see what is behind that cold inscrutable face.

Tonight we are going on another of our marches, at the end of which we are supposed to surprise the boys and shoot them up just as they are preparing their morning coffee – but it never happens.

23 February 1961

We have been sitting in the bushes for three days just above a small crossroads of mountain paths. During the three days none of us has moved except to crawl into the bushes for a pee or whatever as Nature dictates. The nights are cold and damp and we awake in the dirty grey of the morning with stiff limbs and iced blood in our veins. I am running out of cigarettes. Fresh rations arrived this morning and were distributed to us in the bushes – coffee, beer and oranges. Very welcome, good organization for a change.

The circle of our troops is getting tighter around the valley and the constant firing of shots at night keeps the Arabs on the move. Sooner or later they will fall into one of our ambushes. Night falls and we stay put.

The Next Day
Darkness has come again and we prepare ourselves mentally
for the fourth night in the bushes. We have shared the last
cigarette. A system of sentries has been set up to enable some of
us to get some sleep. One man sits at the actual junction of the
two *pistes* and he is relieved every two hours. There is a *chef de
guard* who organizes the relief and apart from these two, the
rest of us can kip. This will make the night hours more relaxing.

I have just learned that I am on guard from 11 p.m. until
1 a.m. – tonight!

25 February 1961
The trap is sprung. I was sitting at the crossroads behind a rock,
quiet and relaxed, just after midnight, when suddenly in the
stillness of the night I heard the unmistakable sound of metal
on stone. It came from the path which climbed up the mountain
through dense bush on my left. And then I began to pick up the
sound of people moving stealthily down the path.

They were coming towards me. The beginnings of panic set
in – I thought my breathing was far too heavy and I put my
handkerchief in my mouth. Visibility was nil and anyway I
could not see up the path without considerable movement
because of the rock behind which I had positioned myself.

They came gradually closer, moving incredibly slowly. I
hoped to Christ they weren't going to circle round behind me
and shoot me in the back. It sounded as though there were
about five in the party and as I gently cocked my sub-machine-
gun, I began to feel shaky but resolved. When you are about to
shoot five people coming around the corner you tend to sweat a
little, whoever you may be. The thought of your gun jamming is
too horrible to dwell on, and the thought of not killing them all
before your magazine is empty brings on an unendurable thirst.
The only compensation is the fact that it is dark and you will
be aiming at their backs. The form is to let them go past you
and then give it to them from behind. To shoot them from the
front is unnecessarily sporting and could lead to a charge being
laid against you for attempted suicide.

They must have been about twenty yards up the path from
me when Pudoll appeared next to me. He was the *chef de guard*

and doing his rounds. He was not a guy for whom I had very much time in normal circumstances, but right now I welcomed any company. He got the message in a flash and had probably heard the Arabs moving around himself. He was armed only with a pistol and he leaned across in the darkness and took my automatic and at the same time tapped my grenades.

So he was going to use the gun and I was going to throw the grenades. I had four and Pudoll handed me two more. I would like to have aroused the rest of the section, but any movement by us would have alerted the Arabs and they would have been gone in a second. There was nothing to do but wait.

Slowly, agonizingly slowly, they came down the path, pausing sometimes for a full five minutes. It only needed one sleeping legionnaire to cough or snore and they would have flown. They know every crease in the valley and every bush. Their movements were fantastic and I found myself doubting whether I had heard them at all. But little sounds make big noises at night and the whisper of a leaf told of their approach.

I could feel them now on the other side of the rock, not ten yards away, and I had held my breath for the last ten minutes. Pudoll touched my arm in an energetic gesture and I pulled the pin. They heard the fizz and turned in a frantic scramble back the way they had come.

My first grenade was already in the air above the rock and the pin of the second already out. Pudoll waited for the blast, stepped out from behind the rock, and poured lead up the valley into the night and the backs of the fleeing Arabs. The second grenade followed the first a moment later and Pudoll, now flat on his stomach, continued firing.

By this time everybody in the camp was wrenched into life and voices were yelling, and with the gunfire and grenades shattering the eardrums the whole place was in complete pandemonium. I threw one more grenade as far and long as I could up the path and then Pudoll frantically screamed at me to stop as he went careering up the path in hot pursuit. I went after him but I was unarmed and there wasn't much that I could do. He was just ahead of me and I heard him stop and fire a burst – very close – a man died. He yelled at me to get the gun and ran on. I hoped he was thinking about his ammunition as he had only taken two of my magazines from me and the way he was using the gun he was soon going to be running short of bullets.

It was in the end all over quite swiftly. People were milling around and torches had come into play so that it looked like some sort of funeral procession. Everybody seemed to have been involved and people further up the path were still firing some time afterwards. This can become quite dangerous. It was ages before anybody was really able to throw light on what had actually happened. Two Arabs were dead and a third was found later some distance away. If there had been others, they had disappeared and no trace was to be found. The trap had finally shut.

We returned to Philippeville leaving behind dead Arabs unburied, some memories, and the ghost of Demar. The *foyer* was packed to capacity tonight as it always is when the regiment returns. We sang until our throats were raw and we drank beer until it was coming out of our ears.

27 February 1961
It was *quartier libre* and I went into town, crawled around the bars and *bordels*, and crawled home – not a wiser man!

28 February 1961
Grueber reported that he had lost his *sac marin* full of kit, claiming that it had been stolen. Much more likely that he's sold it and this is just to cover his arse. The entire company as a result was subjected to the most intensive kit inspection of all time. We spread every single item we had on the parade-ground and a sergeant called from a checklist for everything we had ever been issued with from toothbrush upwards. Missing articles were listed and each man will automatically be debited for the replacement. The review lasted four and a half hours – Grueber's kit was not found – but several people with more gear than they had originally been issued with had to surrender it to those in want. The balance was restored slightly.

Letter from Jennifer telling me all about her new fiancé – Guards officer – very pukka! She's going to feel terrible when she receives the watch I sent her – I hope she squirms!

2 March 1961
I was on patrol duty this evening in Philippeville and there occurred a remarkable incident. I was sitting outside one of the *bordels* on a truck – the sergeant, head of the patrol, was inside having a few drinks, when somebody came out and told me there was an English civilian inside – an event unheard of.

I got the somebody to go in and drag the Englishman out, which he did, and thus I met Martin Fisher.

Fisher, with little persuasion, went back inside and got a couple of litres of red and we sat on the back of the truck and compared notes. He is a radio officer on a Greek ship that is in the harbour for a day or two. I asked him why he was on a Greek ship and was given the explanation that in the Merchant Navy one is not restricted to any national carrier and it is quite often the case that seamen work on multinational lines depending on where opportunities arise for their particular specialities and how the money is. I told him that I had once been in the Merchant Navy and had worked my way to South America on a tramp steamer. He asked me what shipping line and I said, 'The South American Saint Line', and he said, 'My God, it wasn't the *Saint Arvans*, was it?'

I said, 'Yes it was, how the hell did you know that?'

And then the incredible coincidence. He said, 'Because I went on the *Saint Arvans* too – and I was also the galley boy – it was the first ship I ever sailed on.'

He had sailed the year before me. So here were two ex galley boys from the *Saint Arvans*, a dirty little insignificant tramp steamer, sitting on the back of a truck outside a brothel in a nondescript unknown North African town – and surely not another Englishman within miles. If that doesn't prove the world is round then I don't know what does.

Nine Days Later
We are leaving for Batna tomorrow – the lorries are loaded and ready. The barracks are now completely bare save for the steel bunks and the straw mattresses. It's rather like the end of term at school but without thoughts of holidays. It's always sad leaving Philippeville, for although there is nothing particularly attractive here, it is at least civilization – shops, civilians, bricks

and mortar instead of tents, cars instead of mules, and so on. The sea helps somewhat to make this place human. In normal circumstances the beaches here would be a miracle – miles and miles of white sand. Great place for a holiday – maybe one day in twenty years' time.

16 March 1961

We drove south all day and camped just south of Biskra. The mountain tops are still snow covered. When the sun has dropped there is the familiar sight of fires glowing in the evening dark, around which the shadowy figures sit hunched over the mugs of hot soup with eyes focused on tins of beans still sitting in the flames cooking. Stomachs rumble in approval.

This morning we were up at dawn and drove further south for about four hours into the sector of Rhoufi. This is the country of the dead – barren mountains, red-brown in colour, dust-covered and pockmarked with wispy scrub. No tree could survive here – there is a mass of boulder clay and rocks all over the land. This is a wilderness of ghastly dryness – the mere sight of this land is thirst-making – tempered in the early morning by an icy wind, but when the sun gets up it is a different story.

The lorries eventually stopped and we piled out above the most magnificent gorge – practically a crevasse as though someone had taken an enormous knife and gashed the plain. This is Rhoufi. The gorge of Rhoufi is a complete wonder. The sides are sheer and rounded – the river below flows in an enormous crescent, so the walls are like the interior of the Coliseum.

A path three feet wide clings to the side of the gorge and we followed it down towards the river. Far below one could see small square-shaped Arab dwellings on the river bank, built close against the rock face – caves had been hewn out of the rock and were used as stables for the donkeys. Some of the little houses halfway down, built snugly against the gorge walls, had their front door on the path, three feet from a straight plunge of a hundred feet to wet death. Dusty Arabs sat outside their doors like sheep and watched us with expressionless eyes. Their wives sat apart in batches and rows as they always do when we come, looking like crows perched on a branch in their black garbs of rag.

We descended to the bottom of this incredible gorge, crossed the river and climbed up the other side. In front of us was a mountain range of barren rock and sand stretching up to the sky and up we went.

Hour after hour we plodded on and the sun came up in a vicious blaze of heat burning down on our heads and backs and its reflection from the hard ground blasted our faces. Many fell out and turning at one point I could see stragglers way behind, Caulier at the rear. L'Hospitallier kept going like a dynamo in front, marching as ever at a spanking pace. Every time we reached a summit it was only to see another appear from nowhere looming over us. Behind and below we could see the ocean of hills stretching to the horizon – the gorge of Rhoufi looked like a hairline against the flat plain way below us.

At about 4.30 in the afternoon the 2nd Company some two miles to the west came under attack from fellagha well entrenched in caves at the top of one of the million hills. The 3rd and the 4th Companies, flanking the 2nd on either side, moved inwards as a pincer and leaned our fire power on the caves – it was a day for the light machine-guns and the mortars – the *voltigeurs* with their sub-machine-pistols watched and waited to move in for the kill. In fact it was the 2nd Company that gradually moved closer in while we offered cover fire. Five Arabs surrendered, emerging with hands high, fifteen are dead, and we have a good collection of machine-pistols, Brens, and even two Thompsons. There seems to be an abundance of British weapons in the Arab armoury, believed to be left-overs from Suez five years ago when the French and British made their bid for the Canal – alas too brief – and Eden withdrew! The 4th Company lost three legionnaires and the 2nd two legionnaires and two N.C.O.s – several wounded. Our day to be lucky – not a scratch. It was over by seven in the evening.

In view of the march in front of us when we started out this morning and assuming it was going to be a jaunt up and down the same day, we had left our packs containing food and sleeping gear at the bottom under guard. It was now too late to wander down before nightfall (a night march down would almost certainly be very hazardous not only because of the terrain but because of possible ambush by the fell) so we prepared for a night on the hill. Most of us had finished our water and we were dying of thirst, ravenous with hunger and beginning to feel the cold. Eventually helicopters arrived supposedly bringing our *sacs* but unfortunately there was a balls-up: they brought the *sacs* from another company and so promptly flew off again to deliver the goods to the proper destination.

Darkness came swiftly and we faced a freezing night on the mountain top, and worse no food and water. Around us there were patches of snow nestling out of the sun's rays, which helped solve the water problem but little else. At around eleven o'clock the 2nd Company, even more tired than we, if that is possible, moved to our assistance. They shared their meagre rations and it was one *toile de tente* draped over two people – a pathetic barrier against the cold. It was a night of little sleep. Lashed by the wind, we all lay huddled up sharing the warmth of each other's bodies and pleased to shiver for the added warmth generated from the movement of blood in frozen veins.

Grey drawn faces and sunken eyes met the dawn and for once we looked forward to the first rays of the sun.

We came slowly down, searching every shrub and the many caves as we did so. It was a laborious descent and took us seven hours. Our feet were bloody by the end of it and the miserable faces around me, dried and cracked from the wind, told their story. We found a cache with clothes, shoes and food but no other rewards for our efforts. It was good to be down at last and to get to our *sacs* and the food we should have had the previous day.

We are camped for the night on the flat plain overlooking the gorge of Rhoufi, very tired men – I have two hours' guard starting at midnight.

29 March 1961
We stayed where we were *en alerte* throughout the next day and our bodies yielded the last drops of moisture to the sun. There was not a branch or a leaf of shade. There are signs of over-fatigue among the men and infection of one sort or another, particularly boils, is common. This is the result of malnutrition – too long on tinned sardines and canned cheese – too long in the same stinking clothes, too long without soap and water on our bodies which absorb dried sweat and grime for weeks on

end. By the evening of that day I was sweating buckets from fever and the night was freezing.

The next day we returned to our new advanced base camp just outside Batna. The tents were up when we arrived but we had hardly unpacked our gear when we were ordered to take them down again. There was a general change in plan and we were to return to Philippeville at first light the following day.

We did, and it was for the purpose of a parade for a five-star general. He arrived three hours late, during which time we were kept standing on the parade-ground while a pathetic band from the regular army played 'Colonel Bogey' over and over again in a desperate bid to keep us and themselves awake. The General had been gone scarcely five minutes when we started preparing to go south again. And at three the next morning, dark and miserable, we set off back to God-damned Batna. We stopped just before the village of Mac-Mahon and in torrential rain we made camp working until midnight. Metal poles, huge canvasses, thousands of tent pegs and ropes, fingers and thumbs and all the while the rain pouring down our damn necks and everything flooded.

The day following was my twenty-first birthday and I spent it digging latrines and drains in a blizzard. In the evening they opened a small *foyer* tent but everybody was broke. Hirschfeld found a few francs and insisted on buying me a couple of beers to celebrate my birthday and then out of the blue I received a telegram. Somehow it had got through the network of barriers that hamper the complicated communication system of the Legion. It was from my old chums, the Deerstalkers. The Deerstalkers was a club I had formed at school and was the union of nine good men and true. We had arranged to meet once a year for a dinner. One thing was certain, I wasn't going to make it this year. Anyway here was their cable pitched into the desert from the other side of the world. Fantastic effort, fantastic memory, fantastic people. To be remembered by friends in a God-forsaken spot in the Aurès Mountains is really something.

This morning we arrived at first light at an Arab *douar*, through which we went like hungry barracuda. All of the villagers were rounded up, searched and questioned. Those without identity cards were taken away for more detailed interrogation. In the *mechtas* we searched every cranny, using knives to pick at the walls, looking for secret hiding-places. This is the place where the Arabs often put their guns and knives. All this is done with caution as it is not uncommon to find a *mechta* booby-trapped.

We found nothing of interest and were lifted out by helicopters to another terrain where the 4th Company had found caves. Volunteers were called for to go down into these caves and as an experienced potholer I thought I should volunteer, but by the time I got to the head of the line three men were already down and I was kept in reserve. It turned out that there was nothing inside – much ado about nothing! A general from the regular army was in the sector and arrived in a helicopter. He congratulated the three volunteers for going into the caves and cited all three on the spot for the Croix de Valeur Militaire – rather a pity I wasn't a bit quicker – or perhaps that the General wasn't around when I was doing my stuff at Chélia.

We returned to camp this evening – we are grateful for our sleeping-bags tonight. Nobody who has been there will forget the cold at night in the Aurès Mountains. When the sun dips below the mountain tops the temperature drops like a stone and the men with fever start to shake.

31 March 1961
There was a Communion service in one of the tents today which is something rare indeed and I went along. It was a good service – a splendid priest, full of enthusiasm. There's something very rewarding in watching a priest give an address and run a service for six people as though he were doing it for five hundred.

2 April 1961
Easter Sunday – and what an Easter. It started like just another ordinary bloody day. Up at 4 a.m. and into the hills. We had covered fifteen miles by lunchtime. It seemed as though this was to be the end and we finished off our water while we waited for the trucks – they never came. Suddenly excited shouts to prepare ourselves for *héliportage*. We rapidly formed small groups and waited for the helicopters. Apparently a company of French regular paratroopers, '*bérets rouges*', had been ambushed in a gorge some distance away. Within minutes the sky was buzzing with helicopters and we were whisked to the scene of the

action. At first we were held back in reserve just behind the
gorge where it was all happening. We could hear the machine-
guns in the valley on the other side. The noise was deafening.

We were advised to finish what grub we had as it would be
some time before we would pause again. Greco from the 4th
Section and myself were sitting on a small hillock eating a tin of
sardines from where we could see our 2nd Company frantically
trying to bail out the regulars, dead and wounded, from the
trap in which they were enmeshed. One side of the gorge was a
vertical rock face covered with caves and faults and somewhere
in this the fellagha were sitting showering a vicious crossfire on
to the other side of the gorge where the 2nd Company were
placed and simultaneously they were raining bullets on the boys
trapped in the bottom of the gorge.

Suddenly Greco and I were blasted by a machine-gun burst
– bullets everywhere and dust flying up all around us – no hits
and we frantically tried to bury ourselves in the ground lying
flat behind a blade of grass. The bullets stopped coming for a
second and we literally threw ourselves back down the hill to
the safety of the valley behind us. That was very close indeed
and very exciting. As Churchill once said, 'There's nothing
quite so exhilarating in life as to be shot at without result.'
Minutes later we were up and over again, this time with caution,
and we deployed ourselves along the crest of a hill from which
we had a commanding view of the situation. We passed some
regulars on the way, looking bedraggled and tired as they licked
their wounds thankful to be out of the line of fire. We asked for
water as we passed since most of us were dry, but they were not
letting go. That's gratitude for you!

Once in position we ranged in on the Arab side of the gorge
and fired our guns until our fingers ached. Difficult to pinpoint
where they were because of all the smoke so the firing was
chancy at best. We received it back as soon as they became
aware of our presence and their machine-guns were deadly – the
4th Section were caught on the top moving over open ground
and lost seven men to the Arab machine-guns in as many
seconds. Cries of agony from some of the wounded – medics
rushing madly to assist – morphine and dressings being applied.
Noise everywhere – continuous machine-gun fire, shouting of
orders, screams from the wounded.

We shot it out with the fell all afternoon – rifle barrels boiling and Sten guns sizzling. Two dive-bombers came to our assistance and hammered the gorge with rockets and napalm, all to no avail – the Arabs never stopped firing. Choppers circled overhead and ceaselessly machine-gunned the Arab positions without apparent success. The Arab side of the gorge became a flaming hell and it was incredible that they could continue to live in it. But they did, and defiantly responded to every bomb with a blast of machine-gun fire.

Night came and the firing never ceased – Nord planes flew over dropping flares to keep the arena lighted and the battle went on into the night. We were dead tired from the previous day's marching, thirsty as hell and ready to eat grass from hunger – but the Arabs must have been feeling it too.

We had the gorge completely surrounded and just before midnight we all received fresh ammunition brought in by helicopters – no food, of course, just bullets. Firing died down at three in the morning but not before a helicopter had crashed into the flaming gorge – either the pilot had been hit or the air current from the roasting gorge had somehow created an air vacuum. The planes kept flying non-stop all night dropping flares and we stayed in our foxholes and watched. The fellagha would have to move during the night or face certain death in the morning, and we strained our eyes in the dim lights of the flares for signs of movement.

Morning came creeping through with agonizing slowness. I had slept some moments, alternating with Caulier, whom I suspected of winding his watch forward (I didn't have one) when it was his turn to keep watch.

We began to ease forward slowly with caution but there was no shooting and when we arrived on the other side of the valley among the rocks we found four rifles and seven dead fell. One had lost his entire face (probably burnt by napalm) and his whole head was one black throbbing mass of flies feeding on the open oozing sun-blackened flesh. The rest had flown. It appeared that they had escaped along a narrow corniche in the gorge, which we had been unable to see from our side. We had seventeen dead and forty-six wounded. Most of the wounded had been hit while attempting to bring out the regulars – the same regulars who refused us water and cigarettes the night before.

It was a day for the fellagha and an unforgettable day and night for us. Happy Easter! Towards midday helicopters arrived, this time laden with food – even painted eggs! We gorged ourselves and then spent a long afternoon patrolling the area for signs of the boys – nothing.

In the early evening we began the long march back to the spot where it had all started yesterday and where we had intended picking up the lorries. Caulier collapsed from exhaustion on the march and has been put on full *corvée* and night guard for his pains for two weeks. At last I think I've got this marching routine sewn up. I find it much easier, or rather no worse than the others now.

We arrived back at Mac-Mahon and a warm and welcome soup in the evening. Letter from Allister – good news – and a cheery card from Christy.

I have got a very sinister rash right across my stomach and down my leg – it looks like a thousand blisters – Starry is quite concerned about it, obviously does not know what it is, and I am to report '*consultant*' tomorrow.

4 April 1961

I went to the infirmary and was inspected by the '*médecin-chef*', a young captain who announced a diagnosis of *zona anormal*, whatever that is, and he consigned me to the infirmary. Here I received a series of injections – antibiotics, penicillin, etc. – and multicoloured tablets galore and the blisters have been painted with gentian violet. By lunchtime I had a temperature of 103 degrees and the rash was itching to blazes. More tablets and injections.

The chap in the next bed to mine has got malaria and when he is on a cold spell he goes under a heap of blankets out of sight and has great shivering spasms accompanied by terrible groans. Poor lad.

Ten Days Later

I spent ten days in the infirmary, most of the time swallowing aureomycin tablets in enormous quantities and being given two injections a day of emetine and strychnine. The days were long and boring for the most part until I started to get well and then I was able to catch up on my reading. Anski sent me a library of books and I feasted on Hemingway, Steinbeck, Waugh, Lawrence Durrell, John Masters and others. Never have I had such a concentrated diet of reading, but then I don't recall being ill before either.

I returned to the company the day before yesterday and felt like a rag I was so weak. It was impossible to stop sweating with every tiny exertion I made and I fear that I am still far from my normal self.

Today I was back on operations. We spent last night in the trucks on the road and this morning we stopped and camped just to the south of Philippeville. We had hardly finished putting up the tents before we set off again in the lorries into the hills. When the trucks came to a halt, I was feeling so ill I didn't have enough strength to get my sack off the back of the truck. We started on the march and Sergeant Papke had to pull me up the first hill. All through the day I felt absolutely ghastly, my legs were like water and I was running a high fever into the bargain. Papke was fantastic. He pulled me up the hills for hour after hour. His only complaint was against the medics who had let me out of the hospital far too early and in a condition that was ten times worse than that in which I had been when I went in. It was a long, long day without any let-up at all and some time in the late afternoon my head started to go round and round in circles and everything went blank. When I woke up, I was on my back and Baudouin, the company medic, was pumping a needle into my arm. L'Hospitallier was furious about the whole thing and said I shouldn't have been marching for at least another week after having passed twelve days in the infirmary being stuffed full of antibiotics.

I am now in a condition which is known as '*fatigue générale*' and the only cure is some local leave. Papke mentioned the possibility this evening and so, whilst I feel completely dead and thoroughly miserable, there is a tiny spark of hope that something good may come out of all this. A little bit of leave is something I could really use. Meanwhile we are on the top of this mountain and tomorrow the operation goes on, so it promises to be a day as agonizing as the one which I have just managed to survive today.

PART SIX

Treason

22 April 1961

Six days have passed in the bush. I feel slightly better. They have been days of routine operations and then suddenly today there has been a change in events and there is complete confusion.

The morning began as any other when we returned to Philippeville and unloaded the trucks in the usual way. Then we received a counter-order to load again and prepare for departure. The orders were then changed again and again and by noon it was obvious that unusual happenings were near at hand. Whispers of a *coup* against de Gaulle were heard and some said he had been assassinated. And then this evening some facts. It appears that the 1st Legion Para Regiment has taken over Algiers and occupied all the key government offices and annexed the radio. Announcements over the radio declare '*Algérie française*' and state in triumphant tones that the army in North Africa will resist de Gaulle's attempts to give independence to this country. This *putsch* is apparently led by a group of army generals headed by Maurice Challe, with Salan very much behind it, aided by Generals Gardy (one-time Inspector-General of the Legion), Zeller and Jouhaud. The operation is spearheaded by the 1st Legion Para Regiment under the command of Major Saint-Marc in the absence of Colonel Giraud, who is on leave in France. Various regular

paratroop regiments are involved and also the 1st and 2nd
Legion Cavalry Regiments. Our position seems unclear and
presumably Damusez, our C.O., is watching events before
deciding which way to spring.

The French radio meanwhile declares in solemn tones that
the military action here is criminal and treasonous.

By late evening the atmosphere was wild but we waited. The
prospect of being involved in a *putsch*, a *coup d'état*, a civil war
almost, has a certain fascination to say the least and is hardly
an everyday occurrence. Apparently there is a possibility
that we might be dropped on France. Excruciating thought
to be dropped on Paris – everybody is going out of their
minds with the excitement but still we don't know which
way the cat Damusez will jump. He is immensely unpopular
with his men and with his officers too. By comparison, the
second in command, Gabirot, is adored. For some time now
there have been rumblings against de Gaulle's avowed policy to
hand over to the Algerians. This represents a clear double-cross
and a sell-out to the army and the *pieds noirs* here in North
Africa, de Gaulle having previously so firmly supported the
efforts to put down the rebels.

And now it has come to this. De Gaulle's voice orders the
army back into line as it thunders over the French radio – and
we wait for orders, sitting on the fence. Sunday approaches – it
looks like a long weekend.

The Next Day
In the middle of the night we were aroused and ordered to
collect our equipment and board the trucks. In a long column
the regiment drove due west towards Algiers, three hundred
miles away. Gabirot was in command and apparently Damusez
was still abed when we left. We had none of us slept a wink, and
each man was buried well into his greatcoat and *foulard* and his
own private thoughts – thoughts of Paris, Maxim's, imagine
landing with a parachute on the Arc de Triomphe or even on
the Tour Eiffel (not so good) – imagine the reaction to all this
in England. Friends at home would be wondering precisely
where I was in all the chaos and what I was doing – they would
never feel the reality of sitting on the back of a truck in the
middle of the night huddled against the night wind.

Dawn came slowly through, cold and slate grey – and then suddenly it was day and sun. Thousands and thousands of Europeans lined the roads madly cheering us through. Car horns hooted and hooted – three short blasts and two long (*Al-gé-rie franç-caise*) – again and again. Teeming crowds of wild faces laughing and yelling, pushing and shoving in a great heaving morass of bodies. Our trucks were barges floating in a sea of faces and waving arms. They loved us, they raved for us. They have never shown this emotion before and I suspect its depth is not substantial, but we must seem to them to be their saviours. They believe we are between them and the terrible will of the great awe-inspiring monster, de Gaulle. So many people – every town, large and small, produced its European population in total for us. The entrance of the Allies into Paris at the end of the war could not have received a more enthusiastic welcome.

In all this there is one amazing, incomprehensible fact. One question has not yet been answered at all clearly and that is, which side are we really on?

We crawled through the outskirts of Algiers in the late evening and occupied barracks of French regulars who appear to have temporarily disappeared – still unbelievably no attempt at explanation by an officer. This credits us with nil intelligence. They assume we will just obey orders as we have always done; so we remain at the mercy of rumour based on snatches of information from transistor radios. Nobody has yet officially told us whether we are for de Gaulle or against him, or indeed that there is a *coup* at all. In this our officers are grievously at fault.

The Following Day

First thing this morning we drove to the airport and our role became immediately clear. We were to occupy the airport, which was held by French marines, and they weren't having any of it. So we were given wooden batons, heavy, with sharp points, and in one long line we slowly eased into the marines, pushing them forward like bolshie rams. They frequently turned and attacked with aggression. This was met in many cases with savage beatings and it became a sad and shoddy business. Marine officers were pushed around by our officers –

there were scenes of officers yelling at each other with questions of loyalty and accusations of traitor and so on. L'Hospitallier bust his baton on the head of one of the marines. Gradually they were herded out of the airport premises and we were in control of the base from which we will apparently make the drop on Paris.

The evening has come. A kind of stalemate appears to have been reached. De Gaulle has brought up tanks in France and threatened to shoot parachutists out of the air if a drop is made. This has dampened some of yesterday's thoughts of dancing in Paris and put prospects of dinner at Maxim's tomorrow night slightly further away.

The army is completely divided and we appear to be very much a minority. Surprisingly enough in spite of this minority, Challe with eight regiments appears to have control at the moment in Algeria. That means a lot of people are on the fence. The question is, what next? The total armed forces in Algeria are probably 150,000 – the Legion numbers 30,000. What is also surprising is that only a very small part of the Legion seems to be involved. We are not clear whether those who are not with us are against or surplus to requirement or what. The French forces in France itself must be fairly limited, so a united military front from this side would succeed. The next step that Challe will take must surely be a move on France if the objective is the removal of de Gaulle and all that he stands for. The alternative is stalemate and in this case Challe may be able to keep what he has – if, and only if, the other 120,000 troops around him throw in their lot with him. If they do not, then this operation is not going to be remembered for its long duration. We could of course have a siege.

Night has come and we are sleeping in the hangars – talk, talk, but no news that is firm or indicative of what is happening. Maybe Challe and Salan, who has now arrived from Spain, are bargaining or frantically trying to persuade the as yet uncommitted to join them. I wonder what will happen if this *putsch* does not succeed and what our own position will be – perhaps we'll be disbanded and all sent home. Nice thought to sleep on!

25 April 1961

The impetus of the *coup* seems to have petered out. No move forward must mean obstacles and opposition. *Coups d'état* are actions of speed if there is to be success. No word from authority – signs of bewilderment are apparent – planes tried to land today but were prevented from doing so by our tanks – but where are the planes to mobilize us? The air force in Africa under the command of Jouhaud must be an essential ingredient of Challe's plan, otherwise why use paratroops, and yet no sign of them!

Throughout the day there was a never-ending stream of reports coming through, all conflicting with each other. Heard some comments from the B.B.C. – apparently we are at the gates of Paris! Reports say that the air force commanders will not co-operate if there is likelihood of resistance in France, as this was supposed to be a bloodless *coup*. Without aircraft Challe is done for.

26 April 1961

Challe and Salan have fled – the party is over and all is lost. Some of our officers have also disappeared. We began the long slow trek back to Philippeville.

The 1st Legion Para Regiment has been officially disbanded. They have blown up their barracks at Zeralda. It was the most magnificent *quartier* in the French army, which they built themselves from scratch, brick by brick, in the tradition of the Legion.

The Following Day

Our trucks drove eastward throughout the day, back along the road we came so little time ago – gone the cheering crowds, glowing faces of adoration – gone the sea of waving arms, the triumphant trumpets, hooting horns blaring around us like regimental bands before victorious armies. Instead, sullen silence in the streets – sinister atmosphere as Arabs slink along the sidewalks. They do not smile but smiling they are. Europeans sit behind their padlocked doors and count the ticking of the clock that beats out the time until their final departure, which must now be certain. How quickly turns the wheel of fate!

27 April 1961

We arrived back at Philippeville to find ourselves blocked from our own *quartier* – it was probably feared that we also would blow the place to pieces. We have been invited to take up residence in the hills and we have made camp about two miles behind Philippeville in a wood. Tomorrow will be interesting.

Pay-day is now overdue and there is considerable unhappiness about this.

From what we can gather from snatches of radio broadcasts and newspapers, the Legion is being cited as the root of all the trouble. We are to be the scapegoats for the rest of the French army. Damusez, the cat who jumped the right way, has gone to France – he will report on his officers and their behaviour and their futures will be determined.

28 April 1961

We have been given three days to clear all our gear out of Camp Pehaut. Our trucks have been confiscated and each company is left with one jeep and a Dodge. Captain Branca, our new commanding officer of but a few months, has disappeared and so have a number of other officers and senior N.C.O.s. It is not clear whether they have deserted or gone to face the music in France. Rumours continue of desertions from other Legion regiments and there is talk of the formation of a secret army. The 14th and 18th Regular Para Regiments have been axed. All is happening fast and intelligence reports through the grapevine are conflicting and numerous.

On our journeys to Camp Pehaut to collect our kit we pass through the regular army *quartier* – loud cheers and beer are thrown at us – we have some friends left after all.

Damusez has returned and has been appointed commanding officer of the 25th Division – big news for him – a little loyalty obviously pays dividends.

29 April 1961

Restlessness hangs over the camp like a hot sticky day. The officers look drawn and fidgety. I wonder what's passing through L'Hospitallier's mind. He's commanding the company at the moment in the long or short or permanent absence of Branca. He can hardly feel that he was not involved, however, and the pendulum may swing back at any time. The boys in France are probably collecting information as fast as possible right now and L'Hospitallier must know it. Visions of Mark Antony and Octavius pricking the names before Philippi, 'These many then shall die.' I don't envy him at all. And what of us? There still exists the possibility that the Legion might be completely disbanded and sent back 'from whence it came'. This will come as good news to many, including me – I need the break.

30 April 1961

Today was La Fête de Camerone and surely the most sober environment for Camerone since 1863 – prisoners of our camp in this wood halfway up the mountain overlooking Philippe-ville, our home town. No passes were issued so we just sat in misery on the hill and guzzled the extra food and beer that was issued to cheer our sinking spirits. We have still not been paid. Despair is turning to disgust within the ranks and rumblings continue that could well erupt if things are not put right soon.

Branca has reappeared. He is a strange man – very cold and aloof, unsmiling and of few words. Perhaps he is preoccupied with other things. It is said that he is very much a sympathizer of the *pieds noirs*. He was born in North Africa and is a great buddy of Gabirot. He was acting as Gabirot's right-hand man when we went to Algiers.

3 May 1961

The war is still on and we have been sent back to the Aurès Mountains on operations.

Talks have started at Évian with the Arabs. De Gaulle's offer of independence remains the same; it's on, provided the French retain rights to the oil and their naval base at Mers el-Kébir. The Arabs are holding out for total independence without any 'buts' so both sides are keeping up the pressure in the hills hoping that the other will eventually yield. The long arm of de Gaulle reached into these lonely mountains and plucked Branca and Gabirot from our midst today. We were patrolling through the bushes when the helicopter that was to whisk them back to the airport and France passed over our heads. It circled round and round above us as we stood to attention at 'present arms' in farewell and then it hovered for a second and was gone. Sad, because of what they represent to us as officers, and very fine officers the Legion has always had.

Traditionally only the first six who pass out of the military academy, Saint-Cyr, may elect to go to a Legion regiment. We get the best. True, they keep their distance and do not exactly have a parental approach in their dealings with us, but I believe they love us well. And now one by one they are being taken from us to face the ignominy of a court martial after all the years they have spent in the service of their country.

Two Days Later

We were suddenly ordered to return to Camp Pehaut yesterday. Can it be that all is forgiven? I think not, but we have now at last been paid. I have received a letter from Anthony containing a lot of cuttings from the English press on the insurrection, including the Giles cartoon reproduced here. They certainly gave the *putsch* some coverage.

Damusez handed over the regiment to his successor, Colonel Channel, in a grand parade today. There is an overwhelming feeling of good riddance at Damusez's departure but Channel is viewed with some suspicion as he is obviously a Gaullist and therefore a potential enemy. He has nevertheless seen good service with the Legion and is said to have behaved well at Dien Bien Phu in 1954. I remember seeing him at Mascara once. He was in charge of all Legion training. He's a big man and looks like a large friendly bear, but he's liable to break your neck if he gives you a gentle shake by the shoulder. He wandered around the camp in a getting-to-know-you casual way this afternoon, chatting incessantly as he walked. He seems peaceful and harmless enough but he's a tough old bastard and his eyes are as cold as steel.

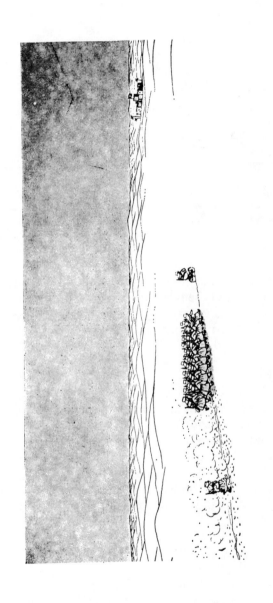

"Well—bang goes our week-end in Paris."

(By courtesy of the *Daily Express*)

PART SEVEN

A Taste of Liberty

18 May 1961

We have been back in the mountains for two weeks on normal operations. Then out of the blue this evening Papke announced that I had been given twenty days' leave at the Philippeville rest camp and I am off in tomorrow's convoy. Fantastic news – and boy, do I need the rest – I'm covered in sores and boils.

The Next Day

The convoy left base camp as morning assembly was just starting. L'Hospitallier gave me a short spiel and shook hands and wished me a good leave.

Three of us are on leave. We drove merrily down to Philippeville sitting on the back of a Simca truck, pouring beer down our parched throats all the way and thinking of those poor bastards back in the mountains marching their arses off. We arrived at Philippeville in the early evening.

20 May 1961

We packed our gear and went into Philippeville to Camp Mangin, which is the leave centre.

Camp Mangin is a three-storeyed army barrack – high ceilings, single-storey bunks – clean and conveniently slap in the centre of town. We are allowed to come and go as we please and although we have to check in once a day we have a permanent *passe de nuit*. I feel free for the first time in a long while.

A great sensation to be able to wander in and out of Mangin at will. Philippeville in daylight is quite a civilized place with people going about their business, women buying groceries – it all seems so abnormally normal. My pockets are virtually empty and *geld* is anxiously awaited. In the meantime, entertainment is restricted to movies and the *salon du thé*, where the waitress, Chantal, whom I met last time we were in Philippeville, is the pull rather than any particular craving for tea.

I chatted to her quite a bit today and received coquettish smiles and glances as she darted in and around the tables with a word and a smile for everybody. I think the smiles I get are slightly warmer than those she gives to the others. There are, however, some problems on this one. Apparently she is married to an adjutant who is in the regular French army, serving in the south somewhere. This probably means that smiles are going to be the maximum return from my pursuance of this relationship, apart from a gut full of tea every day.

24 May 1961

Letter from J. Seems like the first in a long time.

Beautiful day, passed lunching on the beach at Stora looking at Philippeville's best lovelies. They all seem frightened of legionnaires and making contact with civilians is going to be one hell of a task.

29 May 1961

Interesting developments. I got into conversation with a young civilian chap on the beach called Alain Moreau and he introduced me to a couple of girls: José something or other and Nicole Barbolosie. Nicole is stunning. She looks about twenty years old but is probably younger – they always are. She has a mass of dark hair that sweeps down round her face and rests softly on her shoulders. She has a figure that makes my knees ache, and a deep tan. We chatted idly on the beach and later they both went home, but we met again in the evening and strolled up and down the promenade.

She is infatuated by the fact that I am English. She is studying at the *lycée* and thinks I will help her pass her English exams.

I am encouraging this line of thinking and I have arranged another meeting as soon as possible in order to assist her in her studies. After the promenade I went to the *salon du thé* and for once felt tremendously relaxed with Chantal. She was in great form and amazed me by agreeing to a suggestion which I threw out casually that she join me on the beach tomorrow. Why does everything always happen at once? I must be careful how I juggle the balls in case I drop both.

News at Mangin is that a regular soldier has been knifed by an Arab and we have been alerted to go around in pairs particularly at night. The Arabs flexing their muscles a bit could mean 'plenty trouble'.

The Next Day

I rushed to the beach at Stora and was just beginning to despair when she appeared – Chantal. She is almost the complete opposite of Nicole in that she has long fair hair and blue eyes. She is twenty-six and much more mature than Nicole – very French – quick in her movements, petite and chic but graceful – a smile that completely swallows me and the touch of her hand sends my temperature through the roof.

What does one do on a hot day on white sand with blue cool water and a beautiful girl? It was like a typical cigarette ad: running into the water, laughing, splashing, ducking, contact; with contact the beginning of electricity and then flopping down all wet on towels to lie in the sun – fingers touching – looks that told each other that we both want the same thing. I took her to dinner at a small French restaurant called the Casino. We were the only two in the place and the *patron* got the message. A table on the balcony with the sea lapping the rocks ten feet below us; little check tablecloth, candles and soft music – an evening I shall never forget. We told our lives to each other. She had problems with her husband – divorce was round the corner. I believed her. Was I naïve? I didn't give a damn either way. We walked back to Philippeville – slowly – stopping every three minutes to look at the moon with its silver light shining a path on the water straight to us – we looked at each other. If love does not need to be qualified by time, then this was love of the moment that was most beautiful. It took us three long hours to get back to Philippeville and in the late hours of an early morning I saw her to her door – no more. We had neither of us pretended that there would be from the beginning – but there will be if this goes on.

31 May 1961
All day on the beach with Nicole and José. I took Raoul along. He is a Belgian on leave from the 4th Company. Nicole introduced me to a friend of hers, Christian Serve, and he has asked me to lunch at his house tomorrow.

1 June 1961
I received a warm welcome from the Serves on taking my first steps into a French colonial home. They will never know how much pleasure it gave me to be treated as a civilian and not as a legionnaire. Christian has charming parents. I wish they could put Nicole's mother's thinking right. Apparently she would die if she knew her daughter was going out with a legionnaire. I walked Nicole home in the early evening – her hand in mine – shy glances, eyes meet – smiles, just like a couple of college kids, but I love it.

2 June 1961
These wonderful days will not last except in my memory. Not because of Nicole or Chantal themselves, but because they stand out as a period of refreshing happiness in a tough dry part of my life.

I lay on the beach all day with Nicole and in the evening we walked along the cliffs above the town. She told me much about herself. Her father sounds fearful and mother sounds pretty terrifying too. Apparently the parents fight like dogs. Nicole told me that she had mentioned me to her mother as being a friend of Christian's and she got a cautionary lecture. I left her later, as usual, when her mother demands her presence at home and I wandered off, and really quite by surprise found myself at the *salon du thé*. Chantal was packing up for the day, her evening off. We went to the cinema and necked, and then I took her home. I think I'm mixed up.

3 June 1961
Raoul has decided that I am becoming too civilized and that there is a danger I will forget the realities of our situation, so

this evening we went off to the B.M.C. On arrival we had problems with an Arab who tried to push us outside as we were entering one of the *bordels*. Out we all went and as quick as a flash the Arab produced a vicious-looking knife.

Raoul and I were quite relaxed, perhaps a trifle over-relaxed as we'd had some soothing liquor by this time. We circled our boy slowly, looking for an opening. This was outside the *bordel* and very quickly we had a crowd of spectators.

In one moment, as the Arab was between us, I threw my kepi at him and swung a kick at his wrist – I missed, but he was distracted from Raoul for a second who also swung a long round kick which caught him in the small of the back. He gave a yell and went tearing up the narrow street having dropped his knife. Raoul went after him like a greyhound and caught him and then dropped him with a lightning chop at the back of the neck. The M.P.s arrived in ten seconds – regular army – red-beret parachutists. We gave an account of ourselves and were immediately cleared. The Arab squirmed in the gutter but did not get up. I was thunder-struck when the sergeant in charge of the patrol suddenly uttered a series of oaths and gave him a savage kick straight in the teeth with his boot – full force. The Arab's head went back to the full and then toppled forward. He was out cold as a dead trout and his mouth ran red with blood from broken teeth. We went back to the *bordel*.

The realities of our situation are quite clear again.

7 June 1961

There have been more incidents in town with Arabs and the military. The little skirmish Raoul and I had the other night seems to have precipitated a series of fights which are becoming a nightly event.

Captain Ferrer assembled us all in the afternoon and gave a warning that all leave would be cancelled if the trouble with the Arabs did not cease immediately. This is a little rough as it is by no means always we who start the trouble. It is now *interdit* to go to the Arab quarter or to the B.M.C. area unless there are two or three of us together.

Rumours that de Gaulle is still planning repercussions for us persist. There is one school that believes the Legion, which is now considered to be a threat to national security, will be reduced from thirty to twenty thousand Ten thousand of us to be sent home! This sounds much too good to be true.

I had arranged to meet Nicole near the station this evening. The road behind the station has a path off it that leads up into the hills overlooking the town and this we followed for an hour or two.

We sat on the hillside in the cool of the evening with a sea breeze from the Mediterranean fanning us and looked at the roof-tops and the blue sea and each other. I think we are in love – it feels so to me.

The Following Day

I was up with the first cock's crow and racing to the beach – a day in each other's arms, a day in the sunshine – blue sea – other people blurred and shapeless – and the wonderful feeling that I am loved as much as I love her.

She left in the evening as always and disappeared into the crowd. But her spirit stayed and, though wrenched in two, I still felt warm and returned to the barracks at Mangin and went to bed. I have never felt better. The body's condition is determined by the condition of the mind.

11 June 1961

We had a picnic on the beach at Jeanne d'Arc with the Serves and their other friends. Nicole did not come and I was only half alive. I wonder if there is some friction between the Serve family and Nicole's. There is something slightly amiss but I cannot focus on it. I was quite relieved when evening came and I quickly changed at Mangin and went to la Place. I wondered what I would do if she did not come? She came, as beautiful as ever. We took our walk up the hill behind the station – the same way as before – when it is like this one does not seek the slightest change in anything.

The Next Day

We lay on the beach all morning and twiddled our toes in the sand – the hot sun beat down on our backs but we were content to lie and look at each other and touch hands and lips – she had to go to town at eleven o'clock and I stayed. Ten minutes later out of the blue Chantal arrived – this town is getting smaller every day. There are two people I am not keen to bump into when I am with Nicole – one is her mother and the other is Chantal – I suppose one day it will happen and the balloon will go up with a terrible bang.

13 June 1961
I will always remember the beach at Stora and those warm days lying in the sun with my lovely Nicole.

I saw Chantal again in the evening after Nicole had gone. She came up behind me in the street and I realized that I felt nothing for her. Perhaps one can only really love one person at a time.

Maraskal, who was with me, was impressed by the fact that I was a friend of Chantal's. She is apparently the pin-up of the Legion and half the French army too if the numbers in her little tea salon are anything to go by. It is always packed to the brim and those boys aren't in there for tea.

14 June 1961
After a long drive along the coast road with Christian, his girl-friend Hélène, and Nicole, trouble finally came this evening. Nicole and I were walking up the crowded high street, on the way to her home, holding hands and chatting. Suddenly Nicole's mother was standing before us. Nicole froze as she caught her breath and I got the blast, never to be forgotten, in loud ringing tones that brought the high street to a standstill, cars and all. Had I been starkers and in the process of raping Nicole I could hardly have brought more hostility upon myself. She screamed, '*Monsieur, je vous en prie, vous à un côté de la route et ma fille à l'autre.*' I lifted my hat and started to make feeble flustered utterances but she was already heading in the opposite direction dragging a terrified Nicole with her.

Christ, what to do! There is no way I am going to get through to that mother. What a lovely reputation we legionnaires must have to provoke this kind of reaction in people.

What a bloody awful bitch – I had dinner at the Serves' and drowned everything in champagne.

16 June 1961
The beach was an empty desert – she did not come and I waited

all day knowing that she wouldn't and in the evening I went into town and quietly got pissed out of my mind.

17 June 1961

I went to the beach with Christian and his friends as he had said that he would persuade Nicole's mother to let her come with them – but he was not successful. He brought a letter from her in which she said that she would be at the promenade in the evening and so she was – with her bloody mother.

The mother looks like a ravaged Indian squaw, or perhaps that's only how I see her. She was a sheet of steel between us. And tomorrow I must return to Camp Pehaut, my leave is over. It was a dream after all, just as I expected.

18 June 1961

Sunday – I was awoken at four in the morning and bundled into a truck which took me up to the camp. I had twenty-four hours' guard before me and needed to be immaculate and on parade by 0630 for Adjutant-chef Berggruen.

I spent my periods of guard on top of a hill overlooking the sea and I saw Nicole all through the day in the blue water below me and loathed the Legion. I became very tired as the day went on and this evening I was delighted to see Robin White, who has just returned from Sidi-bel-Abbès. He produced a *bidon* of wine which we drank to celebrate his return.

It is now midnight and I am in very big trouble indeed. I fear the wine did me little good particularly as I was feeling so tired. I went to do my stint on guard at 10 p.m. There is a small hut at the top of the hill where the sentry stands, against which is a box, and as I stood in the darkness fanned by a sea breeze I gradually became drowsier until finally I sat on the box. The next thing I knew a gun was sticking into my temple. There is nothing like the cold hard metal of a pistol on one's skin in the middle of the night to bring you back to a compelling and immediate present. The sergeant doing the rounds had crept up and caught me very much off guard. I have now finished my stint, but he will report me tomorrow and I will be for the high jump. I am not looking forward to it at all and suddenly from being so tired I've never felt so wide awake in my life. What a way to finish leave.

1 July 1961

Twelve days have passed – twelve long days in a Legion prison. I hardly remember when it all began. The morning after my guard duty I was last to leave the guardroom – I had rolled up my sleeping gear feeling very uneasy indeed. There was no sign of the guard sergeant. I could not believe I was going to get away with it, and I was right. Berggruen was waiting for me outside – standing like a mountain in the path – feet apart. He called me over and I saluted and stood to attention in the prescribed manner.

A hail of punches to face and gut put me on the ground in a couple of seconds and screams of '*Debout!*' brought me to my feet and to attention again in the prescribed manner; and again I felt Berggruen's fist hammering home. This happened three times, by the end of which I was a mess.

Berggruen wears rings on his fingers which cut my cheek almost to the bone.

It was then '*au coiffeur*' – *boule à zéro* – shaven head and so into prison uniform: denims held together by string, no buttons, boots without laces, and then two hours' *pelote*. Metal helmet without the inside on bald head, a rucksack filled with stones on my back, with wire armbands instead of straps, and then running round and round like a horse in a circus with a sergeant in the middle tooting on his whistle – one blast forward roll, two blasts *marche canard* (knees bend), three blasts crawl. This for two hours – good for the gut – good for the bile! God, how I hated the sergeant with his whistle and that bastard Berggruen and the lot of them – but I went at it flat out. I felt I was on parade for the Brits – we can take anything this crappy army can hand out! I rolled furiously and enjoyed the stones in my back – I couldn't feel them and I could have run for another six hours.

After an hour and a half, the sergeant suddenly yelled out in English, 'Keep smiling, Johnny.' I think he meant it and meant it well – he was not enjoying what he had to do and I suddenly liked him for it. He kept the gaps between the whistle as long as he could so I just had to jog, except when Berggruen came from time to time to enjoy the sport.

After the sport I was made to stand against the barrack wall

to await the arrival of the C.O., by whom I was to be charged.
I stood for two hours in the baking sun, which got ever hotter
and beat down on my naked scalp, with a piece of paper between
my nose and the wall – rigid at attention under the observation
of a guard armed with a sub-machine-gun. The paper must not
fall – it does not because it sticks on the sweat. Eventually I was
frog-marched in front of a captain to be charged with being
found in a position in which I was unable to fulfil my duties on
guard properly, etc. etc. etc. Serious – very serious in any army,
let alone the Legion. I had no comments to make and was given
fifteen days' prison.

All the prisoners, of which there were about fifteen, were
assembled and bundled into trucks, always under guard, which
took us to a quarry where we spent the day swinging sledge-
hammers, breaking up great rocks of marble and loading it on to
trucks. It was heavy work and the hot June sun burned down
mercilessly. We returned in the evening to an hour of *la pelote*
– sport!

This was the daily routine and, if it did nothing else, it
toughened the palms of the hands and strengthened the back
muscles. At the end of each day we paraded for the flag ceremony
and then filed into the prison itself – a Nissen hut with barbed
wire all round – a concrete floor and one blanket per head and
nothing more – but I always slept the sleep of the dead.

There are a number of prison rules which have to be learned
as fast as possible or the wrath of Berggruen is likely to fall like
a ton of hammer blows at any time and from any direction;
these include:

Prisoners will move at all times at the double.

Prisoners will stand to attention and remove their hats when
    N.C.O.s pass their proximity.

Prisoners will not stand still at any time except when urinat-
    ing.

Prisoners will not talk except when addressed by a guard or
    an N.C.O.

Prisoners will not smoke.

My thoughts were never far from Nicole during the time in
prison. With the sea in view, the feeling of space and freedom is
close at hand and heightened the effect of captivity. I used to
imagine her seeing me as a prisoner and it made me sad to

think how sad she would be – now that is really feeling sorry for oneself! As a matter of fact, I think I was. We were all as brown as chocolate and as fit as any man could be. We were healthy too and strong and one had the feeling that one could take a lot of punishment – certainly anything they could hand out. We had a good bunch inside too. We shared our cigarettes and the odd beer that was smuggled into the prison by chums.

Every prisoner gets the same treatment no matter what the crime, the only differential is the length of stay. The crimes were multitudinous: desertion, indiscipline, theft, etc. There was a corporal doing time for having chucked a hand grenade into a bar where he had been overcharged – he was rather splendid!

Those who had done time in civilian life said generally that a Legion prison is ten times worse than anything one could expect to find outside – but in fact on reflection I think there was something good about it.

I caught the first convoy to the regiment, now camped fifty miles west of Philippeville in the hills above a small coastal town called Collo. Very good reception when I got back – everybody delighted to see me. I think the prison sentence has really made me one of the boys!

We have a new company commander called Jais and a new section head, Second Lieutenant Benoît. Benoît is not one of the old school at all – probably fresh from Saint-Cyr. This is a good recommendation but he's rather bouncy and obviously delighted with himself. We will see how he shapes up.

PART EIGHT

Back to the Front

31 August 1961

We have been in the mountains for a month and today returned to Philippeville. Long drive in the trucks – passing through little Arab villages with their squalid dwellings built of sticks and straw and flung together with dung and mud. Sewage runs through the centre of the village – open drains of filth. Kids in rags play in the drains and are covered with open sores and scabs with flies all over them disfiguring their faces. One little girl I saw had her entire mouth thick with flies all round it. She must have grown tired of brushing them away, for she made no sign of being aware of them. She was standing in a dishevelled little dress, covered in dry mud, and her hair was matted and thick with dust. Her big brown innocent eyes looked up at our trucks as we sat and scoffed our tinned sardines and drank our beer. I passed her a can of cheese which she took in her tiny outstretched hand after I had spent several minutes persuading her to come near. She clutched it and turned and ran off to show delighted parents. She must have been about four. Thank God for the warm sun, this in the winter would be terrifying!

The elders look philosophical. The men sit outside the huts, idly chewing their *chique* and chatting away. The women work carrying bundles of sticks on their bent backs with their faces expressionless, neither happy nor sad but just blank and lined

with a million creases; valleys gouged out by years of crying –
dry tears, for there is no moisture left in those old faces.
They look like dried dates that have fallen from the palms
and been left in the sand to be slowly withered away by the
wind.

Dead sheep litter the compounds and half-dead cows and
donkeys stand and stare with their legs tied together so they
cannot run away. Their noses occasionally sweep the dry
dusty ground, but there is not a blade of grass left nor has there
been for years. They represent transport and when their
ravaged bodies can no longer keep their bones together they
will represent the evening meal.

This is the path through Algeria. The lives and existence of
these people are in stark contrast to that of the French with
their rich farms bursting with bright yellow oranges and vines
and splendid mansions. The Arabs' lives are without a trace of
colour and they move from day to day like human rats in a
world of dehydrated poverty. The French say they will not help
themselves and God says something about it too; but in truth
what chance have they of cutting out a slice of French cake?
The hot dry sirocco blows across the village, burns the nostrils
and stings the eyes and the dust is whipped up into a thousand
eddies. It finds its way into every little cranny, every sore and
every wrinkled brow and their whole world is brown and
moistureless – poor devils, but I wonder if it will be any better
when the French leave.

3 September 1961

We spent two days at Camp Pehaut during which we were
unable to get into town because of endless kit inspections and
tours of guard duty and then we left for operations in the south.
We are now camped in the Aurès Mountains somewhere
between Medina and Rhoufi. The company is out on ops. I
have remained behind because I have a boil on my back as big
as a ping-pong ball.

5 September 1961

The long arm of the law has at last reached out to clutch the
lesser offenders in the *putsch* and L'Hospitallier has gone back
to France with the last remaining officers who took part. I am

sorry to see him go. We have tramped many miles together along the same road. I have a great respect for him. He was a fine officer. The final summons has probably come to him as something of a relief. There is nothing that strains a man more than uncertainty in front of knowledge that something bad is coming. When the worst is known and recognized, then and only then can one begin marshalling the inner strength required to face it.

So now we are staffed with new officers and they look new too. They do not have the stamp that is the mark of experience in the Djebel, and they do not look like men who have seen death at close quarters.

7 September 1961

The boil on my back has infected the area around the base of my spine and all the glands too, so it was time to report sick. In the infirmary tent I met the medic, a grossly overweight Belgian who looked not unlike King Farouk, wore dark glasses, and was covered in greasy sweat. He was more like a butcher than a medic and that is exactly what he turned out to be. I stripped off my shirt and lay face down on a camp-bed and he got two mirrors out so that I could see what the problem was; and I certainly had a problem. The boil was more like a tennis ball than a ping-pong ball and it was surrounded by a great circle of angry red skin which covered an area the size of a saucer.

Farouk told me to put my beret in my mouth and bite on it and then he got to work. He put his beefy hands around the boil and squeezed for all he was worth. Jesus Christ, the agony! I thought he was breaking my back. With the groans of agony from me and the grunts of effort from him, we must have sounded like a couple of dying elephants. The boil burst with a bang sending the core, the size of a stone, up to the top of the tent and leaving a crater in my back which would hold five pounds' worth of half-crowns.

Farouk then filled the crater with a *mèche* soaked in iodine or something similar, like hydrochloric acid, and it was all over – except for the standard injection that follows everything and consists of about a quart of penicillin.

Three Days Later

My boil is nearly healed. The Legion methods of cure have got something after all.

It is now the evening. We are camped at 6,000 feet high above Medina and have prepared ourselves for the night up here.

Hasko was bitten by a scorpion a couple of hours ago. It was lurking under a boulder that he tried to pick up. He has been evacuated by helicopter. This is scorpion country, arid and dry and covered in stones and rocks. They love it. We have ambush work to do tonight and it's bloody cold.

The Next Day

We were up two hours before the dawn patrolling through the hills. We must have covered thirty miles this day. Occasionally we came across little clusters of Arab *mechtas* on our way which we searched with fine-tooth combs. The women of the villages are all rounded up like cattle when we arrive; the men disappear at the first sign of our coming. This often means they are in league with the fell.

The normal course of events in these villages which are supporting the fellagha is for the legionnaires to wring the necks of the chickens and stuff them into their *musettes*. Livestock are set free and the *mechtas* are then burned to the ground. The order to burn the huts came in each case from a captain of the Deuxième Bureau who was with us and presumably knew that these were the dwellings either of fellagha themselves or sympathizers. In one group of huts at which we arrived very early in the morning a small chow dog ran out barking and made straight for Hirschfeld. Hirschfeld lifted his L-shaped shovel high above his head and brought it down with tremendous force on the back of the dog's neck practically severing it. The dog was stone dead. It was a gruesome beginning to a day, if not a sinister one.

Just before noon we came across some *mechtas*, and this time the men had not had time to flee. Under questioning by the officer of the Deuxième they refused to admit that they had any dealings with the fell and in fact they had very little to say at all. This all changed when they were put inside one of the huts and it was set ablaze. They started to scream blue murder and when we let them out we couldn't stop them talking.

One of them was finally elected as spokesman and he said he could lead us to a cache that was filled with arms, and so off we set. We followed him over hills and plains and valleys for about fifteen miles, at the end of which time he said he couldn't find it. We had all stopped and were lying about waiting for the order to move on while the Arab explained his problems to the Deuxième captain. I was sitting just above the Arab who was jabbering away to the officer and waving his arms around in desperation. They were below me on the side of a small valley with a dried-out stream bed at the bottom.

Suddenly the officer grabbed a sub-machine-gun off a legionnaire standing near him and as the Arab started to scream in protest he kicked him in the side and sent him rolling down the hill. The machine-gun came quickly up to the officer's shoulder and he squirted bullets into the writhing body of the Arab as he rolled down into the dried bed of the stream. When he reached the bottom he was as dead as the stones around him. We left him. We had a long walk back and in between us and our lorries was a mountain barrier 5,000 feet high. Nobody mourned the Arab – it was too hot and we were too tired.

We have no souls, we have no feelings, our senses are dead – dead like the dead corpse in the stream. Is this really me?

A Week Later

The pattern of every day is the same. The dawn rise and the march for hours to our positions for the *fouillage*. The pause for coffee and a chunk of tinned cheese and then on again. Though we are tireless machines and can march for many miles, we are not infallible in the heat and even the best machines have their off days. Even Theo fell one day. I never thought I would see that.

We are often short of water and there is nothing worse than camping down for the night with parched throats knowing at the same time that there will be no water for coffee in the morning. But we are as tough as leather and our sinewy bodies, devoid of any trace of fat, have the qualities of the mule and the camel combined. We can march for miles in the sweltering heat of the day or in the cold of the night when the rain sometimes falls for hours on end. We no longer feel the pain in our backs from carrying our *sacs* and there are no nerves in our feet where the burst blisters suppurate. Sometimes we don't see our feet for days as it is considered unwise to be without one's boots on at night.

We had a skirmish with the Arabs one hot afternoon but their shot-guns were no match for our machine-guns that day and we were victorious. But we overlooked one of them and he gave Hallard in the 4th Section a double blast from his shot-gun in the gut. I watched Hallard as he lay on his back and life flickered in him like a light bulb with a faulty connection – God knows how he stayed alive. The medics covered him with antiseptic powder, but half his stomach was out and they could do nothing except wait for the helicopter. He died on the way to hospital. We never caught the guy who shot him.

And we killed a mule one day. What a sorry, sordid incident that was. We had been out all day and the rain had not ceased for a second, and as the light was failing and we were coming down into a valley, there was the mule. It looked like the loneliest thing in the world. Benoît tried to kill it with his pistol and Hirschfeld joined in with his sub-machine-gun. I was seventy yards away and yelled at them in vain to shoot it behind the ear. Stupid ignorant bastards – they just kept firing at it, and a guffaw of laughter went up as each burst of bullets hammered into the poor brute's side. It staggered around in bewildered agony, groping for life and stubbornly refusing to die. Finally it fell and with a little twitch it breathed its last and lay still – food for the jackals that night. We continued on our way leaving behind a little incident that left a monument of something shabby and dirty in my mind.

19 September 1961

We are camped for the night overlooking the magnificent plain of Biskra; a hundred kilometres wide and stretching into nothing on the night horizon – perfect flatness with not a tree to be seen.

> The stars are setting and the caravan
> Starts for the dawn of nothing – Oh, make haste!

For what? This is a country that I could love, for its mountains that climb to the sky and its valleys that disappear into the

▲ **Legionnaires on the march**

◄ **On parade on Camerone Day**

Appel!
▼

Boarding the planes for our first jump

'Pour encourager les autres'

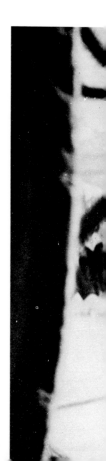

The moment of truth

Stardom

Mud . . .

. . . and snow

The fellagha position on Easter Sunday, 1961

The Aurès Mountains

Wilderness

An Arab *douar*

Three members of our island expedition

Keratta

The Moroccan border . . .

. . . and the Tunisian b

The sixty-foot dive

Combat course

Dropping into the trees

Building the road

Fellagha prisoners

Legionnaire Simon Murray

centre of the earth. It is stark and wild and incredibly beautiful.
A place for a man and a dog and a gun in times of peace.

Hasko, who has recovered from his scorpion bite, and I
pooled our little packets of dehydrated soup this evening and
then the bastard drank the lot while I was doing an hour's
guard. He said he thought I'd already had some before I went
on guard but he knew damn well I hadn't. He's a slob but he's
kept me charged with cigarettes for the last two days so I let
it go. I have discovered that warm rum and powdered lemonade
crystals make a very pleasant evening drink, particularly when
your balls are freezing off at the top of a mountain on the edge
of the plain of Biskra.

26 September 1961
We climbed up and down the hills all day today and I had a
terrible stomach ache. The medic has diagnosed it as 'rien'. It's
probably appendicitis but why should he worry, it's my gut
not his.

The Next Day
My stomach ache has gone. The medic must have been right
– amazing!

2 October 1961
I had a letter from Anthony this morning announcing that
Jennifer has broken off her engagement. That's the first piece
of good news around here for some time.

3 October 1961
We left at first light and as our trucks were moving off hundreds
of Arab children emerged from the cluster of huts and poured
over the ground like ants, stopping every few seconds to rum-
mage in the grass and rocks where our tents had been. I wonder
what we left behind – a watch or two, a few cents and a photograph or a magazine and some ammunition.

We drove north-west to Batna and then followed the main
national highway, Route 3, up through Constantine and then
west to Mila. On arrival we were immediately lifted into the hills
by helicopters and surprised a small group of fellagha in a

village. They were caught red-handed with their weapons and they made no attempt to resist.

Just before we entered the village Pilato approached Sergeant Papke and asked permission to 'handle' the women. Papke gave him hell, which was good to see. I was somewhat surprised to see Pilato actually asking permission. He's an evil little shit. His dark face is full of points and sharpness like a rat's. It's pinched and taut – he is a man to keep in front of you at all times. Papke's reaction was typical of him. He's a straight man and a decent one, but I think he's in a minority and Pilato was obviously surprised at being refused. Some of the stories I have heard about the treatment given to women on these outings are pretty horrendous.

The day was nearly over when God gave Hirschfeld two more lives. He was passing under a tree when he heard the metallic click of a trigger hammer falling on an empty chamber – twice. He looked up to see an Arab with a shot-gun pointing at him. The unfortunate Arab had given Hirschfeld both barrels in the back but both cartridges had failed him and it cost him his life.

He jumped down from the tree, all smiles, gabbling a profusion of greetings and suggesting eternal friendship. '*Monsieur, camarade, nous les amis; Vive la Légion! Vive la France! monsieur!*' But he was unconvincing with his double-barrelled sawn-off shot-gun still in his hands. Nobody had ever come closer to his ticket than Hirschfeld a few seconds earlier and he was going to make sure this man never had an opportunity to try again. He emptied half the magazine of his sub-machine-gun into him and the Arab died in convulsions writhing like an eel on the end of a line. This was the end of the line.

11 October 1961

This was a hell of a day!

We came in from the hills some time after eight o'clock in the evening. It was after supper when we had settled down in our tents to books, poker, beer and chit-chat when it happened. There was suddenly a colossal explosion like a bomb which shook us rigid. We were all paralysed for about five seconds and then the spell broke and as one man we dashed outside into the darkness. Fifteen yards away the tent of the *compagnie portée* was a smoking wreck. We leapt at it, tearing it apart with knives and hands, and as the tent flaps came off we were confronted with a ghastly scene.

Jeeps came careering in from all sides and beamed their head-lights on to the terrible mess. Ten men had been sitting in the tent minutes earlier. They had just come in from operations and one of them when taking off his webbing had unclipped a grenade and the pin had somehow caught and been extracted. (This transpired some hours afterwards.) We all carry our grenades dangling from our webbing and it has struck me before that it could be dangerous, particularly when we are fighting our way through thick bush. Anyway it was an Ameri-can grenade with a two-second fuse and in two seconds it went off.

As we entered the tent it was like a painting of hell or the *mise en scène* of a grisly theatrical drama. Bodies were lying all over the place – some started to stir and there were dreadful groans. Some lay on their camp-beds where they had perhaps been reading, others lay sprawled on the floor. Nobody had been spared. One man lay half off the bed on his back with his head on the floor and his stomach and guts all over his chest – another had just a bloody mess where his leg had been. The compression in the tent must have added to the damage. *Infirmiers* rushed about and people fell over themselves in the darkness in the desperate scramble to help. It was a pitiful sight but the sheer horror of it jelled the emotions. Of the ten men in the tent four were killed outright and the others are walking on a tightrope for life.

Christ, how life can suddenly take a turn – I'll remember tonight when things are going well.

1 November 1961
We are back in Philippeville and today is the seventh anniversary of the beginning of the Arab uprising. In consequence of this we are *en alerte*, anticipating demonstrations. We moved trucks and men into the main square in the town during the day but there was no trouble. There are reports this evening of riots in Algiers. Sixty-seven Arabs have been killed and there have been several incidents of plastic-bomb explosions, but no details are given of who was responsible. We are leaving for the Tunisian

frontier in a couple of days. Suddenly I'm bored with Philippeville and I'm looking forward to getting back to the mountains.

4 November 1961

We drove east into the morning sun, through Bône and then to a small town on the coast called La Calle. The weather changed and we arrived in a thunderstorm which did little to help strained tempers as we put up the tents. Benoît volunteered his section (us) to go out on a night patrol along the frontier. He certainly picks his moments for glory!

The regiment is spread along the frontier over a distance of about fifty miles, each company operating somewhat independently. The frontier itself is exactly the same in appearance as that with Morocco, with barbed wire and mines all over the place. Very unfriendly stuff! In between the two frontiers there is a no-man's-land as on the Moroccan side and in the middle of this is a hill which keeps the two opposing factions out of sight. The distance between the frontiers is about a mile and a half as the crow flies. On the other side of the hill the Arabs have amassed a substantial armed force, and Ben Bella, their great hero, is also there awaiting the glorious return to Algeria, when independence finally comes. It is possible that they may not be prepared to wait that long, which is of course one of the reasons we are here.

18 November 1961

We were hauled out of our sacks at three o'clock this morning and rushed to the wire. The fell had blasted their way through with bangalores. They made several well synchronized breaks at different points and in the confusion and darkness they scored a 100 per cent success. Dive-bombers and artillery spent the rest of the morning blasting the no-man's-land area which seemed pointless after the birds had already flown.

21 November 1961

Up until now we have not ventured into the no-man's-land area. It appears, however, that the Arabs have now moved closer and are installed just behind the line of hills that runs down the centre between the two frontiers. This obviously brings them much nearer to our wire and the nearer they can get the easier it is for them to make their night runs into Algeria.

Although we keep up a regular barrage of artillery we already know from practical experience that this can be in-effective against a well-dug-in installation. It has been decided therefore that we will launch an attack on the hill tomorrow night.

24 November 1961

We stole out of our camp at midnight – no lorries, no noise. The artillery had been pounding the hill all day in the hopes of reducing some of the opposition we were most certainly going to confront. This was going to be a big one and the entire regiment was participating, plus some elements of the regular army.

Dawn found us crouched just below the crest of the hill awaiting the order to rush over the top. Adrenalin was pushing the blood through the veins at maximum speed and keeping out the damp cold of the early morning. Then through the grey-ness came the sight of nine B26 bombers, at first a drone and then a roar as they thundered low over our heads towards Tunisia. Seconds later they dropped their load on top of the hill with an almighty crunch that shook the ground around us. And then immediately afterwards the solemn thumping of the guns began in the rear and the swishing shells seemed to pass through the hair on our heads as they followed the line of the bombers and landed with shattering blasts on the other side of the hill.

The bombardment continued for two hours and then silence – a sinister silence if ever there was one. Suddenly the quiet word to prepare to move forward. A quick bite of chocolate and we were on our way. The smack when it came shook us rigid. We had hardly covered ten yards when the skies opened and mortar shells started falling like God-damned raindrops. Hectic chaos – nowhere to hide, no rocks to dive under. We were in the open like ducks on a pond. But in hitting us the fell had shown their hand and the radios were buzzing their positions back to our guns and the artillery came into play again. Thank heavens the fell didn't have any artillery.

The immediate damage to us was bad. The *compagnie d'appui* (light artillery) appeared to have taken the brunt of the fell mortars. All around me guys were in trouble, some screaming for help, others lying deathly still. There was not much time to focus on this for we were suddenly running forward up the hill, going for our lives.

Gradually we pushed them back out of no-man's-land and into Tunisia – and we followed them across the frontier all through the long day, well into Bourguiba's land – and we didn't give a stuff whether we offended him or not – we had cleared the ground. But we can never finish the job because we can never hit them hard enough, for without the ropes behind them there is no resistance and they can ride our punches.

Next Day

We rested and licked our wounds. Many have received shrapnel damage from the mortars. Captain Jais liked our performance yesterday and has registered his approval by offering drinks to the entire company. The more I see of Jais the more I like him. He's good with people and that's all that counts at the end of the day.

Pay-day. I spent half the day playing toss-the-penny with old Theo and he practically cleaned me out. Theo is splendid on pay-days; by midday his eyes are completely out of focus and he epitomizes the meaning of being blind drunk.

Several Days Later

We have been on routine operations over the last few days patrolling the wire during the day and sitting in ambush in no-man's-land at night. Not much movement from the fell. They are obviously licking their wounds too. We moved our base once and it was our turn to be next to the *bordel*. What a wonderful life it all is!

I had a long chat with Sergeant Bockemier in the *foyer* one day. He's a sort of company secretary, normally rather quiet and slightly sinister as though he is the only one with confidential information. He opened up a little. He was a P.O.W. during the war just outside Bury in Lancashire so he knows the North well. He talked about his time working on a farm and about porridge and cornflakes. He obviously rather enjoyed it and certainly had a much better time than our guys in Colditz. He told me that I had the highest I.Q. in the company, which doesn't say much for my colleagues. It would bring tears to the eyes of all who taught me at Bedford. He also told me that I had been proposed for Corporal School by Prat-Marca, Glasser and Willemin but in each case it had been turned down by the Deuxième Bureau. No reason is given on my file but there appear to be a number of question marks on me about who I am and what the hell I am doing here. I'm not surprised it's got them guessing – it's got me completely confused. I've been regarded as a potential deserter since day one and apparently they still expect me to make a move sooner or later.

12 December 1961

We rose at 3 a.m. It has been raining for eight days and everything is drenched: our sleeping-bags and our tents, inside and out. Our clothes are soaked through and through and we shiver hard in the black wet mornings when we rise. It is not easy to be cheerful. There's no reason to be anyway.

It was time for another go at the hill to push the Arabs off their nests again. It's like a game of grandmother's footsteps. French military tactics are sometimes difficult to follow, but I suppose they did produce Clemenceau and Napoleon.

The action was similar to the last time we went on this jaunt but our nerves were of stronger stuff having been tempered in the fire once before. The Arabs had not really dug themselves in firmly and our artillery and the B26 bombers were much more devastating in their effects this time. We soon had them on the run but not before they had done considerable damage with a couple of well-placed machine-guns. They missed me by inches with one burst and hit the man running along two yards from me. He was hit in the knee and I've never seen anyone in such agony. There was a medic on hand. We pulled the guy into a ditch and the medic pumped morphine into him. I ran on wondering when it was going to be me, and my knees felt very exposed.

We moved the Arabs back again with our superiority of numbers and firepower and then like last time we turned our backs on them and struggled wearily home through the mud and the rain. What's it all about?

14 December 1961

I received two parcels today. One was from my brother Anthony and contained a thermos flask and the other was from Loris and Leila full of Fortnum's best. They will never know what it all means to me because when I see them and tell them, the circumstances will be so different that they will never be able to imagine how it was. The thermos means that I can go on ambushes at night in the cold wet mountains and be fortified with warm tea laced with cognac. This is gold-mine stuff. I took all the food over to Georges Penco in the 4th Company who is fast becoming a good chum and we got stuck into it. Georges is going to Corporal School in a month or so and he's pleased about it. He speaks English fluently and, in his own words, he is fed up with being fucked around by corporals and sergeants all day and he feels it's time he had a go at it – it makes a lot of sense.

We talked about *La Quille* as always and our plans for making millions when we get back into civilian life. *La Quille* was the name of a ship that used to take prisoners off Devil's Island when they had finished their time. Here *La Quille* refers to being demobilized or '*libérable!*'

18 December 1961

Operations continue, so does the rain and so do our nightly treks into no-man's-land where we sit in ambush all night freezing to death and see not a soul. There are some minor improvements.

We have been issued with thermo packs that one sticks inside one's shirt and they generate heat when a cord is pulled. They are large envelopes filled with chemicals which react to produce the heat and they are most welcome on ambush parties. There is also an improvement in the tinned rations we take with us on operations. Until now we have usually been issued with individual rations. There is an 'E' type, standing for European, and an 'M' type, standing for Muslim. We get whichever is available at a particular time. The 'E' type contains a small tin of beef, a tin of cheese, and one of sardines. There is also a bar of chocolate, a tiny packet of dehydrated soup, two packets of lemonade crystals, a packet of coffee powder, a small bottle of cognac '*eau-de-vie*' and some loo paper. The Muslim ration has

tuna fish instead of the beef and doesn't have the cognac or the
loo paper! Anyway we are now being issued with collective
rations with a much wider variety of tinned food and it is bliss
to be off those dreadful sardines.

The Next Day
We drove south-west all day towards Sétif through rain, snow
and wind and pitched camp in the evening high up in the
Kabylie Mountains. Faces were purple and swollen with the
cold and eyes were staring stones in red sockets from the wind.
In the darkness with frozen fingers we somehow put up the
tents. We managed to get two of the bigger ones up into which
the officers piled and we left the rest until morning. We are near
a village called Bordj-Bou-Arreridj, somewhere in the middle of
nowhere. By the time the lorries had finished churning around,
the entire camp was a field of mud and the misery was complete.

This is the moment when one needs morale; this is the time
when it pays to hold on to yourself, when everything is perfectly
bloody and conditions are impossible, when one is an inch from
letting go completely. Character comes through in moments like
this and those without fibre bend.

It is dark and difficult to see and the opportunity to slink
away from the work is easy. This is when all hands are needed
and every effort from each man makes the final task that much
easier. Those who lurk in the shadows of the night or don't pull
their weight jeopardize the entire operation.

Coldness is enemy number one – hunger and heat are toler-
able but cold kills morale. The misery of crawling into a
sleeping-bag which is wet and sodden in total blackness on top
of a mountain with the rain pissing down and the wind howling
and people with great galumphing mud-choked boots wandering around tripping over each other, with boxes and poles and
equipment lying everywhere in total chaos, is without parallel.
And when on top of that somebody tells you that you are on
guard duty from 0300 until 0400, well then you throw.

22 December 1961
Christmas approaches. Each tent has its crib and decorations
for the festivities. There is one large tent called the *salle de fête*
where performers and would-be cabaret artists will make us

laugh on Christmas Eve. It is competitive stuff with each section trying to outdo the others in its festive display with ingenious lighting effects and coloured paper. Outside the wind howls across the mountains like a lonely wolf and the rain pours down – Christmas will be cold comfort in this.

Christmas Eve
We toured the hills to make sure the enemy kept their distance while we had our fun – and it was as well we did, for we had a head-on *accrochage* with a band of fellagha. It was just after midday when thoughts were turning for home. We were on one side of a shallow valley with a stream forty yards in front of us and the ground sloping up to rocky hills above on the other side. Suddenly, as always, there was small-arms fire from our flank and the flat staccato chatter of sub-machine-guns. The boys on our right had surprised a group of fell and they ran straight across our line like gazelles.

Everybody opened up, and with no trees for camouflage their protection was sparse grass and the odd boulder. Five of them died under the murderous fire. The others had stayed in their cache and slowly emerged to surrender. They came out of a hole in the ground, arms held high, looking beaten but very much alive.

They must be tough to live like rabbits in their underground warrens. Their cavern contained clothing, a radio, and food for a brigade plus armaments for a regiment – Stens, Brens, binoculars, compasses, the lot. A massive haul and an excellent note on which to begin Christmas.

Everybody was in great form and we returned to camp in good spirits ready to celebrate.

The interior of each tent is quite fantastic, almost beautiful. So much effort has been made to create this it is hard to believe that rough hands of legionnaires have been at work. We assembled in the evening in the *salle de fête*. Colonel Channel on his rounds of the companies came to wish us well. The Germans sang '*Stille Nacht*' as only the Germans can and the atmosphere was one of friendship and goodwill, contrasting so greatly with the cold outside and the death in the afternoon.

Captain Jais gave out a present to each man in the company, with a warm handshake and a message of good wishes. The presents were radios, cameras, watches, electric razors and other things, financed by the profits of the *foyer* – a painless way to finance welfare. When that was over each section returned to its own tent and sat down to a magnificent dinner. That a field kitchen can produce such food in these hills is quite incredible – roast pork and chicken, salads and beans, cakes and cheeses – sensational.

We as a section were armed with twenty bottles of wine, four bottles of rum, six bottles of cognac, several bottles of Martini and Cinzano, and twenty-four cases of beer; something over 300 bottles in all and there are twenty-four men in the section. We drowned out the night cold and we drowned out the memories of another world. We sang our hearts out and drank until it came out of our ears. I remember doing the rounds of the other tents to pass greetings to friends. Everybody is constantly on the move, drifting from tent to tent, arriving in each case to hails of welcome and offers of drink.

Koch and I had a duet going singing 'Seven Lonely Days' and 'Tom Dooley' – tremendous success in all the sections. Koch can harmonize anything and I must confess it really did sound quite good. We earned lots of drinks in appreciation.

I was still going well at five o'clock in the morning when it was my turn to do guard duty. I was well armed spiritually and wandered around the hills outside the tent with my mind in a daze too far gone to be sobered by the cold – what a moment for an attack by the fell – but the crack over the knuckles this afternoon had cooled their enthusiasm for a bun-fight. At six I was relieved and clambered slowly into my sleeping-bag. Christmas Eve was over for another year – a new year was fast approaching and I slept the deep sleep of a contented man.

25 December 1961

Christmas Day was, as always in the Legion, a sad day. The eve of Christmas is the day, the day of Christmas is a nightmare. Hungover heads completely obliterate the Christmas spirit. Memories of other Christmases are washed away in the streams of last night's alcohol. A cold day, devoid of laughter, devoid of the spirit of Christmas, devoid of everything. These are the mountains of the moon that surround us; featureless, no trees, no grass, just cold hard rock, ice and snow and frozen mud.

And around me humans with frozen minds and aching heads.
Cold – it's so bloody cold, that is the problem.

The Next Day
Two companies went out on ops. They ran slap into trouble
similar to our little fracas on Christmas Eve. The camp is full
of Arab prisoners. They are being questioned and whilst I have
not seen it the word is that they are being persuaded to give
information with the old generator method.

27 December 1961
There is a small outpost about ten miles from here occupied by
a company of Harkis. The officers are French but the ranks are
formed from Arab regulars serving in the French army. Last
night the Harkis rose up and slaughtered their officers and then
fled. Visions of the Indian Mutiny! We spent the day tramping
through the hills in pursuit. They are fleet of foot and these
mountains are a wilderness. We are sleeping out tonight and
will pursue the Harkis tomorrow at crack of dawn. The snow is
falling, the night is black and only shivering generates warmth.

The Following Day
Snow turned to drizzle and we continued to put one foot in
front of the other mile after mile. Not a sign or a smell of those
boys – they have melted with the snow and we have no hope of
catching them because darkness falls early in these hills. We
returned to camp in the evening to warm soup and shovelled it
down our throats.

Out of the blue a Christmas card from Nicole reviving a
furnace, fanning the flames of starved affection, bringing her
suddenly close to mind. No address on the card so I wrote to
Christian Serve and asked him to establish contact again.
Anticipation has put me back on fine form. How quickly the
tempo of emotions is changed by the falling flakes of snow or
the receipt of a piece of paper.

30 December 1961
Short patrol – more festivities are coming and we don't want
to be caught with our knickers down!

31 December 1961

Celebrations. Much mirth, singing and laughter. A thousand times better than Christmas; controlled; not a debauched total immersion in alcohol. We got through a lot, but without agony.

The dawn of 1962 is at hand and 1961 dies in the evening darkness. Good riddance – but I am still on the near side of the hill and have not yet completed half the journey. Sobering thought but time is nevertheless moving on and there is the first glimmer of light on the distant horizon. This year has been a long one – my twenty-first!

1962

1 January 1962

A holiday in the Legion! There was an assembly of the company in the main tent. Jais reviewed the year and told us what a good lot of guys we were. We drank toasts to ourselves, the Legion, France, de Gaulle, and several other things of greatness. There was much singing of '*Le Boudin*' and '*Le Képi blanc*' and so on and then shouts for volunteers to stand on the table and sing.

Then to my embarrassment there were yells for 'Johnny *et* Koch', repeated over and over again like supporters at a football match. Jais called us forward, Koch and myself, and we leapt to the table and sang. Heaven knows what we sang, I don't think I want to remember but with Koch's fantastic harmonizing it sounded quite good apparently. Yells and bellowing of applause and shouts for more – amazing what alcohol can do to people's ears! General toast to us both and more gulping of liquid. Terrific stuff, I really enjoyed it. The day was super relaxed and everybody appeared on good form. Steffen was magnificent with his face covered in black boot polish, a huge beret on his head and sunglasses; he staggered around with a candle in his hand calling himself '*le Roi de Bougie*'. Charlie Chauvin went to bed last night in a stupor and woke up this morning naked. We told him he'd been rogered during his unconsciousness; lots of eyewitnesses as to the best spectacle in years congratulated him on being a part of it. He spent the day going round pouncing on suspects – saying, '*C'était toi qui m'as encoulé hier?*' He couldn't find the culprit – there wasn't one, but he'll never really know.

2 January 1962

Today we are serious again and business begins anew. We were up with the dawn and tramped the hills all day. Yesterday's quick breath was a fantasy, just hard concentrated relaxation; a pause in the endless strides we make trekking through the months, the years, in these lonely mountains.

It is six in the evening and we have paused for the night. I am on a corniche with my sleeping-bag laid down on the hard ground inviting sleep much needed. The sun has dropped behind the pinnacled horizon, and the sky glows red in the distance while nearer it is blue and then purple and jet black above and behind. Below me and around me the fires of an army flicker over an enormous area. The valley sweeps down below and up the other side, dark now in the shadow of the falling light but illuminated by all the fires like a procession of burning torches in the night. Little groups cluster round the fires; a shadow leans forward to put on a can of beans or coffee and moves back to disappear again into the blackness. Night falls quickly like a final curtain and muffled voices drone softly into eventual silence. Fires are stamped out – another day has passed over my shoulder and it is time to snuggle down into my sleeping-bag. It is time to rest before I hoist tomorrow on my back – Christ, it's a long journey!

The Next Day

A parcel from Anskie stuffed with food. It's the labels on the chocolate and the stamps on the brown paper and the realization that this was wrapped by friendly hands in a warm home in England that feed my system like no other feast has ever done. The simple things in life produce the real peaks of pleasure – never to be forgotten ever. What a lesson. Baudouin is impressed with the quality of the stuff in my parcels, which he reckons have 'de la classe', and he now refers to me as '*Milord John*'.

6 January 1962

Up at 1.45 a.m., that is to say just after we were down. We drove due east in the trucks through the black cold night and took the National Route 5 to Sétif. From Sétif we travelled due north along Route 9 and after five hours we were in the gorge of Kerrata.

The winding, twisting road through the gorge was built by the Legion many years ago and a huge plaque carved into the rock at the side of the road bears witness. The gorge itself is a miracle to see. From the road vertical sides of sheer rock stretch to the sky. An unbelievable formation, a fault without parallel; just a staggering quirk of nature that strained our necks and eyes in wonder. And then the horrifying idea of climbing up! A goat, or God knows what, had traced a zigzag path up the side, and this we took in long file, with knees on chins and backs bent double weighed down by sacks. We climbed to the sky and all the while the rain drizzled down. The clouds were on the upper reaches and we trod warily in the mist; a slip would be the last, of that there was no doubt.

Eventually we reached the summit and, as surprised as we, were a bunch of Arabs camped on the top and caught unawares. They were quickly away and the clouds hindered efforts to catch them. Plaumann had the machine-gun and I had the ammo. We rammed it on a rock and I fed in the bands of rounds and Plaumann squeezed out the bullets – chattering gunfire echoing round the hills. The boys were away but only by the skin of their teeth, saved by the weather. There was a little *mechta* nearby in which they had been sheltering before we surprised them and we burned it. Their sentry must have been dozing and for this he'll pay with his life when they pause to assess the situation. Their code is strict and so is their discipline. Without it they're dead!

We poured over the hills in pursuit but there was no hope of finding them in the clouds and we began the descent at the day's end. On the way down in a valley we came across some orange trees on which we fell like locusts – to tired limbs and dry throats they were like no fruit I had ever tasted before. We filled our bellies and carried on down, arriving at the bottom of the gorge in darkness, soaked through to the bone. We found some deserted barracks with straw on the floor and we passed the night there.

18 January 1962

We rose at dawn under sheets of rain and drove back to

Philippeville. Met up with Robin White in the evening; swapped our news as we supped our ale. I think Robin would in many ways prefer to be operational rather than stick at base camp. He doesn't know what he's missing, I'd swap with him any time.

20 January 1962

The Arabs are kicking up. These things are cyclic and the beginning of the year signals the build-up of tension that usually explodes into manifestations and riots.

There is a curfew at 1100. The plastic-bomb season is with us again. The hand of Arabs, the hand of the O.A.S.? Who knows? who cares? What an agony this separation has been for the French and indeed perhaps much more so for the Arabs. I went into town – it was like a morgue. The bars and bistros were shuttered and barred – a few francs extra business cannot compensate for the risk of a grenade through your window. It was as dead and silent as a ghost town. I wandered round the empty streets, maybe hoping by some weird twist of fate or some miracle that I would meet Nicole – but no way was it to be or could it be and I am old enough to know better than to think that there was even a possibility.

> We are the music makers,
>   We are the dreamers of dreams,
>   Wandering by lone sea-breakers,
>   And sitting by desolate streams.

An empty beer can was lying in the gutter. I changed my course slightly and kicked it hard up the empty street, bouncing and clanging, echoing against the stone walls of the empty houses – everybody had gone home except me.

25 January 1962

We had *parade* and *défilé* today for Commandant Ferrer who is leaving the regiment after thirty-two years' service. That's a long time to be in the Legion. Masses of Médailles Militaires were distributed; morale boosters to discourage us from going to the O.A.S. – or maybe a sign that the war is really drawing to a close and it's now or never?

30 January 1962

'*Rapportez au commandant de compagnie!*' No reason given, just told to appear before Jais at 0900. He reviewed my *livret matricule* – my personal file. He noted that I had refused initially to volunteer to become a paratrooper, which is regarded as *mauvaise volonté*. He also noted that I was very much a spectator and was somehow not 100 per cent committed to the Legion – or at least this had been his impression in the past, but events at Christmas had changed his opinion. He then asked if I had any ambitions in the Legion. I nearly said, 'Yes – to get out', but thought better of it. The upshot of it all is that he is thinking of sending me to Corporal School in the future and he wanted to know my reaction. I was very non-committal about the whole thing – some time in the future maybe, but right at the moment I don't feel like being a corporal or anything else for that matter.

3 February 1962

Operations have officially been suspended for ten days while negotiations continue to intensify at Évian. In spite of this we are going out tomorrow into the mountains behind Philippeville where it is believed that there is a fellagha hospital – the temptation is too much!

4 February 1962

Left camp at 0700 – the rain was torrential. The going was abysmally slow, the bush almost impenetrable. We covered two miles in six hours, slashing with our *coupe-coupe* every inch of the way. Eventually we came upon the fellagha camp, lately abandoned, but the light was fading fast when we arrived and pursuit would have been useless. Their camp was superb, with huts buried in the undergrowth with neatly and expertly thatched roofs. Inside, the huts were bone dry after five days of rain. There were oil-lamps and a few pots and pans but nothing of interest. We burnt it to the ground and returned to camp, arriving well into the night, soaked, cold and miserable.

6 February 1962

Long speech to the nation by le Général – strong stuff. 'Algeria must be led to self-government by the wisdom of the French and the two countries will remain friendly thereafter with the Arabs independent and the French holding long-term marketing rights to the oil and gas.' It all goes down like a lead balloon with the *pieds noirs*! They are totally unconvinced and must now recognize that the sands of time are really running out for them; but they are going to drag this out one way or another and there's going to be lots of trouble before they leave.

There is a general strike throughout Algeria. Arabs and French alike, all seem to have joined in. Shops, trains, postal services, and even the bars, have all ceased to function. Open doors are an invitation to plastic bombs. It's not clear from which direction they are coming, whether it's an O.A.S. token of existence or Arabs hustling de Gaulle right up until the end; but coming they are and in ever-increasing quantities.

The O.A.S. are growing in number daily and they are clearly a force to be reckoned with. There is little sympathy or support for them in France but they have a million people behind them over here. I do not think they have the power to prevent the inevitable but they have the will and strength to delay it.

22 February 1962

Two years completed. Who said I wouldn't stick it?

The desertion rate is rising. One presumes they are going to join the O.A.S. The radio reported today that the O.A.S. are using legionnaires as assassins and they cited the case of a legionnaire who has been tried and sentenced to ten years' prison for killing a lawyer. Ten years sounds lenient – the lawyer must have been an Arab!

Two Days Later

Chauvin lost his cool with Corporal Meyer today and took a swing at him. For his trouble he is sleeping in a '*tombeau*' tonight. When a man is given a *tombeau* as a punishment, he digs a hole in the ground the shape and size of a coffin, and he sleeps in it. In the summer it is death by incineration, in the winter it is death by drowning. Chauvin will be freezing tonight and if it rains he's a candidate for pneumonia.

Two Days Later

Yesterday I took a stroll through the small Arab village which
is just beside our camp. The Arabs are quiet and suspicious but
not aggressive or surly. There are very few males except small
boys and grandfathers. The men have gone to the hills to wait
for the great day when they can return to their homes without
being subjected to the threats and violence of us soldiers or
indeed the fellagha. They have been sandwiched between us for
too long now. I never cease to be amazed at what I see in these
little villages. The poverty is so absolute. The houses of mud and
sticks tightly cramped together look so vulnerable; freezing in
winter and sweat heaps in the summer. The rain washes through
the village in rivulets, through the huts – nobody notices. There
is mud everywhere and everybody is clothed in rags which hang
on bodies that are thin and undernourished. There is one brick
building in the village – it is the school, now used as a cowshed,
but I suppose the French meant well when they built it. There
are little plots of arable land along the banks of the river where
an attempt is made to grow rice and higher up on the hillside
there are some olive trees. But there is no drainage system and
the rains come and wash everything away in time.

It is a sobering reflection to realize that this country, still so
poor and stark with its people still so utterly ignorant, is but one
tiny step from donning the weighty mantle of independence.
And tonight we and they will be in the hills sitting by the path in
the darkness with our guns. There is still time for them and us
to die for the cause.

A Week Later

The talking continues at Évian and the fighting continues here
in the mountains, in the desert and in the streets. The O.A.S.

appear to be the stumbling block to a settlement at Évian, which is precisely what they want to be.

There were 200 plastic-bomb explosions in Algiers yesterday. One bomb exploded in a school full of children and whilst there were many Arab children in the school it was predominantly occupied by French children. This has brought a cry of anguish and outrage from France. And it has inevitably produced at last some retaliation from the Arabs. Since they cannot rely on protection from the French *gendarmerie* or the army they have taken their own line of defence. A car full of Arabs roared through the centre of Algiers today with machine-guns sticking out of all four windows firing at random at anything resembling a European. Over forty people were killed and many more wounded. I do not condone it, but I understand it.

We killed a wild boar today and roasted it over hot ashes. The most delicious meat in the world, well marinated in gallons of red wine.

'Cessez-le-Feu'

It is 18 March 1962 and the ceasefire has finally been announced after seven years of agony. Hopes for some come true and dreams are fulfilled. For others, it is the loss of everything they have worked and lived for, the end of a lifetime and the dawn of a new beginning, in many cases from scratch.

But it is not the hour of independence yet and for the O.A.S. It may still be only the starting point. We are still losing deserters on a daily basis and that means the O.A.S. is still recruiting.

So the war is finished in the mountains, but the battle in the streets may be about to begin.

PART NINE

Interlude

20 April 1962

We are camped a hundred miles south of Khenchela. Below us the desert stretches like the sea to a blank horizon and to the north are the Aurès Mountains reaching to the sky. The place is utter desolation. A hot dry wind has been blowing hard from the south for four days. The red dust of the desert is in our sacks, in our food, in our weapons, in our eyes and ears and in our nostrils. Our saliva glands have ceased to function, we have lost our appetites, and at the end of the day we dissolve a packet of dehydrated soup in half a mug of water and force it down our throats.

We have been on patrol for nine days. Under the terms of the ceasefire the fellagha are allowed to carry arms in certain sectors, in others they are not. This is one of the sectors where they cannot be armed and for this reason they are not here. I am sure we are proving something by being here ourselves but I cannot put my finger on it.

The radio broadcasts a daily roll-call of casualties as the plastic bombs of the O.A.S. deal out destruction in the principal cities. Algiers was a bloodbath two days ago. Some Europeans were attacked while walking in the forbidden city. There was a riot. French soldiers arrived and panicked and fired into the crowd. Fifty people were killed and a hundred and thirty wounded.

The French army cannot control the O.A.S. but I do not think that de Gaulle will use the Legion. It is doubtful that his confidence in us has yet been restored so we will be kept away from the cities and used as a last resort.

The French army has demobilized all its loyal Arab troops who have immediately been recruited into the new Algerian army. So eventually it will be the Algerian army that is left to deal with the O.A.S.

But the O.A.S. has been doing its own recruiting. We are still losing deserters steadily. The situation gets worse rather than better.

A Week Later
There has been yet another referendum in France. The question asked simply whether or not Algeria should be given independence. The result was an unequivocal '*Oui*'. So that is that.

28 April 1962
Camerone is approaching again. Each company is preparing a series of stalls. Some Spaniards have got hold of a young bull and Legionnaire Nalda has promised to fight it. I remember the fiasco at Mascara when they had a bullfight. I do not suppose this will be very different but it is a talking-point and it has brought the bookmakers to life. The bull is odds-on favourite.

29 April 1962
General Salan, who led the *putsch* with Challe, was captured in Algiers today. They say that he has been a restraining influence on the O.A.S. and that without him they will step up the offensive.

Camerone
We had a big parade in the morning. Lots of brass arrived and we were inspected by a four-star general. Senior officers from regular army units in the area came with their wives to see how the legionnaire animals lived. The main event, the bullfight, got under way just after lunch in front of a huge crowd. The bullring was surrounded by bales of straw, behind which the crowd were pressed four deep. Nalda was dressed immaculately and

after several vodkas he eventually staggered into the ring. A roar went up from the crowd and the bull promptly charged. Nalda panicked and, having seen the bull, I didn't blame him. Twenty Spaniards leapt into the ring to save the honour of Spain and attacked the bull with bottles, brooms and pickaxe handles. The bull went berserk and charged headlong through the straw bales and was last seen going for its life down the main street of the village of Telergma.

At this moment in time Steffen and I decided to take advantage of the general pandemonium to slip out of camp and head for Constantine. Constantine is about twenty miles from Telergma and in no time we were sitting in the back of a car having hitched a lift, racing for the great town.

The move was not thought through in depth or we would probably not have gone. If we were caught we would almost certainly face charges of desertion and obviously be suspected of going to the O.A.S. Constantine is known as an O.A.S. stronghold. Anyway, these thoughts did not enter our minds until much later and we had a great day.

We were approached in a bar in the evening by a civilian wearing a parachutist *brevet* in his lapel, who introduced himself as an officer of the O.A.S. He said there was work to be done and that if we were interested he could arrange papers for us immediately. He guaranteed repatriation to any country we cared to nominate after two years. Tempting stuff in some ways. We said we would consider it and outside the bar decided that if we could not get a lift back to Telergma that night we would take up the offer. We got a lift – but only halfway. Night was falling when we began walking the last ten miles.

Just before we arrived at Telergma we got a lift from a regular army major. A good man. With his help we managed to get through the Legion patrols operating in and around Telergma.

When we got into the village we were confronted by a sight of total devastation that was absolutely unbelievable, something along the lines of Warsaw in 1942.

The people in the town had been warned of the coming of Camerone and had been advised to keep the bars and bistros open and to trust to luck. But they had not followed this wise council and when the drunken regiment descended on the town in the evening they were most unhappy to find all doors barred.

This was bad psychology and the legionnaires took grievous offence at the insult; they destroyed the town.

Shop windows were smashed, the bars were all forced open and the bottles broken and Telergma was an unsafe place to be if one was not a legionnaire. It was a complete disaster area. The patrol ran haywire in every direction but they were totally outnumbered and unable to cope.

When Steffen and I got out of the major's car we could see a long column of some hundred legionnaires staggering down the main street back to camp with various items of booty slung over their shoulders – tables, hat stands, radios, bottles, chairs – and six people were actually carrying a juke-box. Ninety per cent of them were out of their minds and in the dim glow of the street lights it looked like some weird medieval procession.

It began to pour with rain but this did nothing to dampen the spirit of the party and back at the camp things were well out of control. Everybody converged on the regimental bordello where the N.C.O.s were trying to keep the legionnaires out because it was officially after time for the rank and file. Bottles started flying and mob orators threw the crowd into a frenzy – they started to pull the tent down and with a great rousing cheer and a 'Heave-ho' it crashed. The bar was upended and the bottles and glasses destroyed and thrown into the air. The noise was like a volcano erupting.

The whores fled into the darkness and pouring rain, screaming blue murder, with twenty men pounding after each one of them. Everybody was drenched, and it looked as though they were standing under an oil-well strike. The storming of the Bastille had nothing on this.

And then somebody threw a couple of offensive grenades into the crowd and serious fighting broke out. Many of the N.C.O.s got hidings that were long overdue. The situation was inflammatory now and very dangerous – and then the patrol arrived with reinforcements in about ten jeeps, all with sirens going at full volume. Mass exodus – people running like hell into the night – the military police swinging their batons – the fun was over.

The Next Day

Yesterday's toll: fifteen legionnaires missing with six submachine-guns, two jeeps and a Dodge truck. Belgian Joe from the 4th Company is one of the missing. And the late news is that eighteen of our boys in the base company in Philippeville are missing, along with two radios, nine sub-machine-guns and three vehicles. All leave is cancelled.

3 May 1962
They took us on a forced march for thirty-five miles yesterday and marched us back today. The entire regiment participated. This was their way of drying us out. The heat was staggering. Nine men are in a coma and apparently someone in the 4th Company has had a heart attack and is either dead or dying. We must be getting out of condition with all this ceasefire stuff.

5 May 1962
Steffen and Charlie Noi are leaving tomorrow. *La Quille* after five years. Willie would never have joined the O.A.S. the other day in Constantine, he was just going through the motions – so was I.

We had a party for them that went on until they dropped. They are both out of their minds with joy at the prospects of leaving. They declare that they will never return. But everybody says that and yet so many of them do not make it in civilian life and back they come as soon as they have swallowed their pride. Making it on the outside is a tremendous challenge. To return is to have failed and many of those that do return volunteer for other regiments in the hope that their old chums will not know that they have come back. On occasions we discuss someone who has left and we imagine him breezing down the Champs-Élysées with three girls on each arm but in fact he may well be sweating it out in Djibouti or Madagascar or some other Legion outpost.

Anyway, it is *adios* to Willie. I liked him well and will miss his humour. The Legion breaks down barriers of preconceived ideas and misconceptions about people and in their place sometimes generates a great spirit of comradeship. So has it been with Willie and me. But at the end of each man's time he goes on his way and the friendship that was dissolves with each passing day into a faded memory. One of our songs says '*pour oublier il faut partir*' – but I will never forget, completely.

Ten Days Later

We have been on operations south of Djidjelli for the last week near Texanna in the great oued Gen-gen. We left behind Willie and Charlie Noi, waving their arms off. I wonder what the future holds for them.

Although we go through the motions of operations, we do not expect to find anything. It is all a farce. Certainly if there is some sanity in it, it is beyond my comprehension. We just keep staggering up and down the hills like mindless mules.

Grueber collapsed on the march today. Out cold in the stifling heat. Nobody mourned the event – he is poison.

Three Weeks Later

We have moved all our gear from Philippeville to Telergma. Yesterday I went into Philippeville, probably for the last time. I met someone in a bar who by chance knew the Serves and some of their friends. In fact he seemed to know everybody in town. He confirmed that the Serves have gone to France. Everybody has gone as far as I can determine, the place is a morgue. And early this morning we marched out through the gates of Camp Pehaut for the last time singing the song of the 2nd Parachute Regiment. The sea was in front of us as we marched down the hill to the main road where our lorries were waiting; the camp was behind us, already only a memory by the time we got to the bottom of the hill. We drove to Telergma. The Philippeville chapter is over. I had some good times there and I will remember them always.

6 June 1962

Time moves forward ever more slowly as we drift towards independence. Now that it is inevitable I want it to happen speedily so that we can make a clean break and start the next phase of our lives here. Waiting for it to happen is like running on the spot.

We have been on the Tunisian frontier for ten days. The first convoy of fellagha have been allowed to enter from Tunisia. The frontier was opened for two days. Thousands of Arabs on foot and a column of trucks and cars stretching to the horizon crawled through all day and all night for those forty-eight hours.

And when the doors were shut again we spread ourselves along the wire for miles and lay in silence through the night to make sure they did not abuse the welcome.

There are definite signs already that the Europeans will have an uncomfortable time here once the Algerians have regained control. Too much hatred has been produced over these last years for it to be erased by the signing of a document of peace. Revenge is human. When we left Philippeville a small unit remained behind to do the final clearing up. On the last night two legionnaires were attacked in Philippeville. One got away, the other was decapitated.

White was in the last truck to leave Philippeville. He said that on the final day a bunch of them went to the town cemetery and weeded the grass around the Legion graves. That's the last weeding those graves will get. Not until the grass has grown over them and they have disappeared forever will the Arabs be finally satisfied.

And one day in Souk-Ahras I felt their antagonism in a strange environment. Pavlicic and I were in town. It was a Sunday afternoon and we came to a large mosque which we decided to enter out of curiosity. We removed our boots and showed much respect by bowing very low to the holy man who came forward as we entered. We were wearing our para uniforms and though the various elders were clearly astonished to see us, they beckoned us to come and sit within their circle on a rug in the middle of the floor. We were in a hall strewn with fabulous carpets on which people sat or kneeled in apparent meditation. The elders were splendid and, masking their incredulity behind their long white beards, they offered their hands in a gesture of friendship. We sat and talked about religion and we agreed that all of us had our own different ways of worship, but common to all was the belief in one divine being. They were good people and totally genuine in what they said. I felt no animosity at all. On the contrary, I think they felt about us as I felt about them. There was goodwill in the air. But not for long. An Arab suddenly came forward and whispered to us that there was a patrol outside and trouble was brewing and that we had best leave immediately. We bade our farewells to those worthy people and hastily put on our boots.

Outside we were startled to see an enormous crowd of Arabs

and the expression on their faces was none too friendly. The goodwill atmosphere was gone completely and I was preparing for the worst. I think in that moment Pavlicic and I were about as near our demise as it is possible to be without actually going overboard. And then the door of the mosque swung open and the senior of the elders came out and in front of the crowd he shook our hands in farewell and friendship. We were very relieved indeed and seeing the old man's blessing the crowd grudgingly made an opening for us. We walked slowly through, resisting the temptation to break into a run. And eventually we were round the corner out of sight and we ran like hell. It will be some time before I go into a mosque uninvited again.

15 June 1962

Three corporals and eight legionnaires have been arrested for running arms to the O.A.S. This has been going on for some time. The minimum sentence they can expect is seven years in a civilian prison. A civilian sentence does not count against Legion service and they can at the discretion of the Legion be dragged back afterwards to finish their time in the ranks. Something to look forward to when they are inside.

And on top of that some staggering news from Marseille: Willie Steffen and Charlie Noi have been arrested for holding up a bank with sub-machine-guns. It just does not make any sense at all. It is so crazy that it has to be true. Whether or not they had been put up to it by the O.A.S., as has been suggested, still does not make it remotely comprehensible to me. Only a few weeks ago they were rejoicing at the prospect of freedom, a new start, and now they have pissed it all against the wall. Madness.

So when I think of old Willie in the future I won't imagine him quaffing ale by the gallon in Heidelberg, dancing with the frauleins on the table, as I would like to have done. Instead I will think of him in a cell behind bars. He is a wild man with so much spirit. Ten years in gaol will kill him. He was like so many others here; they are on the surface of life and I suppose I am too. It is because we have no responsibility. There is no worry. And at the same time there is no care.

Willie will care even less when he gets out and then it will be too late – he will be dead forever.

2 July 1962
Independence Day. After so long it has finally come, in spite of everybody and everything. Seven years of fighting is over. The world is beginning to learn that independence from the big powers comes by force alone.

The result is always the same in the end. Why don't the colonial powers negotiate earlier and get a better deal? The French have ended this one with a lease on the naval base at Mers el-Kébir and the oil rights in Sahara for a period of five years and then it will all be over after more than a century of investment.

There was no move or gesture from the O.A.S. today. It would seem futile for them to continue now. They must recognize that it is finished. The Arabs are in a state of euphoria. The new Algerian flag hangs from every window and in the streets people are dancing with joy.

A Month Later
The day after independence was hoisted we had a jump involving twenty aircraft. God knows what the Arabs felt as they looked up to the sky and saw hundreds of paratroopers descending upon them. That was my twenty-fifth jump. Since then nothing has happened and we are just drifting along without any indication as to what our next move will be.

When peace comes after fighting and war there is jubilation, often on both sides. People return to their homes and pick up their lives where they left them before the war started and they prepare to begin again. There is a meaning in their lives once more. In the Legion this is not so, the opposite is true. Life comes to a halt. Suddenly there is no purpose, there is no direction. Bewilderment is quickly superseded by boredom, which is itself overtaken by a rapid decline in morale. Discontent follows and the system begins to rot.

The war has finished in Algeria and the energy that has driven the fighting machinery of the Legion for so long needs to be channelled into some new enterprise. Energy that is not released is potentially explosive. The remaining French colonies are few in number and as far as I am aware they are free of trouble. So there is nothing for us there. There is talk of a movement towards independence in Madagascar but the French may not be prepared to go through it all again. It has been a long slog and a costly one through Indo-China and North Africa, even though they have used legionnaires.

Morale is low and there is no ebb in the desertion rate. I don't know now whether the O.A.S. is still recruiting or whether the deserters are making their own way home.

There are many new faces around these days, which proves the Legion is still recruiting anyway. Two Englishmen have arrived called Kenny something and Bob Wilson. Kenny is an ex-private soldier from a British parachute regiment and Wilson has been an officer. He is an interesting character, puts on a bit of an act I think and is probably not what he seems. Having said that, I enjoy his company and it is good to have reinforcements that do not look as if they will let the side down. They are both in the 2nd Company.

There are some new people in the section too and many of the old hands have suddenly disappeared. Perhaps it was not so sudden, but I have only just noticed. Now that we are no longer in the hills all the time one is getting to know more people in the regiment. Their faces are familiar but we have never stopped in one place long enough to say 'hello' before.

Carlsen has re-emerged after so long. I used to chat to him sometimes in the *foyer* in Philippeville. He is Danish, speaks English when he is half sober, which is seldom these days, and is generally a cheery soul. And there is a splendid new Hungarian in our section. Young and tough as a bullock and he doesn't give a stuff about anything. That is an attitude I find I have always admired. I think I do care about things but I would like to be able not to. This fellow's name is Huber. He has threatened to kill Corporal Guhl, which is another reason I like him. I will like him more if he does.

We spend most of our evenings in the crowded *foyer* drinking gallons of ale and singing German marching songs. Few people go into town these days. It is crawling with Arab soldiers all armed to the teeth. They carry their sub-machine-guns like gentlemen in the city of London carry their umbrellas. Our military police carry only batons now. The shoe is very much on the other foot.

Chief Corporal Kroll, who is one of the old school, has been

in the wars lately. We had a practice operational jump the other
day and we were instructed to keep down when we landed. Kroll
disobeyed this order and collected eight days in prison. He had
no sooner come out and was celebrating in the *bordel* when he
was again in trouble. He was supposed to be on duty in the
bordel, a sinecure that N.C.O.s do on a rota basis, but he managed
with the aid of a case of champagne to get himself and all the
whores drunk. When it was found that the tipsy whores could
not perform, there was a riot. Somebody grabbed the cash box
and ran off with it and Kroll fired his pistol several times into
the air in indignation. Kroll is now safely back inside doing
another eight days. He has done well over a hundred days in his
time.

In the regulations of the French army it states that if a man
receives more than eight days' prison during his service he must
pass a special tribunal before he can be awarded a certificate of
good conduct on demobilization. After the words 'eight days'
it says in brackets, '*La Légion étrangère, cent-cinquante jours*'.
It must be getting quite close for old Kroll.

Legionnaire Ledermann was also involved in the incident in
the *bordel*. Ledermann is always around when trouble and drink
are together. He came out of it somewhat worse than Kroll
because he has no protective N.C.O. stripes and he is now sleeping in a *tombeau* every night. He has also been beaten up. He is
down to three teeth and I would not put money on their chances
of lasting much more than a month or two.

20 August 1962
Kroll has done it again. Each section in the company has its own
mess tent and over a period of time these mess tents have become extremely acceptable places in which to eat and drink.
They started out with the basics and then after a time members
of a particular section subscribed to buy table-cloths, plates and
glasses. Then this was followed by the acquisition of stoves and
a bar and they became places where one could buy beer in the
evening or bacon and eggs in the morning. In fact within no
time at all we had quite a flourishing little business going in our
section and all the other sections envied us our luxury. The bar
made a profit and on special occasions money was taken out of
a caisse to finance an *apéritif* for the section. Members of the

section could also negotiate interest-free loans from the barman when they were short of cash. And then suddenly two days ago, out of the blue, Benoît ordered it to be closed down. No reasons given. Most of the section were out on orders when this message came through but Kroll and one or two others were in the bar as usual, boosting the profits. They didn't like what they heard at all and to show their displeasure they took it upon themselves to destroy the whole bloody place. They smashed all the plates and glasses and then started on the bottles and they didn't let up until they had torn the table-cloths to shreds. The general reception to this outburst from the rest of the section, once we had heard the reason why, was good. The wreckers were congratulated on a job well done. That would have been the end of the affair, but Caulier with his big mouth started bragging about it and eventually, spurred on a little by Corporal Guhl perhaps, it got back to Benoît. Benoît interpreted it for what it was – a demonstration against authority. In short, a rebellion.

We got just enough warning that the authorities were planning a counter-attack for us to agree that the whole section was involved and that we would stand together. Only Grueber refused to agree to this.

The warning was accurate and the following day the balloon went up. When the authorities saw that they were faced with a united section, they started individual interrogation. By the time the first six had been interviewed, the cat was out of the bag – blown by Corporal Guhl.

Guhl is the epitome of what one imagines a good German corporal should be. He obeys orders to the letter, is incapable of any deviation from guidelines set, irrespective of any change in circumstances, and is part of the machinery that made the German army what it was.

Anyway, the upshot of it all is eight days each for the plate smashers, which is now on its way up to the colonel with a request for doubling. The punishments for the N.C.O.s involved are somewhat harsher. Kroll has been made to sign a paper forfeiting his parachute *brevet* and he is to be thrown out of the regiment, stripped of his rank and collects fifteen days' prison into the bargain. This in spite of the fact that he is one of the most highly decorated men in the company. He has the Médaille Militaire and the Croix de Valeur Militaire with three stars and a palm. Starry, who was going to Corporal School, has been banned forever so that he can never rise above the rank of private. Theo and Caulier are inside. One bit of good news is that Slymer was involved. He has been stripped of his corporal stripes, collects fifteen days and will then change companies. I hope that is the last we see of him.

I think the officers have over-reacted to this whole thing. Although I was not there at the time, I can imagine exactly what happened. The boys just got carried away a little, that's all. This punishment is unnecessarily harsh. For the rest, the *réfectoire* is closed and we take all our meals standing to attention in the sun and we are on hard labour from sun-up to sun-down until further notice. In addition we have barrack and kit inspections every morning and evening.

We have just heard tonight that the eight days has gone to thirty, not fifteen. That's heavy stuff for smashing a few plates. *Vive la Légion!*

2 September 1962

The Arabs are still ecstatic with their new-found liberty. I wonder what's so different about it. They are seizing French property and carving it up amongst themselves. Later they will look back and wonder where it all disappeared. The O.A.S. maintain a low profile. Our desertion rate climbs steadily every week. We go quietly about our business: drill, inspections, football, weapon cleaning, inspection and back to drill. Morale continues to slide; nothing happens.

I was late for *appel* last night. I had been drinking with old Carlsen. Tandoi stood in for me and was counted twice so I was all right. Carlsen was not so lucky. I went over to his company later and found him sitting in a barrel of water under guard. He was quite happy at the time, but he is miserable today. He has spent the day cleaning lavatories with a toothbrush and a bar of soap. Not a great way to pass the time of day. I am in Tandoi's debt.

Georges Penco has returned from Corporal School and is now sporting two green stripes on his arm. He feels better and his voice is a little louder.

8 September 1962

Idle days continue to move slowly past. There is time for reading and even more for thinking – time to take stock of one's life. Realizing that I have two more years and more to go, I realize simultaneously that it is too early to plan. But it is not too early to dream and that is a source of great pleasure.

When I finish here I will be approaching my twenty-fifth birthday. That is a sobering thought. My youth will have passed me by – not so slowly that is for sure. I will have no qualifications and no experience that is readily marketable. What to do? Friends with whom I was at school will have finished university and obtained their degrees and will be years ahead of me.

I do not even begin to know what I would like to do, although I am aware of several things that I would like not to do. Perhaps it is by a process of elimination that one eventually stumbles on the thing that gives one the most satisfaction in life. The great thing is to keep on moving forward and to keep on looking.

We are quite a strong little band of English-speaking people in the regiment now. Carlsen, when he is coherent, is a member of our band and there is another Swedish fellow called Leif who always drinks with us. Then there are Kenny, Bob Wilson and White. We all go to the *foyer* every night. Often there is no money among us and we draw lots to decide who will get the beer. The loser must use his reputation to obtain credit from his friends or he must sell something or he must go to the lenders, but he must get some beer. To fail is to become an outcast.

Wilson continues to somehow just miss with me. He is a nice guy but he is still pretending to be what he is not. This is so unnecessary because it belittles him. He should know by now that in the Legion all men start equal and what has gone before contributes nothing to one's standing. Here you are as you are. Perhaps it is too early to judge, I may well be wrong.

9 September 1962

It is evening and we are waiting for *appel*. Friend Ledermann, who has been drinking continuously since last night and probably still is unless he is unconscious, has so far failed to appear. He has about three minutes in which to get here. There is a reception committee waiting for him led by Corporal Guhl. He and the other corporals are obviously looking forward to beating the hell out of Ledermann if he is late. They may not, for the mood among the men is sour and it would not take much to incite a riot. Poor old Ledermann he is always in the shit. He is a liar and a thief and a leech-like beggar without the slightest trace of self-respect, but in spite of everything I like him.

He is down to two teeth, he looks about sixty-five although he is scarcely twenty-eight, and he has been beaten up so many times that his mind is now cracked.

I cannot begin to imagine where Ledermann will end up. There is not the slightest hope for him. His life here is spent between the bars and the prison – poor lost soul, poor miserable bastard. But he does not stop to think, so the misery of his plight has not yet caught up with him – but it will.

A Week Later
Ledermann is still in prison with two more days to go. We are planning a little celebration for him when he gets out. Carlsen has been appointed storekeeper in his company and he now sleeps in a separate tent with all the stores. He has made this into his own private den and it is known as the British Club.

24 September 1962
Something happened in Carlsen's tent today that has left me wondering who I am and whether I have become something very different to what I thought I was. I do not understand my reaction, or lack of reaction, to this incredible incident.

Carlsen has a cat and it ate his lunch which was sitting on a plate in his tent, while he was guzzling beer. I was with him also guzzling beer but I was still sober whereas Carlsen was already his normal glassy-eyed self. When he saw the cat had eaten his food, he grabbed it by the neck and held it at arm's length by one hand while he screamed oaths at it.

After a minute or so I suddenly realized that he was strangling it and I sat mesmerized and fascinated. That cat's body was hanging down and then almost in slow motion it bent its body and back legs up and over Carlsen's wrist and with a quivering motion dug its claws deep into his forearm and slowly tore the flesh in a long searing gash. Carlsen never moved. His face was taut and covered in sweat and his eyes remained fixed on the cat as he continued to hold it in his outstretched hand, squeezing the life out of it with every bit of strength he had. I didn't move a single inch, nor could I. And the cat continued to claw at the flesh on Carlsen's arm, ripping it to shreds so that it was bloody and torn as raw meat. It was as ghastly a sight as one could ever see and still I did not move. And then suddenly after an age he dropped the half-dead cat on the ground and grabbed his sheath knife lying on the table and rammed it through the breast of the cat as it lay on its back and skewered it to the floor and held it there. In slow motion again the cat's four legs came up, quivering and trembling over Carlsen's wrist, and tore his bloody arm almost to the bone in its last desperate effort to save itself.

Carlsen registered no pain and his face was fixed and grim and deathly pale and wet. He withdrew the knife and smashed the heel of his boot hard down on the cat's head – again and again until eventually it ceased to move. I left the tent without a word and wandered back to my company. I felt nothing toward Carlsen, nor did I feel anything in particular for the cat. I felt nothing. My emotions were dead and yet my mind told me that I had witnessed a scene of unimaginable horror.

I cannot believe that this is me; that my senses have been dulled to this extent, that I am so past caring about anything or that my values have disappeared. What are my values? Christ, what a thought.

Three Weeks On

If you take the main road out of Oran, west along the coast, you pass the huge naval base of Mers el-Kébir and about twenty miles further on you come to the small town of Aïn el-Turck, which has little to offer except a dingy hotel, four or five bars, a main street covered in dust and a deserted beach. Ten miles beyond Aïn el-Turck is the village of Bou-Sfer which offers still less. Nobody lives in Bou-Sfer now, it is a ghost town with a number of shacks and small brick buildings that were once holiday homes of the French people living in Oran. The coastal beaches are among the most unspoilt and beautiful that one could ever hope to come across, but the beauty is chilled by the empty gaping houses of the village. They create an atmosphere of disquiet as though something bad once happened here and everybody has gone away to forget. A road leads out of the village up the hill onto a flat coastal plain that stretches for miles and miles to the foothills of blue mountains on the distant horizon. This plain is the site of our camp.

When we came here just three short weeks ago there was nothing but dust and dead vines; old vines with gnarled roots that had burrowed their way deep into the soil over the years.

For the last thirty days we have attacked these vines with picks and shovels, working from dawn till dusk in long extended lines. Sometimes there are as many as two hundred men in the line slowly moving forward with their bodies flowing up and down with every swing of the pick, like waves breaking on the shore. It is an amazing sight; everything is moving all the time.

At lunch there is a break and a jeep drives along the column dropping off rations which we gobble up and then it's *au boulot* again. The fighting machine has become the bulldozer. We have the energy and the discipline and there is no problem of maintenance or need for spare parts, except occasionally when a pickaxe handle can take no more and it snaps in two.

And we have now created an enormous dust bowl over which we have spread our tents. There is nothing here except dust and tents. In places the dust is four inches deep. One drop of rain will turn the place into a quagmire in which we will all flounder and submerge forever.

With the passage of time this camp, which now resembles a nomad's paradise, will become a network of tarmac roads, telephone wires and drains. Modern barracks will replace the tents and concrete will replace the mud floors inside them. The perimeter of the camp is six miles, around which there will be an impregnable barrage of barbed wire and mines and there will be an airstrip which will be our lifeline to the outside world if the Arabs do decide they want to get rid of us. Grass will grow and there will be gardens and trees and we will once more have reclaimed land back from Nature. This will be a French oasis in Algeria.

That, we are told, is the future. The present is the sweat and the dust and the boredom of it all. A new corporal has arrived in the section and it turns out that he did *instruction* with me at Mascara. I remember him as being very much a loner, quieter than most, and what little I saw of him I liked. His name is

Trainée. He is Italian. He remembered me well and surprised me by saying that he had heard that I had been killed at Medina. The way I feel right now that might not have been such a bad thing.

16 October 1962

I received a letter today from my old friend, Alister Hall. He is going to Italy with his fiancée, Julia, and his mother. They will be staying at his parents' villa and he thinks he could slip across for a few days in spite of the frantic tide of opposition that he is facing from the two ladies. It just so happens that I am due for a spot of local leave and a rest centre has already been organized down in Bou-Sfer. I would much prefer Aïn el-Turck but we are only allowed there on Sundays.

The idea of old Al coming over here is just simply unbelievable. I feel a new man. I have sent a letter back and told him to get on his horse. But I do not believe for one second he will come. It's the thought of it that makes me feel good.

Three Days Later

My leave is on, beginning the day after tomorrow. Although I will have to stay in Bou-Sfer, I can get a pass to Aïn el-Turck each day until ten in the evening. I have written to Alister and told him that he is booked into the Hotel Saint Maurice in Aïn el-Turck. The people who run it are a rather nice French family who have been there for years. The owner's granddaughter is a twenty-year-old bombshell called Jacqueline. I told them the booking could not be regarded as firm and that if my friend arrived it should be regarded as nothing short of a miracle. They understand the position but as there is only one other guest in the hotel, they do not expect overbooking to be a problem.

It is just possible that Alister will come. If it were anybody else I would probably not have bothered to make the booking. But he is a very special chum and I know that if our positions were reversed I would come over to see him, no matter what.

21 October 1962

Fantastic, unbelievable, staggering news – he's coming! Jais summoned me from Bou-Sfer this evening and presented me with a cable. It said simply, 'Arriving Oran 1930 on 22/10 –

Alister.' That's tomorrow. It is inconceivable that he will actually be here tomorrow.

Jais asked me hundreds of questions about who he was and what was happening. I told him that he was an officer of the 21st Lancers on leave, that he was an old friend and that I would like to spend the rest of my leave in Aïn el-Turck. No deal. But he did ring up Major Debiré, who agreed that I could spend tomorrow night in town. They are obviously anxious not to create a precedent and I suppose the desertion rate over the last few months has not made it any easier to make a decision. Anyway, that's already something of a concession by Legion standards. Jais said he would like to meet Alister while he was here and I promised to bring him up to the camp. That will be an eye opener for Alister. Probably be an eye opener for Jais too.

The Next Evening
When I got to the Saint Maurice hotel, Alister had already arrived. He was sitting at a table by the window in the restaurant already halfway through a bottle of champagne. He was wearing an immaculate tropical suit, one of Hong Kong's best. He looked absolutely splendid. What a meeting! Blücher and Wellington, Stanley and Livingstone, and now Murray and Hall. We looked each other up and down. Impossible to describe the joy, the sensations of the experience as we clasped hands. We had had so many good times together in the past, so many laughs, and now suddenly we were thrown together in a situation neither of us could visualize even though we were actually living it. There was something about it that was totally unreal. I think we were slightly nonplussed by it all for a few seconds. We just did not know where to start. It had been so long, magnified ten times by the change in circumstances. Before, young teenagers finding their feet in London nightclubs in the first rush of excitement after leaving school. Now much older and in a very different setting, foreign to us both. It was momentarily difficult to grasp the sheer reality of it.

We had a great evening – caught up on years of news, talked about all our mutual friends and reminded ourselves of so many good times we had seen in the past. I was suddenly transplanted back in England. The Legion was over and I was back home.

Never will I forget this evening. We talked all night without a moment's pause. And I will remember thinking what a fantastic friend I had in him and what a great man he was to have come. How many other people would go to Algeria to see a friend in the Foreign Legion?

23 October 1962

We got a ride on a regular army truck up to our camp first thing in the morning. Through the main entrance into the camp itself, the subject of all eyes. Alister looking miles out of place sporting a charcoal-grey tropical suit. We arrived at Jais' tent and I made the introductions. Jais was charming. He had nil English and Alister had no French, but through me we got messages of goodwill across.

Eventually Alister put in a request that his good friend Murray be allowed to stay in Aïn el-Turck for a few days. This was going to be terribly important and would of course make or break Alister's trip. He put up a convincing case explaining that he had come all this way and could not believe that the Legion would not allow me the necessary time off. He gave his word as an Englishman and an officer that I would not run away and I added mine to it.

Jais obviously wanted to give me the necessary permission but he did not have the authority, so he wound the handle of his camp telephone and got onto Debiré. After a lot of talk the answer was finally 'No'. It was a shattering blow.

We bade farewell to Jais and then Hall made an immediate line for Debiré's tent. He was not going to be put off. I was feeling distinctly uneasy because any rebound could only land on one person. It was obvious by this stage that the boys were going to treat this English officer with respect, courtesy and friendship, but if there was going to be any trouble it was going to come down squarely on my neck as soon as Alister left.

We marched past a bewildered sentry into the commanding officer's tent and Hall demanded to see the C.O. The Legion is just not equipped to handle this sort of thing. Debiré is acting number two at the moment while Colonel Channel is away on leave and the acting C.O. is Commandant Arnaut de Foyard. De Foyard is someone with whom as a legionnaire I had no contact whatsoever, but his reputation as a first-class officer and a first-rate man was unequalled in the Legion and well known to me. He was made of the stuff that men admire, and in the regiment he had the respect of every man.

After a lot of commotion, Hall was eventually ushered into de Foyard's *bureau* where he was confronted by the great man himself and Debiré. I was left outside. They were in there for an hour and got on famously. Drinks all round and discussion on the merits of the English cavalry and the Foreign Legion made the base for mutual admiration. I gave Hall very good marks. These men were veterans and to make one's number with them is no easy task at all. I was somehow proud of the fact that my team had come through too. They did not let me down and created no less of an impression on Hall than he did on them.

The upshot of it all was that the decision was reversed and I was given five days' leave in Aïn el-Turck. De Foyard called me into his office without Alister and I met him at close quarters for the first time. He said he had heard a lot about me and liked what he had heard. That went down very well indeed! I thought that he was about to make me a captain. He said he wanted to make it absolutely clear that he had authorized the leave in Aïn el-Turck not because of the arrival of my friend, but because of my service record to date. That was great psychology and he earned my total respect in that instant. There are some people who spark feelings of rapport at the first meeting, and such was de Foyard. Not because he was giving me a good deal, but because of what I saw in him. People who have power and use it wisely and with perception are rare birds and when you stand before them you feel good.

When we came out of the C.O.'s tent we ran into Chief Sergeant Grandys and I introduced Alister to him. Grandys is Polish and I had told him before that Alister was coming. He was delighted to meet this English officer and invited us to join him later in the N.C.O.s' mess for drinks. I had forgotten how much the Poles love the Brits.

And so a couple of hours later there we were in the N.C.O.s' mess knocking back beer with the best of them. They could not have been more hospitable. All of them: the Germans, the Italians, the Spanish, the Hungarians and the Poles. These hard-faced Legion veterans treated Alister as though he was one of them. Many of them spoke English. Alister I think must have been in a daze by it all, he was enjoying himself so much. I just

watched in wonder at the continued incongruity of it. It made
no sense at all, and yet it was happening. I remember thinking
that Alister was going to be able to dine out on this one for the
rest of his life. Who could possibly trump a story like this?

Eventually it was time to move and Grandys drove us to Aïn
el-Turck in his bright-blue convertible Chevrolet. Adjutant
Simsky, also Polish and a great chum of Grandys, has invited
us to take coffee with him tomorrow in Aïn el-Turck. Simsky is
the Postmaster General and he drives his jeep through Aïn el-
Turck every day on his way to Oran to get the post. He is the
most splendid man. He fought with the British during the war
and he thinks we as people are the finest in the world – second
only to the Poles perhaps. The British have good friends
scattered far and in strange places. That is worthwhile remem-
bering.

Four Days Later
We have had the time of our lives. Each day begins at nine o'clock
with an aperitif with old Simsky at the Palm Beach bar on the
corner of the main street. We have developed a strong partiality
for Ricard and over the last few days have boosted sales of this
poison to new heights. During the weekdays no legionnaires
come to Aïn el-Turck, so amongst the regular French army
here we have established a reputation as being something
special. On the few occasions when we have come dangerously
close to upsetting the regular army military police, a combination of the Legion and the British army has been enough to
talk our way out of it.

One evening we were in a bar with a bunch of regulars singing
our heads off until two in the morning, with 'You Are My
Sunshine', 'It's a Long Way to Tipperary', 'Sunny Boy', 'Old
Man River', 'Glory, Glory, Alleluia' and the rest of it, when
suddenly it was curfew time and the regulars ran for their lives.
Alister and I were left solo in the middle of the main street.

Along came the M.P.s. The guy in charge was looking for
trouble. He had a long scar down the side of his face which did
not help the atmosphere at all. He was going to be difficult from
the word go. He demanded to see our papers and he was clearly
under the impression that Hall was a Legion deserter. Alister's
papers were back at the hotel, so Scarface ordered us into the

jeep and said he would accompany us there. Hall then got on his high horse and explained that he was an English officer and as such did not travel in the back of a jeep but in front. I didn't like this much because if we were thrown inside and caused trouble after de Foyard had been so damned good to us, it was going to take a lot of explaining. I tried to get Hall to change his mind, but the Ricard had done something to his ears.

We were at an impasse. Scarface was frantically trying to weigh up the situation and he was smart enough to realize that Hall might just be telling the truth, so he refrained from hitting him over the head with his baton.

Eventually we compromised. Scarface and the driver got in the front, I got in the back and Hall walked. We made quite a procession going slowly down the main street.

When we got to the hotel and Hall produced his papers, Scarface was all smiles and invited us to the bar for some more Ricard, which we gladly accepted. The ending was fine but I know from experience that it could have turned out very differently. It taught us one thing and that was that there was some mileage to be had from this 'English officer' bit. They didn't know how to handle it.

We went to the *bordel* one day and the sentry refused to let Alister in as a civilian, so he demanded to see the regular army officer commanding the garrison. This was dangerous stuff and our necks were now out quite a long way. At least mine was. I was dying for something to come along and make me disappear. Anyway we were eventually paraded in front of this regular army colonel to whom Hall sold a line about being an English officer on leave with a particular interest in studying the French bordello system which he was planning to introduce into the 21st Lancers. The fellow bought the whole thing and gave Alister a special pass and in we went. I should record for the benefit of the lovely Julia waiting for him in southern Italy that nothing happened inside. We merely had a look and a few drinks.

We went to Oran once. I was in civilian clothes and felt better than I have done in three years. And we became great friends of Toto at the Saint Maurice. Toto is the sort of 'every man' at the hotel. He holds it together. Checks the catering, organizes the staff, looks after the guests and in fact runs the place. He invited us to his little house one day, where we met his family and some of his friends. We talked into the early hours of the following day about Algeria, its problems and its people.

And we have also grown very fond of Abdel Kadar, who runs a little bar in the main street. He is a splendid man with a huge Mexican-type drooping moustache and he serves the most delicious *moules à la marinière* I have ever tasted.

In these few days I have come to like these local people enormously. We sat and talked politics to six Arabs one night in Abdel Kadar's bar and I felt for the first time that I had come to know them. There was no hostility in them and there was none in me. On the contrary, I think they are fine people and I like them.

Everything has happened so very fast. Al leaves tomorrow. Grandys has offered to drive him to Oran. These four days have been the most enjoyable that I can remember. We have not stopped laughing. I have never felt so relaxed and free. I wonder what Alister will make of it when he gets back to England. He will never believe that it all happened, nor I think will I. He has learnt some French which may convince him that he was here. Some of his French has been very useful to us. The most over-used phrase he had was '*Mon ami, le Commandant*'. For the most part his English was in use and I had to translate. His favourite expressions are: 'Look, Murray, put this guy right. Get it across to him that I am an English officer and I demand that . . .' or 'Can you get a jeep organized?' And 'Christ, this Ricard goes through you like a dose of salts!'

This evening we went up to the camp again. Grandys and Simsky had invited us for drinks again at the N.C.O.s' mess. As last time, we were well received and they could not have been better hosts. Hall loved it. And afterwards I took him over to the *foyer* tent of the other ranks. It was packed to the brim. Everybody was singing, shoving and guzzling beer. The atmosphere is that of a mining camp. And Hall, immaculate, sitting among all these fellows was an incredible sight. He was not fazed by it and kept his cool and so did they. All it needed was just one bastard in there who might want to make trouble; but not a bit of it, they were all terrific. I was somewhat relieved when it was over. I think they were all good to Alister because they were curious, because they are by nature not deliberately unkind, and above all because he was my friend. This I will appreciate always and many of the harsh words I have used about the people here I regret. One cannot generalize and one must be slow to judge.

28 October 1962
Alister left at 10.30 after a final drink at the Palm Beach with old Simsky. Grandys was there in his splendid limousine to take him off in style. The parting was a real wrench. He took with him England, my friends and values and everything they represent to me. As the car disappeared around the corner I was back in the Legion with a bang, one hundred per cent solo again; still a stranger here after all this time and I know now that I will never be anything else.

Two Weeks Later
It has been raining for three days. The tents are knee-deep in water. All the drains we have dug over the past few weeks are now torrential rivers that have flooded their banks, and the whole area looks like the mouth of the Mississippi. Auxiliary pumps work in vain through the night and human chains with buckets stretch in lines from every tent. On top of that we keep digging ditches ever deeper. Mud and slime everywhere, that slides back into the ditch every time you try to shovel it out. Hour after hour we battle away without the slightest hope of winning against the bloody water. Everything is soaking in the morning when we rise. We suspend our boots from the eaves of the tent at night but they are still full of water the next day. They would be even if one hung them upside down. There is no stopping this stuff.

There are signs that in time we will be able to master the situation. We have started building a network of roads through the camp and concrete platforms for our tents. This is a monumental task and the Legion is the perfect force for it. Cheap, resourceful and indefatigable. Each morning after assembly the plumbers, the artisans, the carpenters and those with a skill or trade of some kind are separated from the rest of us and we, the rump, are then divided into labour groups. Sometimes we go into the hills and spend our day digging for gravel or sand or loading trucks with rocks, which we bring back to the road and bash to gravel with heavy sledge-hammers. At other times we are assigned to cement making and spend the day shovelling sand and gravel into a cement mixer. We often work by the lights of the lorries well into the night. This happens because they have mixed too much bloody cement and it has to be used or because they begin casting a new platform which has to be finished to ensure good bonding.

The work on the main road through the camp is the toughest. Each company is responsible for a section of it and it has become competitive. One day we filled fifty trucks with rocks and brought them back, dumped them on the road and hammered them into gravel with exactly fifteen minutes' break during the whole God-damned day. The corporals stand over us drinking their beer and egging us on. In spite of all this as the road develops one cannot help feeling a certain amount of satisfaction. It's a hell of a job that we are doing with no tools other than our picks and shovels, our sweat and muscle. The Egyptians couldn't touch us for productivity.

12 November 1962
The rain goes on – conditions deteriorate – Stalingrad. It's cold now as the winter rushes in. Morale drops with the drop in temperature.

13 November 1962
The 1st Regiment of the Legion infantry has left for France. They will form a new base at Aubagne. The name of Sidi-bel-Abbès will still always be synonymous with the Legion, but nothing of the Legion remains there now, except perhaps an immortal spirit. The huge monument to the dead that every legionnaire knows so well has been removed to France piece by piece and it will be reassembled in Aubagne. I am glad about this. To have lost it forever would have been a tragedy. This departure heralds the end for the Legion in Algeria after more than 130 years.

15 November 1962
Yesterday I was supposed to be on *corvée soupe* duty in the evening but I didn't show because I was drinking in the *foyer*. When I got back to the tent there were three corporals waiting

for me: Guhl, Sot Garcia, who makes me throw up every time I look at him, and Hebert. Hebert is normally not a bad chap as corporals go, but he was right off form last night. They each in turn gave me a week's extra duty for the one offence. I decided there and then that it was about time I became a corporal and put in an immediate request to see the commanding officer in the morning. They didn't like this as they assumed that I was going to complain about the punishment I had received and I refused to give my reasons for wanting to see the C.O.

I got into a good slanging match with the three of them until Hebert suddenly said that if he had any more lip from me, he'd take me outside and knock my teeth out. I gave him some more lip and rather regretted it as I did so. Hebert is six feet five inches tall and he is very tough. He once bit another fellow's ear half off during a fight and he claims this is his speciality. Anyway it was too late and he called me outside.

In the Legion when you are called out you go, no matter what you feel about your teeth or ears, because if you do not you are a dead man, condemned forever as a coward, and they will never let you forget it. So out I went.

However, before I got to the end of the tent, Tandoi, who is becoming very much a buddy these days, and Huber jumped in my path and said if I moved another step I would get hell from them. These two guys are also very tough and I dived between them but fortunately they were too quick and down we went in a heap. A tremendous struggle ensued in which I came off worst. But I was prevented from going outside, thank God, and my honour was saved. This is of course what Tandoi and Huber had in mind. It is a face-saver you use on a friend if you really feel that he is going to get murdered. I think old Hebert was quite relieved too. He's not a bully and he would have been very unpopluar beating up somebody who hardly comes up to his navel. It just so happens that I'm quite tough too and whilst I think he probably would have killed me eventually, it would have been a slow process and I would have left him with a fair share of souvenirs.

Meanwhile Guhl and Garcia went off to see Benoît to complain about my attitude and to get their story in first just in case I was going to complain to the C.O. about them. Guilty consciences.

This morning Benoît called me in and gave me eight days. Crime? Requesting permission to see the C.O. without first asking Benoît's permission to do so. He then proceeded to give me a lecture about last night's scandal. All this was because he presumed along with his wretched corporals that I was going to lodge a complaint about victimization or something. As if I would. When he finally dried up I told him that some months ago Jais had asked me if I was interested in going to Corporal School, that I had declined, but I had now changed my mind and wanted to tell him so.

Benoît was flabbergasted and I had the pleasure of seeing him feel bloody stupid; he knew I saw how he felt and he also knew that it was giving me quite a lot of satisfaction. He is very unimpressive. He said he thought I was perhaps still a bit young. I'm older than he is, for Christ's sake! I said I had not the slightest intention of signing on, so it was now or never. He agreed finally that I could see Jais and I have now done so. I will be going to the next Corporal Training School sometime in the middle of next year.

16 November 1962

Hasko has been caught stealing. I'm surprised. I knew he was a rogue and a bounder but I would not have thought he would steal here. Only very rare breeds of thief do that. He is now in prison, having been half murdered beforehand.

We have had seven deserters in the last two days. There is little news about the O.A.S. these days, although there is still a working underground recruitment operation in the regiment. I have had no further approaches since Constantine.

Twenty new recruits arrived in the regiment today. Some compensation for the deserters. Two of them are already doing eight days' prison for smoking while waiting for their first interview with their C.O. That's the sort of welcome that only the Legion can produce.

One of our trucks has crashed on the way back from Mers el-Kébir. Starry was on board. He fractured his leg in thirteen places, broke six ribs, dislocated his shoulder and cracked his skull. He has been flown to France. I don't think we'll see him again, poor old boy. He was one of the good guys.

Wilson is in the infirmary with an outbreak of boils all over his body. I had a long chat with him this evening. He talked about his parents – divorced. He met his father when he was twenty-one, having not seen him since he was five. I wonder if that will happen to me – I have never seen my father.

Wilson asked me what I would think of him if he deserted. We have discussed this many times before. It is a question of balancing out the contract we have signed against the disillusion, the boredom and the mental frustration. It's all so bloody depressing. I said I would think none the less of him if he went. He has further to go than I have, so I sympathize very much with his desire to get the hell out of here, but for my part I'm going to see it through. I couldn't bear the prospect of not being able to go to France in the future without the possibility of being picked up and brought back to finish my time in the Legion.

Three Weeks Later
We have lost 136 deserters in the last four months. Discipline is on the wane, drinking is on the up. Alcoholism is a real problem now. Before, we were always on the move in the mountains and there was never time to stop and think, to assess. Now time is something we have too much of without any means of filling it. Two days ago Huber had a terrific punch-up with Guhl and then today Sot Garcia gave Martinez two days confined to barracks which brought the whole section down on him. In the past Garcia would have gone to the sergeants for support. But he lives in the same tent as us and when the temperature gets to a certain level, anything can happen. Garcia has fled into town.

The work goes on day in and day out with no change in the routine. The main road, which is twenty-five feet wide and eighteen inches deep, is already two miles long. The drainage system throughout the camp is beginning to be effective and our tents are gradually being replaced by steel-framed barracks.

So we have more comfort but at what cost? Bashing rocks, digging ditches, shovelling sand and gravel, loading and un-loading rocks onto lorries, pushing wheel barrows of concrete endlessly along planks all day. Back-breaking work, soulless enterprise yielding no satisfaction. Every day is the exact replica of the one that preceded it. The prospect of doing this for another two years fills me with total despair. I begin to sympathize with people who spend their lives working on the roads; but at least they get paid for it.

10 December 1962
General Lefort, the Inspector-General of the Legion, reviewed his old regiment today and gave us information that might turn out to be that which will save us from insanity. The regiment is to undergo a massive metamorphosis designed to make us the crack unit of the French army, ready to participate in combat operations that may arise in the seventies and eighties. If we do not do this, it is likely that we will eventually disappear as a regiment. The French requirement for ground troops now that they have lost Indo-China and North Africa is going to be considerably less, and the axe will fall on those units that are the least useful. Hence the regiment is going to set about training up specialized sections in underwater combat, demolition, guerrilla warfare, night fighting, special armaments. We will be trained to operate tanks and armoured vehicles, we will be taught to ski and mountaineer, we will become familiar with submarines, we will be sent on survival courses and we will become a highly skilled and dextrous force with multipurpose capability. In addition it has been decided that the regiment will improve its P.R. and we will enter a team for the French army pentathlon and the French shooting championships in the coming year.

This is all terrific stuff. At last someone has come forward with a directive on where we are going. The message has been well received. Morale has in one stroke been given a gigantic shot in the arm. We're back in business. Somebody thinks we can do more than just build bloody roads all day. Suddenly the mountain of the next two years diminishes, there is a feeling of moving forward again. The mind moves back into gear. Christmas is coming. I feel good.

12 December 1962
The Algerian franc that has until now been tied to the French franc is to become an independent currency and will be called the dinar. There is a frantic scramble to change Algerian francs to French francs. It's like a run on the banks. Fortunately I am

not in a position where I need be overconcerned as my total savings at the present time amount to the price of a good night in the *bordel*.

Two Days On
Huge Christmas cake from Jennifer's sister, Gillian. Wilson and I gave it our attention this evening and reduced it to a very fine memory.

17 December 1962
The usual turmoil of Christmas is upon us again as each section tries to outshine the other in the finery of its Christmas decorations.

Baudouin, who is an amusing fellow, has been trying to organize some sketches in order to create an opportunity for himself to demonstrate his acting prowess. He has asked me to assist but it has not been easy because he wants to play the leading role in everything. I have explained to him that he is welcome to do this but that he is unfortunately unequal to the task, not because he cannot act – his whole life is an act – but because he cannot remember any lines for more than five minutes. He does not accept this so we will have to live with a silent hero on the night. He makes me laugh like hell actually so I don't really care what he does.

Christmas Eve 1962
It was lousy. Dead and devoid of spirit. People didn't seem to really try as they have done in previous years. Before it has always been in the mountains and we have been alive and vigorous but now the days of boredom that we have suffered for so long have turned us into soulless robots. The shows went off quite well. Baudouin couldn't remember anything and was therefore very funny. People wolfed their food down in the normal way and drank themselves stupid but there was no feeling in it somehow. So many people are new. Half the old-timers have gone: Koch, Steffen, Auriemma, Charlie Chauvin, Starry, Elch, even that terrible bastard Slymer has gone. Everything seems to have changed. It's all over. There were times when I groaned before but compared to this it was a ball.

I have been promoted to private first class in the Christmas honours list – *quel honneur*! It's taken three years to get one stripe. That's really moving.

I drifted around until about four o'clock in the morning, then I met up with old Bob Wilson. We are becoming good chums, brought together by circumstances. We sat at the side of the road and slowly made our way through a case of beer. And we watched the fights and the forced mirth and the drunken bodies until we could bear it no longer. Then we wandered off and drank some more beer and remained sober.

Christmas Day

Benoît arrived in the section shortly before midday. We drank champagne and all was in order. He left and all was immediately disorder again. I went into Bou-Sfer with Noel and Huber. We were picked up by the M.P.s for being drunk and causing a '*scandale en ville*'. This charge normally merits eight days inside automatically but the spirit of Christmas was on the sergeant in charge of the patrol and he contented himself by bundling us into a truck and carting us back to camp. That was after he had nearly cracked Huber's skull open for resisting arrest.

Huber is about twenty-four years old and if ever anyone was destined to die an alcoholic, it must be him. I don't think anybody realizes how far Huber has gone. Nobody cares anyway; nobody gives a damn, least of all Huber. It's all a laugh. But it's a tragedy because he's a good man and he's just destroying himself in front of our eyes. There is no point in telling him, it would be wasted breath. I started once and he thought it was the funniest thing he'd heard in years.

Noel is an interesting fellow. He is a *pied noir* – very solid, quiet, and highly competent. He has no noticeable allegiances to anyone but Noel. But he will come to no harm, of that he will make absolutely certain. I wonder if he is something to do with the underground recruiting of legionnaires for the O.A.S. There is something about him.

28 December 1962

As a private first class one has a tiny fraction less work to do. This is a fact that is only just discernible to the trained experienced Legionnaire, but it is there. The second-class privates' names are called first when they are looking for volunteers.

I went into Aïn el-Turck today. Nostalgic stuff. Memories of that wonderful week so long ago when Alister was here. I went to our old haunts. Tremendous reception and free drinks from old Abdel Kadar. He was delighted to see me and so was I to see him. He's a fabulous person. Repeat performance at the Palm Beach and then on to the Saint Maurice. Toto went into a state of ecstasy when I arrived, he was so excited, and he went dashing off to break the news to the old madame. They gave me a huge meal and refused to take a penny for it. I think I was nearly ready to cry by the end of the day. These people owe me nothing and yet they have been endlessly kind; they have welcomed me as though I was one of their own family.

The old madame's granddaughter was there today, having just arrived back from France. She was the attention of a number of Legion officers so I was not able to talk to her as long as I would have liked.

31 December 1962
The year ends. No mourners here. All I know is that time, like the hills, is rolling by and I am definitely over the top now. Bob and I had a small private celebration. We toasted the Queen and absent friends, all of whom we introduced individually to each other.

1963 approaches, the dawn of a new existence for us if Lefort meant what he said the other day.

1963

3 January 1963
The selection of a regimental shooting team has begun. The team will be made up of four riflemen and two pistol shots. There will be at least one officer in the unit. That means in round terms as a rifleman I have got to be in the top four of the regiment at best and the top three at worst, if the officer happens to prefer a rifle to a pistol. Each company will send eight men forward for the elimination rounds and prior to that each company will have its own elimination programme.

There will ultimately be several championships among the French troops in Algeria, of which there are still over a hundred thousand at the present time. These will be prequalifying rounds and the best three or four teams will eventually go to France to participate in the final championships of France. The chances of my making it to France do not make them worth considering for a second, but I might just make the regimental team if I really apply myself. I shoot reasonably straight and I have the right temperament. It is pure concentration.

Four Days Later
The company selection is complete. So far so good. I am still in. We met Captain Lafont today. Lafont is the man sworn to produce a regimental rifle team that will win the French championships in the first year. He is a total fanatic, completely and utterly dedicated to his task. He talks shooting all day from sun-up to sun-down and then dreams about it. He is a tough veteran who has made his way to captain from the ranks over some twenty years. He has got decorations to prove that he is an experienced combatant and he has a loud mouth and a volatile temper to go with it. I think I liked him on sight. He's the sort of

roughneck who appeals to me. He's got plenty of common sense with his brawn and I like enthusiasts.

We are forty in number and over the next week Lafont will reduce that number to about eight. The eight will then be moved to a special camp apart from the regiment where they will spend their lives shooting all day. It sounds fantastic and has become terribly important to me. I think this could be my salvation from a lunatic asylum, which is the alternative if I have to go on pushing wheelbarrows much longer.

14 January 1963
The elimination rounds with the pistol are over. Not a chance. A German called Weiss, who was a member of the Bundeswehr shooting team, is first and a little French fellow called Windel is right behind him. It is now the turn of the rifles.

Up until now we have been practising all day. We shoot at two hundred yards with the object of producing the smallest group of ten shots in the target and then we have a rapid-shooting exercise in which we fire ten shots at the target in forty seconds, during which we must change the magazine.

Lafont's excitement and enthusiasm is affecting everybody. He is himself an expert rifle shot, by his own admission, and has shot in the French championships several times before. He was once tenth in the individual order.

16 January 1963
We are down to fifteen and I'm still in.

The Next Day
Sunday. Tandoi's birthday. We went into Aïn el-Turck and celebrated. I saw Jacqueline at the Hotel Saint Maurice. She's hung up on a Legion officer called Lamy which is a bore. So is he, as it happens. I met the local butcher, a splendid little man called Fonfon. He is a great friend of Jacqueline's family (he has been supplying them with their meat for the last fifteen years) and he thinks Lamy is a pain. Jacqueline adores Fonfon and I think I may be able to use this relationship to my advantage. What a dreadful schemer I am. I have suggested casually that the three of us go for a picnic some day. Fonfon thinks this is a splendid idea and Jacqueline is vaguely interested.

Three Days Later

There was a change in plan: the final elimination round for the selection of the rifle team was postponed and on Monday we went into the hills on a field exercise. We stayed out that night and returned the following day. It was then that I discovered to my horror that I had left my glasses behind in the mountains, probably at the old ruin of Bastos farm where we had slept the previous evening. Without my glasses I was a goner in the rifle selection. I was absolutely desperate and I went to see old Grandys. He immediately offered to drive me the twelve odd miles to the farm there and then on the spot but Benoît refused permission. I explained to Benoît that this would blow my chances in the shooting team and that as I was the only member of the company still left in, he might want to reconsider it. He didn't, and what tiny vestige of respect I still had for him died there.

So I resolved to go that night. Tandoi immediately volunteered to come with me, as wandering around in those hills at night can be big trouble if you happen to run into some of the boys on a scalping party. I said I would wake him but I didn't.

I set off at about half an hour before midnight wearing running shoes and a track suit and strapped to my waist I had the comfort of my bayonet. I had no problem getting out of the camp. The mines have not been laid yet, thank God. I think I would have chanced it even if they had been. Fast progress to begin with, then into the hills. Nightmare – I got completely lost and was beginning to really panic. It was a cloudy night and the moon wasn't doing me any favours at all. I climbed to the highest point around, from which I could look back down onto the plain, and after a while I got my bearings. I had studied the map for an hour before leaving until I thought I knew every contour every inch of the way. But once up there it was a very different story indeed. I set off again and eventually hit the path that led to the farm. Christ, was I relieved. And there, lying on the ground where I had slept the previous night, were my specs. I had no time to dance a jig and I turned round and galloped for home. It was downhill now and I just had to keep going straight until I hit the sea; a much easier target than trying to find a tiny broken-down farm ruin in the mountains. I ran back through the night and through the dawn and got into camp just after six. I had covered about twenty-five miles and suddenly I was a dead man. Several people were already up and about and I got some strange glances. They must have thought the mad Johnny English was on a fitness jag.

The prospects of shooting were worrying the hell out of me, but I have never shot better than I did this day. We are down to six and Lafont is going to leave it like that for the time being. He is, of course, one of the six. I am one of the other five. Jesus, what pressure. I can understand the pressure that pro' golfers are under when they shape up for their putts in those golf championships when 100,000 dollars is on the line. Anyway, I am delighted and everything has meaning again. It's something to aim at, something to hold on to.

I received a small parcel from Anski this evening. It was a beautiful little snuff box and inside was earth. A piece of England. On the back was engraved, 'In England's green and pleasant land'. I am overcome completely. She is a very special friend. What fantastic friends I have. Nobody can be as fortunate as I have been in this respect – nobody. Hilaire Belloc wrote:

> No one, in our age and clime,
>   So dusty, spiteful and divided,
> Had such pleasant friends as mine,
>   Or loved them half as much as I did.

That will be my epitaph.

30 January 1963

We are getting down to the serious business of becoming crack riflemen. We shoot all day and every day, weather permitting. Sometimes we are better than the preceding day and it looks like real progress and then the following day we take a step back and nothing goes right. Much depends on what we did the night before. We will not really be making progress until we are consistent. Consistency is the secret. This is the aim. One has to score regularly in the nineties to stand any chance against the competition that we will soon be facing.

We have quite a good bunch of guys. Apart from Windel and Weiss, there are two sergeants, Van de Est and Subera, and two legionnaires, Schmidsdorf and Speis. And then of course there is Lafont and a young lieutenant called Savalle.

Every morning after assembly in the company the boys pick up their shovels and set about the day's work and I pick up my rifle and go off to shoot. My God, how smug I feel!

2 February 1963

Benoît stopped me as I was walking along today and said he'd noticed that I had found my glasses again. I said, 'Yes, I must have been mistaken about leaving them in the hills' – I don't think he likes me very much.

A Month Later

We are already well into the year and it looks like being a good one. Over the last month we have had a ball. We have now been separated from the rest of the regiment and are camped about three miles away. There are seven of us. Lafont comes every morning with Savalle and spends about two hours coaching us and then he returns for three hours in the afternoon. For the rest of the time we are on our own. We have one duty to perform and that is guard, which we do every night. Other than that it is a fantastic existence. We shoot thousands of rounds every day and are becoming consistent in performance.

When Lafont has gone we line all our empty beer bottles up – we have many – and shoot them from the hip at sixty yards. Excellent sport. Van de Est is a splendid character. He's having a great affair with one of the French tarts in the *bordel* called Christianne and she, together with the madame whose name is Janine, comes to our tent every night for a romp and a cuddle. Christianne is a good-looking bird. Janine is an old boot, but she means well and she has plenty of character.

Fonfon has turned out to be a real matchmaker. He has brought Jacqueline and me together in a manner which is totally professional. He comes to our tent every so often and when he can, he brings her too. I wait for the hoot of his car horn in the evening and I run down to the road and there they are and we go off somewhere. Sometimes we go to Aïn el-Turck, sometimes to Les Andelouse where Fonfon lives, and other times we just drive around. Lamy is still in her life but we are moving closer every time we meet.

We went for a picnic one day at Madakh, which was a totally private beautiful place with a beach of white sand that stretched to eternity. We grilled steaks over a fire and listened to the sound of the water on the shore until the late hours. I haven't felt this sort of freedom for so long.

Van de Est is a brick for letting me go because he's sticking his neck right out. If I get picked up by the M.P.s he could be in trouble. I suppose his neck is already out a fair distance with the comings and goings of Christianne and Janine. They have a flat in Aïn el-Turck and he frequently spends the night there, crawling in at five in the morning. His shooting is not improving as fast as it should be and the bags under his eyes look like coal buckets. Subera is getting a little sour about it all. He's jealous as hell and I can't really blame him. Fonfon comes to the tent and brings steaks and lamb chops from time to time and I think this tips the balance and just keeps Subera on side.

3 March 1963

Fonfon told me today that Jacqueline was under some fire from her grandmother for not paying enough attention to Lamy. Lamy eats at the Saint Maurice every night and takes all his buddies along. He is therefore a very good customer and he is there because of Jacqueline. Jacqueline's night wanderings have attracted the attention of her grandmother, who runs the whole family like a military operation, and the red signal is up. Much though she likes me, I am not very good for business. In fact I'm bad for business because they usually feed me on the house. She doesn't know that Jacqueline is with me every other evening and we've got to keep it that way. Apart from anything else, Fonfon would lose the meat-supply contract at the hotel if 'granny' found out that he was our accomplice and she's the best customer he's got. I would also be in trouble if Lamy found out because he'd probably get the military police to ambush me one evening which wouldn't be much fun either. So all in all it's tightrope stuff and I rather enjoy it.

Jacqueline came again this evening. Drove the ten miles from Aïn el-Turck just so that we could be together for a *petit quart d'heure*. Quick plans for next Saturday and then the faithful Fonfon drove her back in time for dinner. Lamy is dining at the hotel again tonight.

5 March 1963
We are approaching our first *concours de tir*. It is vital that we do well for the honour of the regiment and so that we can continue our splendid existence. And also for Lafont too. He will die if we do not do well. I have come to like him tremendously over the last few weeks.

I think we are ready. The triggers on our rifles have been doctored to the finest pressure. We can zero in our rifles from scratch to meet any conditions of weather or light in three shots and we can shoot the tops off beer bottles at fifty yards without knocking the bottles over. Our main enemy will be nerves. It's the first time for us and there is no way round a first time.

9 March 1963
We moved camp to within about two miles of Oran, the site of the competition which begins tomorrow. Fonfon came and picked me up and drove me to Aïn el-Turck. We went to Toto's house. He is also an accomplice, and he went and signalled to Jacqueline. She came running out and flung herself into my arms – and then back into the car again and away into the night. I feel on top of the world.

The Next Day
There are fourteen regiments taking part and this is going to be a three-day marathon. Each man fires four times, twice in precision shooting and twice rapid shooting. It's all very professionally organized. In the precision shooting we get five free shots in which to zero in the rifle. At the target end after a shot has been fired a black pallet comes across the target and indicates the score.

There are various signals that the pallet makes to indicate the precise point of entry. The target has concentric circles going out from the bull's eye numbered down from ten to one. If one hits the nine circle at two o'clock the pallet moves vertically up and down indicating a nine and then it moves backwards and forwards from the centre to the two o'clock position showing that it is a nine at two o'clock. Lying at the side of the man shooting is his scorer who has a miniature target into which he sticks a coloured pin at the point of the hit. Thus one has a close-up of the result and you can see exactly if you are firing off centre. After the first five shots you adjust your sights if, for example, your hits are grouped to the right of the bull, and then you begin.

You have ten minutes to fire ten shots. It's very tense stuff indeed and requires total and complete concentration. Eyes become watery after seven or eight shots and at two hundred yards the black bull, which is a semicircle four centimetres in diameter, is looking very blurred. It needs one fraction of loss of concentration to score a four or a three and you've blown it. To win you have to be consistently in the high eighties. With seven bulls in hand you can throw it all away with a couple of fours and a six. Bang goes sixteen points. On top of this everybody can see how everybody else is shooting and with a huge crowd standing over you the pressure is magnified ten times.

At nine o'clock this morning we had the trigger weigh in. The trigger has to have a certain minimum pressure and the reason for doctoring them is to get this to the finest point without going too far. If the trigger is too fine the gun cannot be used. The rifles were inspected to see that they were all standard and that nobody had built into the foresight a miniature telescopic lens and then we were off.

I shot first and started with four tens and a nine. That means at the halfway stage I was one point off a hundred per cent. It is then that you start sweating because you know it cannot last and when you place the gun to your eye everything is moving. You put it down again and wait a while, but seconds are ticking. My sixth shot was a three and I knew I'd blown it. Crashing disappointment floods through the body in a great wave from head to toe; your gut feels queezy and you suddenly want to pee very badly. But you must take hold of yourself, grip your concentration and force your mind to start thinking positively. You're still on ninety-two with three shots to go. I shot two nines and an eight to give me a final count of eighty-eight. Respectable.

Van de Est shot badly, very badly. The signs of too much Christianne were all over the target. In fact they were off the bloody target.

Schmidsdorf wasn't much better and it looked as though we were heading for disaster. Then the weather turned foul and the wind got up. Various people were in favour of postponing things, including Lafont, but they were overruled. And then a very funny thing happened. Lafont was lying down shooting and doing quite well when a colonel came up and declared a postponement in view of the weather. His boys were obviously not doing very well.

Lafont was furious and turned over on his back protesting wildly. The colonel obviously didn't realize Lafont was an officer because he had taken his epaulettes off to shoot, and told him to belt up. Lafont protested even more then and the colonel told him to stand to attention when addressing a senior officer. At this stage Lafont completely lost control of himself and told the colonel it was he who should bloody well stand to attention when addressing an officer of the Legion of Honour. Tremendous stuff. Threats of duels and all the rest. The colonel finally stormed off saying the general would receive a full report in the morning. Lafont was cheered by one and all and became a national hero on the spot. The shooting ended for the day and we all went off to celebrate Lafont's performance.

Day Two
Pistol shooting in the morning. Windel and Weiss both shot well. And then this afternoon we had our first go at rapid shooting. Van de Est again excelled himself and chalked up a zero score. At the end of the day we were lying in fifth place. This is bad. To qualify for the next championships we have to finish in the first two here. Everybody is depressed, Lafont most of all. I feel a bit sorry for poor old Van de Est. He does too.

The Final Day
We all did our stuff and we came through in second place. Lafont is beside himself with joy. We are all as pleased as punch with ourselves. Windel was placed first in the individual order in precision shooting with pistol and I was placed first in precision with rifle.

We returned to the regiment this evening. The results have been published in the *foyer* and everybody is delighted. Congratulations all round. The regiment is off to a good start in its intentions to improve its P.R. I am the First Rifle in the regiment and will be entitled to wear a gold rifle on my sleeve. How's that for one-upmanship?

14 March 1963

We had a ceremony in the main military stadium at Aïn el-Turck – presentation of prizes and cups by the general (I wonder if he'll catch up with Lafont). He presented me with a gold fountain-pen and said a gold medal was on its way from France. Same thing for Windel. Lafont hosted a champagne lunch at the Saint Maurice hotel (which I hope will increase my kudos with Jacqueline's grandmother) and then we were given passes for the rest of the day.

17 March 1963

We are back at our little camp in the hills preparing for the next competition. Life goes on well. Today was one of the great days of my life. It was perfect. It was beautiful. We drove as always the three of us, Jacqueline, Fonfon and myself, miles into the hills until we came to a wood filled with flowers. I seem to remember the afternoon as one long embrace with Jacqueline. Little Arab children kept bringing us flowers until we had filled Fonfon's car. This is the last Sunday, she returns to France in a couple of days. We laughed so much this day in spite of the sadness over the hill. I'm in love again. What a life.

25 March 1963

My twenty-third birthday. Card from Jacqueline in France. I think it was Hugo who said, 'The greatest happiness in the world is the knowledge that one is loved'. I am a happy man.

27 March 1963

Went over to the regiment. The boys were all in good heart in spite of everything. Tandoi well. Had a few beers with Bob and Kenny. They are still on hard-labour routine every day. My God I'm lucky to have landed this shooting lark.

We are off to Arzew, on the other side of Oran, in a couple of days for the next competition.

Two Days On

Arzew. We are camped in the barracks of the regular French army. These boys live really well by our standards. We have spent today tuning up our weapons. The competition will be stiffer this time but we are a little better prepared to meet it and have the experience of one *concours* behind us – that steadies the nerves.

1 April 1963

We've won! Unbelievable – sensational. We took nine of the twelve medals and one of the cups. Each of us got a gold medal for being in the winning team. I got an additional bronze medal for being placed third in the individual order for the combined result of precision and rapid shooting together. Colonel Channel and Arnaud de Foyard were there and obviously delighted with the results of Lafont's efforts to turn us into a successful team. Van de Est shot well, thank God – I was worried about him. He has either been laying off Christianne or he is improving his stamina.

We now have one more round to go. This will be the final shoot-out of the French forces in Algeria and it will take place in Algiers in about a month's time.

The Next Day

Sunday. I went into Aïn el-Turck and felt very depressed. Could not shake it off. I could not bring myself to go to the Saint Maurice. Abdel Kadar was away in Oran and I sat and drank buckets of Ricard all afternoon. I saw Fonfon briefly in the street but he was in a hurry.

By seven o'clock I was smashed and I missed the last truck back to camp. There's no other way back except in the M.P.s' wagon and the journey is unpleasant and usually preceded by a roughing-up at the hands of the M.P.s. I was in Abdel Kadar's bar half out of my mind when he arrived back from Oran. He was frantic with worry about the M.P.s. They came into the bar and he and two others managed to drag me just in time into his rooms behind until the boys had moved on. Then they bundled me into Abdel's old jalopy and drove me back to camp.

3 April 1963

We are moving our tent back to the regimental compound. This is the end of freedom as we have known it, although we will still pass the time of day on the shooting-range.

Some very bad news: Tandoi has got tuberculosis. He is being

H

shipped back to France and then out probably. There goes a good friend.

5 April 1963

Lamy has been posted to France. Pity it wasn't earlier.

Out of the blue this evening a letter from Nicole. She is living in the South of France in Vence. Quickening of the pulse and revving up of the old emotional system. I wrote back to her with steady hand and mind. It does one ill to over-react to these situations.

8 April 1963

I wonder if we are getting a bit stale. We have been shooting for a long time now. Like the athlete, we must seek always to arrive at peak form on the day of an event. To peak too early is fatal. I think we need a break from it. There are signs of strain. I had a row with Lafont today. He has managed to acquire some new Springfield rifles which are far superior to those we have been using until now. The argument was over a piddling little matter of how best to hold the new rifles when shooting. He worked himself into a tantrum but I knew I was right. Finally I asked him if he wanted to hear what I thought or what I thought he wanted to hear. He understood and slowly came round to the fact that he was wrong. He accepted that he was wrong. This is why we all like him and respect him so much. That is why we would do anything for him.

Easter Sunday

Weiss was out of his mind this evening, having personally consumed two cases of Kronenbourg. We had a punch-up that started out as a friendly rag. I got the better of him because he couldn't focus on anything and then he lost his temper. He took a swing at me that would have knocked my head clean off if it had connected. The tent was beginning to collapse and everybody was involved a few seconds later. It was going to be a murderous business because Weiss out of control is much more dangerous than a charging rhino. Certainly he is much stronger than a rhino. Schmidsdorf saved the day by slamming him over the head from behind with an empty jerrycan. He never knew what hit him.

The pattern of life is unchanging. We shoot all day and drink all night. After *appel* the case of beer is pulled from under the camp-bed and the session begins. Wilson and Kenny often come over. The conversation is always the same: the world and its problems, life and its problems, religion, women and what we will all do when we get out. Sometimes there are variations. Bob talks with enthusiasm about Fascism and the need for a Fascist regime in England as an alternative to depression and decline and the final eclipse of nationalism. He's read history but not enough of it and my answer is that any regime founded on the principle of the suppression of individual freedom is tyrannical and unacceptable. Impasse. We drink some more beer and talk about something else.

21 April 1963

The colonel came to watch us shoot today. Lafont panicked and the whole thing was a shambles. Actually today's performance belies our worth. We are now all crack shots and so we should be. I have several times chalked up ninety-six. That's not easy at two hundred yards. Under Weiss's careful tuition I have become quite handy with a pistol too. When Lafont and the colonel disappeared at lunchtime today I shot twenty bottles of beer at sixty feet with Weiss's Walther in nineteen seconds. That is very satisfying. I bet John Wayne can't do that! We are ready for Algiers.

Ten Days Later

We are leaving for Algiers tomorrow. The ultimate test of our skill with rifles is upon us. On this hinges the trip to France that is so important to all of us. Much has gone into the planning of our days to come in Paris. It would be unbearable if those plans did not materialize.

Camerone has come and gone. Routine now. Sideshows, chariot races, jousting, boxing and drinking. Bou-Sfer was destroyed totally. Over the last few months Bou-Sfer has mushroomed into a sort of grimy shanty town as the parasites and carpet-baggers have set up shops and bars in anticipation of a substantial fall-out of Legion pocket-money. The metamorphosis from deserted village to seaside shanty town has been rapid but subtle. It was suddenly upon us without warning. It was there in the morning having not been there the previous evening. In general it is welcome. We prefer bars and bistros, pinball machines and hookers, to quiet beaches and romantic sunsets.

Anyway, after yesterday it has now been restored to what it was, a quiet peaceful fishing village – which looks as though it has been attacked by a sizeable school of tiger sharks.

The scene at the camp the day after Camerone was one of disaster. Half the regiment seemed to have ended up in the infirmary, the rest were wearing dark glasses. One particular incident occurred which in terms of vengeance was particularly impressive. Wilson gave me the details. There's a man in his company called Vance who fell over at the height of an intoxicating evening and broke his wrist and leg. He was lying screaming on the ground when news of his difficulties came to the attention of his old enemy, Legionnaire Wizzick. Wizzick is smaller than Vance and has been beaten up by him several times in the past. Here was a chance to even the score up a little. He did, by kicking four of Vance's front teeth out as he lay writhing in agony. He apparently had further plans for Vance too but was pulled off before he could execute them. There are some nice guys around here.

And so tomorrow it's our big moment in Algiers. Van de Est is not coming because he has *La Quille* in three days' time. He has decided that he will not be taking Christianne with him. A number of his friends are glad about this. She is certainly the best number in the *bordel*.

One piece of bad news is that the colonel has given Lafont strict instructions that none of us is to be given passes into Algiers. I have heard so much about the place that to leave the Legion without having seen it would be a pity. We might have to do something about this even without a pass. Schmidsdorf has a girlfriend in Algiers and there is nothing that is going to stop him seeing her. He used to be in the 1st Para Regiment and their base at Zeralda was very near Algiers, so he knows it well.

Two Days Later
We are camped in regular army barracks at Maison Carrée a few miles from Algiers. Everything is ready for tomorrow. Lafont commended us to an early night but no sooner had he retired than we went charging into the town of Maison Carrée

and drank ourselves stupid and having done that we went straight to the *bordel*.

The Next Day
Lafont was furious when he heard about our antics last night from Subera. But when the rifle shooting started this morning, it was Schmidsdorf and I who performed. Subera and Lafont were hopeless. At the end of the first day's shooting, having fired once in precision and once in rapid fire, our scores were Lafont 134, Subera 139, Schmidsdorf 141 and myself 174. We are a long way behind and this could be the end of the line this time. We need to be placed in the first three to qualify for France.

The Second Day
We all shot reasonably well, but we have done better so many times before. The whole thing hinges now on our pistol boys, Weiss and Windel. They will shoot tomorrow. For us the pressure is off and Schmidsdorf and I decided we would risk going into Algiers and giving it a whirl.

The Following Evening
The repercussions of last night's folly are upon me. One of the mistakes we made last night – there were many – was to go into town in Legion uniforms. There are no legionnaires within miles of Algiers nor have there been since independence was declared. To appear in the centre of Algiers wearing white kepis was like waving a red flag to a bull. Nothing could have been more conspicuous.

We got a lift into Algiers on the back of a truck and no sooner had we arrived in the centre than Schmidsdorf jumped into a cab and went off to see his girlfriend. That was the last I saw of him. I felt very strange indeed standing in the middle of the town in my Legion kit with thousands of unfriendly eyes staring at me. Anyway it was too late to turn back so I went straight into the nearest bar.

It was jammed with Arabs but surprisingly enough standing at the bar were two Europeans. They offered me a drink and we toasted the Legion and then they explained the circumstances that had led to their presence there. One of them was a retired major from the French army who happened to be in Algiers on a business visit and the other was a Polish gentleman who appeared to be something in the diplomatic field. They had known each other five years before and had met that evening in their hotel by chance and had decided to celebrate the event by crawling round some of their old haunts. I had arrived at the beginning of the crawl and they invited me to join them. I accepted with gratitude and immediately began to feel much more comfortable about the prospects of the evening before me.

Some four hours later we came staggering out of a bar in a back street when our Polish friend was accosted by two Arab thugs in leather jackets who demanded to see his papers. He was a few yards behind the major and me, because he had been paying the bill. He told the Arabs to go to hell and demanded to see their papers before he would show them his. Quite suddenly the street seemed to fill with people who emerged out of the shadows. I turned back to intervene and was voicing my opinion of the Arabs when one of them suddenly jumped forward and slugged me in the mouth. I took a couple of steps backwards and then as he came forward for a follow-up, I kicked him in the crotch with everything I'd got. He subsided quietly with a sigh. I had never done that before and the result was most satisfying.

However, the satisfaction was short-lived, because it triggered an all-out assault by the rest. The whole pack suddenly threw themselves upon us. I remember swinging left and right at the mass of bodies that appeared from everywhere like rats trying to get at one's throat and then down I went with the sheer weight of numbers. There was a second I remember very clearly. There was somebody on top of me and I managed to bring up my leg and I lashed out at his face with the heel of my foot. There was a scream of pain from the man – I had caught him square in the eye. And then a sea of hands were swinging at my face. I fought like hell in desperation to get out from under but it was hopeless and I could feel myself getting weaker and weaker. These boys meant business and I was expecting to feel a knife go between my ribs at any moment. That is a very unpleasant feeling when you are pinned down on your back. I think it was the numbers that saved us, paradoxically. There were so many of them that they could not see clearly enough to put the knife in.

And then suddenly when it seemed that I was done for be-cause I had no strength left, everybody broke up and ran and I found myself looking up at two Arab soldiers holding sub-machine-guns pointing at my head. They had particularly nasty expressions on their faces. At that moment the Polish fellow came running up and I was glad to see him. He'd taken to his heels when the trouble started, yelling, 'Help – Murder – Police!' and all that. I remember thinking that I would have preferred it if he had stayed to give me a hand. The major was flat on his back with a long gash from his eye to the corner of his mouth. He was in a bad way. We lifted him up and followed the Arab police to their headquarters. One of our attackers had remained and was explaining to the police in Arabic how we had started all the trouble.

When we got to the police headquarters the major was dispatched in an ambulance and the Pole and I were interrogated for three hours. Finally they let the Polish fellow go and I began to get nervous. It was obvious that it was me they were after and I was beginning to doubt that I would see the light of day again. I had no pass and I had no papers on me of any sort, not even my identity card. On top of that nobody knew I was there officially. I was praying like hell that the Pole would come through, but having seen his exit when the fighting started, I was having some difficulty keeping my faith intact.

It was four o'clock and I was beginning to feel the bruises on my face and body. I was a complete wreck. My uniform was hanging in shreds. I knew I was really in terrible trouble this time and I was pretty scared. The Arabs kept asking the same futile questions. What was I doing in Algiers? Why had I not got a pass? Why had I not got identity papers? Why did I attack this innocent man in the street?

And then at last four gendarmes arrived. Boy, was I relieved to see them. The Pole was with them and I could have hugged him. It took the gendarmes another hour to negotiate my release and then I was questioned all over again by them. They also wanted to know why I hadn't got a pass or identification papers. I eventually told them the whole story from beginning to end: how the colonel had said no passes were to be issued and that I decided to come anyway. They were quite decent about it but said they would have to make a full report because the atmosphere in Algeria was still very sensitive and the Arabs would certainly be putting in a report themselves. It looked like developing into a nice little political incident.

Eventually we were allowed to go. We went to the hotel to find the major still in one piece with thirty stitches in his face that would be a permanent memento of the evening. We were all slightly intoxicated with relief and we opened a bottle of champagne on the spot. They were both very appreciative of my efforts on their behalf and praised the honour of the Legion and I was equally enthusiastic about them; particularly the Pole for getting the gendarmes to come to the rescue. And we saluted and said our farewells and I got a taxi back to camp. I was suddenly overcome with complete exhaustion. It was six o'clock when I got back. The sentry on duty looked aghast when he saw me, as well he might. My face had swollen to three times its normal size, both eyes were already turning blue-green and my lips were battered blisters. No broken teeth. I collapsed into bed, but not before I had seen that Schmidsdorf was tucked up, soundly asleep with a faint smile on his face. The bastard had obviously had a ball.

The gendarmes didn't get to Lafont until about mid-morning. He was on the shooting range watching Weiss and Windel when they gave him the story. He came into the barracks like a tornado. I was still in bed asleep. What a wakening. I thought he was going to kill me, he was so mad. He was pacing up and down the room shouting his head off, working himself into a froth, yelling and screaming abuse. He was totally insane. He could have had a seizure at any moment. He swore that he would have me put behind bars for a year and he was frantic about what the colonel was going to say let alone the general. Apparently the Arabs had put in a report that I had assaulted an Arab civilian and kicked his eye out and blinded him. Lafont went on and on and I let him rave because I wasn't feeling up to any resistance. He finally told me to consider myself in prison as of that moment and stormed out of the room.

In the afternoon our pistol boys performed badly. If they had done well that might have saved me, but it was not to be. So we came fourth. It was a bitter disappointment after so long. Apparently the first three teams will qualify for France and with three more points we could have made it. Our total number of points exceeds 1,750, so there is a flicker of a chance that we may

be able to go, but I don't think my efforts will have helped senti-
ment in our favour.

This evening I decided to form up to Lafont and I went over
to his rooms. He is a man I have come to like and respect and I
thought I somehow had to try to explain things to him. I wanted
as much as anything else to apologize for dropping him in it with
the colonel, because this I have most certainly done. He was
responsible for us and it will be his lack of control and discipline
that will ultimately be questioned. When I went into his room he
was quite calm and we talked it over. He asked me why I had not
at least come to him for a pass, and I said I knew that he would
have had to refuse and that I was set on going anyway. Matters
would have therefore been worse because I would have disobeyed a direct order. He then said I should have got the hell out
of it as soon as the trouble started and I explained that I could
hardly abandon two civilians and what would be their impression
of the Legion if I had run? He quite liked that. It was a direct hit
on his tremendous pride. He was very good about the whole
thing after that.

He said it was now out of his hands because a report had
already gone to the general commanding the division. One way
or another it would get back to Colonel Channel and one way or
another I was going to prison. It was now open to question
whether or not I would go to the Corporal School. Having said
all that he added that he would put in a good report and mention
the bit about coming to the rescue of civilians – I'll probably get
a medal.

The Next Day
We had the closing ceremony and presentation of medals and
cups. I have been placed third in the individual order for combined precision and rapid shooting and I received a bronze
medal – and I'm damned proud of it. In third place I qualify to
go to the French championships as an individual. Lafont does
not think the colonel will sponsor an individual effort and anyway I'll probably be behind bars.

I think all in all Lafont is quite pleased with the fact that we
have come as far as we have done. If Lafont is reasonably happy,
then I think we all are too.

12 May 1963
Back at Bou-Sfer. Reported in to Captain Jais. He congratulated me on my shooting exploits and then said reluctantly that he had to give me eight days' prison. He told me that Lafont had given me a sterling report, otherwise it would have been longer. Lafont seems to have let himself go in his account of the incident. I was apparently carried away by my sense of tourism when I went into Algiers without a pass and the description of my rescue of two civilians who were under attack from a bunch of Arabs would have turned Sir Lancelot green with envy.

I passed *au coiffeur* in the afternoon and was duly administered with a *boule à zéro* and then with my blanket under my arm I was escorted under guard to the prison. Oscar Kautz, now the senior adjutant in the regiment, was at the stockade to welcome me. I found that I was a bit of a hero as word had already passed round that I was inside for having tried to kill some Arabs. This is being talked about as a battle of epic proportions and will almost certainly find its way into the Legion archives.

In the meantime it is back to *la pelote* and hard labour.

Eight Days Later
Came out today. The routine during my stay was similar to that which they laid on for us in Philippeville. Up at dawn. *Corvée quartier*. Hard labour during the day and then sport in the evening. We took our meals standing to attention which is a new development; otherwise it was just like old times. The security is better than Philippeville and there was no way of smuggling in cigarettes or beer. I've lost nine pounds and I feel fit.

Had a celebration this evening with Weiss, Wilson, Carlsen and Kenny. News has come through that we have qualified to go to France – jubilation.

The Next Day
Summoned to report to Colonel Channel. He was splendid. Congratulated me on the shooting, said he regretted that he had had to put me away for a few days, but that I must appreciate whose fault it was. He told me that the corporal *peloton* was starting in a few days and that I would be joining it. This

means of course that I will not go to France with the shooting team.

26 May 1963
Channel is leaving the regiment and we had a parade for the new man, Colonel Cailloud. Many of us would like to have seen Arnaud de Foyard take over, but he's still only a major, so he must wait a while. General Lefort presided over the ceremonies.

28 May 1963
I have said goodbye to my chums for a while and I am now at the Corporal School. The camp, called Lindless, is situated at 2,000 feet above sea level in the hills five miles from the regiment. We are a band of forty-five men. Our commandant is a youngish looking, hard-faced captain called Mascaro. He is aided by three sergeants: Delgado, Schmidt and Winter.

Mascaro in his opening address left us in no doubts about what we are in for over the next four months. It is the principal aim of the course to make men of us and secondly to make us corporals worthy to serve in the finest regiment in the French army. In the past these N.C.O. training schools have been run through a centralized system that produced corporals for any regiment. This one is being run specifically for the 2nd Para Regiment. It is an in-house effort. The regiment requires twenty corporals and among other things it is the intention of Mascaro and his henchmen to weed out the weaker ones among us as soon as possible. Out of the rest it is intended to make leaders and experts in the art of soldiering. We will be able to find our way around the mountains with or without maps, we will become specialists in the use of weapons, tanks, explosives and sabotage, and we will become Legion N.C.O.s. But first we must become men and before we can administer discipline we must fully understand what discipline is all about and that begins tomorrow.

I've got an uneasy feeling that we are in for a very rough time indeed. There is something about the set-up here that is positively sinister. This is going to be much worse than basic training, of that I am sure.

PART TEN

The Peloton

6 June 1963
We have been here for eight days and my first intuitive feelings
about the place have proved to be well founded. This is a murder
camp; Mascara was a holiday resort by comparison. The day
begins at five o'clock in the morning with a five-mile cross-
country gallop. This is followed by parade and inspection. Our
barracks are inspected morning, noon and again in the evening
at *appel*. More often than not the required standard is not met,
in which case individual punishments are meted out or the
entire barracks are punished as one and the inspection takes
place again at midnight or at four in the morning or whatever
time springs into the mind of the particular sergeant on duty.
Objective one of the N.C.O.s is to keep us short on sleep. This is
the quickest way to break resistance and they mean to break us.

Each day one of us is appointed as the corporal of the day. It
is his job to prepare the duty rosters and get the *peloton* on
parade at the appropriate time and to make sure we are ready
for *appel* in the evening. The night before he has to prepare
numerous charts with the order of the day, the guard roster and
other things and this has to be presented to Delgado after *appel*.
It is an exercise in perfection. Everything has to be to millimetre
precision; the spacing between lines and the width of the mar-
gins. Very few people get it right much before three in the morning. Delgado sees to that.

Our daily programme is not dissimilar in content to that which we had at Mascara except that before we were coming to it for the first time, learning it. Here we are learning how to teach it to other people; we are learning how to be instructors of others.

We spend the afternoons in the hills. Combat training and practical map reading are priorities and in the evenings we return to camp at a forced march. In the Legion if you cannot march further than your men you will never have their respect and you will never lead them.

Apart from Noel, there are few people here that I know. The atmosphere is cool and this again reminds me of the early days when everybody remained independent cells, carefully weighing people up before there was any kind of commitment.

Over the next four months we will be rated and marked for the many different things we do and there will be two intermediate exams and a final test at the end. We will then pass out in order of performance. This is going to be very competitive. There is great prestige in passing out first, like winning the sword of honour at Sandhurst, in addition to which there are very tangible material rewards. The man who passes out first, and he alone, can be considered for promotion to chief corporal. This effectively makes him a lance-sergeant and he ascends to the exalted ranks of those who wear a black kepi instead of a white one. His pay is double that of a corporal, he becomes a member of the very élite chief corporals' mess, he has his own rooms, he has a batman to clean his kit, and life becomes very much more interesting all round. His duties, for instance, include being the duty N.C.O. at the *bordel* which is much more fun than collecting rocks in the hills. So there is going to be a determined struggle for the first prize and, looking around this lot, there are plenty of people here who have the brain and the capacity for it. The competition will be keen.

There is a Frenchman called Daniel Vignaga who is in my estimation a very possible winner, even at this early stage. He is highly intelligent and he is a natural leader. And there are others. Kalushke and Pitzer, both German, are strong contenders. Kalushke is very fit indeed and he is well balanced in terms of personality, good humour, common sense and general ability. Pitzer is much more complex. Totally dedicated, unemotional and no trace of humour. He again stands out as being more intelligent than the rest. He is older than most of the others and will be short on the physical side but he has more than enough between his ears to make up for it. Then there is Eduardo de Soto, who is the accepted leader of a sizeable Spanish contingent. He is more of the mould of Kalushke, not perhaps so much of an extrovert. His dedication to the task is synonymous with his Spanish pride – inflexible. He must be regarded as a strong runner. His relationship with Delgado will be interesting to watch. I do not for one second think that Delgado will do him any favours but the Spanish do have an understanding between themselves that is not common to the other nationalities here.

Apart from the specific tests in sport and the exams that we will do at the end of the *peloton* we will also score points for shooting over the whole four months and for attitude. Attitude and morale are rated higher than any other single factor as point-getters. This may cause upsets for Pitzer because he looks bloody miserable most of the time.

So the scene is set and it is going to be a tough and entertaining battle. There is much to gain and we are all aware of it in terms of net income, prestige and a better existence, to clarify the more materialistic implications. But we are mercenaries after all and none of us are here at this stage for the fun and games. Those dreams were buried years ago.

A Week Later
The battle against fatigue continues to be the toughest part of our lives here. There is no rest, there is never a pause for a second. We ran five miles in full kit with sacks and rifles against the clock this morning and then when we came in at midday it was to find the barracks had been wrecked. The contents of our lockers had been flung in a heap in the centre of the room; our uniforms, shirts, shoes, boots and helmets together with the sheets and blankets from our beds. The beds themselves had been dismantled and also lay strewn in every direction. Twenty packets of soap powder had been thrown over the whole bloody mess and then a hose had been sprayed around the room for fifteen minutes so that everything was flooded. It looked like an earthquake.

We were absolutely dead beat when we arrived back at camp and to be greeted by this was just the last bloody straw. It was the work of Winter. He is different from his colleagues Schmidt and Delgado, who are robust thugs but not without a sense of humour. Winter is a weedy pale specimen of a man with fair hair and watery blue eyes. He has a long thin nose and a weak effeminate mouth. He would make a good number-two man for Belsen or Auschwitz. He is a sadist and he delights in the discomfort of others.

God knows how we got the mess cleared up. We had to have it ready for another inspection at two o'clock. There was no time to wash and dry anything. We just folded everything wet and covered in soapy slime into our lockers. And then this evening after *appel* we had the big wash-up and as usual collapsed into bed at one in the morning.

In the two weeks that we have been here I have had *tenue campagne* on five nights. *Tenue campagne* never finishes before one o'clock.

They have another little punishment for us too, which is to send us after *appel* to the coast where we fill our water-bottles with sea water which we bring back to the sergeant for inspection to prove that we have been there. The sea is five miles away and at night the journey takes five hours. We return at three in the morning. I have had to do this only once so far, but it again hits at the vulnerable spot of tiredness.

On one occasion earlier this week, Schmidt found a mosquito in my helmet at *appel*. Six of us then carried the mosquito outside on a blanket, we were the pallbearers, and I had to dig a hole five feet deep in which we buried it. I then had to make a cross for the grave and paint on it '*Tom Dooley est mort*'. Schmidt thought the whole episode was hysterical and I suppose I might have done too if it had not been one in the morning by the time we were through. We are in the hands of madmen.

25 June 1963

We are fitter than we have ever been in our lives and at the same time we are dead from exhaustion and lack of sleep. The first of our tests and exams is upon us and during this week we will be examined on everything we have learned so far and put through physical tests at the same time. Over the last two weeks we have been preoccupied roaming around the hills at night. The form is that we march in small groups on a given compass bearing, measuring the distance by pacing, and we are ultimately supposed to arrive after about ten miles at a crossroads or a river or something, where a truck is waiting to bring us back to camp. What happens in reality is that we never find the objective or the truck and have to walk back to camp where we surface at dawn. We collect our punishment for failing to find the objective and the day begins with sport. In spite of this we are improving. We can be dropped at night by parachute and using a compass only or sometimes an aerial photograph we can regroup twenty miles away the following morning. That's not bad going in these barren hills where there are very few landmarks to assist. Our map reading is also improving and we can find our way around the hills at night or by day as easily as we can find our way around the barracks. Mascaro will give us a point on the map, twenty miles from Lindless, and say, 'Be there tomorrow at dawn,' and we will be.

We are becoming competent drill instructors. We are becoming familiar with radio equipment, mines and explosives and how to defuse them, armoured cars, an armoury of weapons including Russian, American and German guns and grenades. We can build useful bridges across rivers, spend a few days in the hills without food, living off the land; we can splint a man's leg and carry him single-handed down a hundred-foot precipice and we can survive five weeks with an average of three hours' sleep a night. We can run five miles in full kit in forty-five minutes, we can shin thirty feet up a rope without using our feet, and we can sing all night. The precision of our drill would impress the finest Coldstream Guardsmen and we can march a mule off its feet.

In spite of all this Delgado, Schmidt and Winter think that we are a disgrace to the regiment and the Legion as a whole and over the next few weeks they are determined to whip us into shape. Morale is at an all-time low and many are saying they will not try in the forthcoming tests in the hopes that they will be sent back to the regiment. Against this is the determination of Pitzer, de Soto, Kalushke, Manbar, Vignaga and even Nalda, the famous matador who is also up here with us, and others whose ambition and pride keep them going. And one thing that keeps me going is that I will not be the first to crack, no matter what happens.

And so today we attacked all the tests they had laid on for us with vigour, and although tiredness is all over our faces like smudges of ingrained dirt, we found the energy from somewhere and we ran our races in record times, jumped new distances, climbed ropes higher than ever before, did more press-ups and abdominal exercises than usual, and we had studied our notes and knew our facts. We knew every detail of our weapons, the lengths and weights of the different components and the speeds of the bullets and distances they travel when fired from different guns. We knew all about mines, the different types, and tanks and armaments of every description that we had learned about. We had all done our homework. In spite of everything we had found time to revise.

With a few exceptions this *peloton* comprises a force of men of very high calibre, certainly as a group unequalled by anything I have ever seen in my three years here. And in spite of what Delgado and the others think, I believe we impressed our examiners today. They were N.C.O.s from the regiment and I don't think they expected what they found.

30 June 1963
The tests are over. We went into Bou-Sfer to celebrate and relax for the first time in an age. I met up with Bob and Kenny and poured out all my troubles and told them how bloody it was. They didn't believe me.

The Next Day
The result of the exam and the order to date is first Vignaga. Inexplicably I am second, with Pitzer one point behind. Piva is fourth and right behind him are Soto and Kalushke. Apart from myself, there are no great surprises in the order. It's still wide open and there is a long way to go. Eight men failed to measure up to the minimum standard required and will return to the regiment.

2 July 1963
It's back to normal again. We were out in the hills today with heavy packs and Winter, carrying nothing of course, marched us

back at a terrible pace. I was carrying the twenty-six-pound radio among other things and was probably worse off than anybody. Winter was marching at the head of the column and the curses from behind got louder and louder until he could no longer ignore them. He stopped the march and ordered us to crawl. For a moment I thought discipline would finally crack. Winter was on his own with us and we had all had enough and we hated him. There was a second when anything could have happened. Winter was on a knife-edge. There are some very hard characters around here – but we crawled.

My back is a mess where the radio has been rubbing and my spine feels as though it is broken tonight. And *appel* has been a bloody disaster. Schmidt went wild with all our kit again, throwing it around the room, and then declared that *appel* would be reset for midnight on the parade-ground. So we had to take all our beds and lockers outside and reassemble everything in the same order as it is in the barracks, on the parade-ground. Schmidt passed the inspection with a torch at midnight and said it was unsatisfactory and that he would inspect the barracks at five tomorrow morning. This effectively means that we will have to get up at four to get things ready. I can no longer follow the logical purpose of this. It is pointless and proves absolutely nothing.

4 July 1963
We jumped in the dunes at Cap Falcon. The sand is deceptive and although it looks soft from the air it can be as hard as concrete. Gasser dislocated his spine on landing and Dufour broke his leg. So the *peloton* is over for them. Ten down, thirty left.

I have an enormous boil on my back where the radio has been rubbing. It's like carrying a water-bottle hanging from a nail in the base of the spine. I'm going down to the regiment for the big squeeze tomorrow. I hope they've got rid of Belgian Farouk, I don't think I could face him again.

Interesting incident at *appel* tonight. Schmidt selected a rifle at random from the rack and after a glance down the barrel declared it filthy and asked the owner to step forward. It was Pedro Rodriguez. Pedro is as mad as a hatter, but he is a good soldier. I like him well. He does, however, have a lethal temper and when it explodes he can be very dangerous indeed. Schmidt threw the rifle at him and told him to have it ready for inspection at midnight, and then he turned and walked out of the room.

He got as far as the door when Pedro popped. He went completely berserk and with a long agonized roar like that of a dying lion, he swung the rifle round and round his head by the barrel as though he was throwing the hammer and he flung it full force at the receding back of Sergeant Schmidt. It slammed into the doorpost one inch above Schmidt's head. The whole thing happened in two seconds. The scene was frozen still for a full minute. Nobody moved a muscle, neither Schmidt, Pedro nor anybody else. This was a spectacle unequalled for tension and suspense. Pedro remained rooted to the spot.

And then Schmidt slowly picked up the rifle and advanced on him. In a very quiet voice he said, '*En prison – allez!*' and Pedro marched solemnly off to gaol carrying his blanket, with Schmidt one pace behind him.

5 July 1963

Piva has shown why he came fourth in the exams; he has a creative mind and today he excelled himself. At *appel* Winter sent him to collect sea water in his water-bottle, for having dust on the underside of his boots. He told Piva to wake him on his return in the early morning.

Piva went off into the night but returned ten minutes later and declared he was damned if he was going to get sea water and instead peed into the bottle, added some cold water from the tap, set his alarm for two o'clock and went to bed. At two in the morning he reported to Winter. Winter put his finger in it and tasted it to make sure it was sea water and that was that. Winter has drunk Piva's pee and Piva becomes immortalized among us all. It is a major *coup* and morale has been uplifted a mile.

If by some extraordinary quirk this diary should one day fall into the hands of Winter, all I can say to him is, 'Prost'.

10 July 1963

We have a new commandant, Lieutenant Loridon. No tears for Mascaro. Loridon is quiet but I sense that he is tough. He chews *chique* all day, which he spits out at intervals like the Arabs. He apparently learned the habit when he was a prisoner of the Arabs three years ago. We had a weapons inspection today and he rejected the lot and gave us all three days' *tenue campagne* and two hours' extra drill at lunchtime for the same number of days. The weapons were spotless but I suppose he's making a point.

12 July 1963
Pedro came out of prison, Garbou went in. Garbou is in trouble for refusing to obey an order from Winter. He was in charge of a squad cleaning the washrooms and lavatories and at *appel* Winter rejected their efforts and ordered them to clean the lavatories with toothbrushes for an inspection at midnight. Garbou told him to get stuffed.

The Next Morning
At morning parade Garbou was wheeled out in front of the *peloton* and we were given a tirade by Delgado on the iniquities of refusing a direct order in the Legion. Garbou is a really hard man and is as stubborn as hell too. When he had finished, Delgado ordered Garbou to go to the lavatories and to clean them with a toothbrush as Winter had ordered him to the previous evening.

This was a direct confrontation of rank, but more than that this was a confrontation of two personalities and characters each possessing enormous forcefulness. We watched this drama slowly unfolding before us. It was fascinating and one could feel the intangible forces grappling with each other and neither would yield. I think Delgado was sorry to find himself in this position because I think like us he respects Garbou and his strength of character but he could see no way out. And Garbou faced us all with his tremendous pride and he knew we were all behind him and he was not going to let himself down.

It was a tragedy. It was a terrible waste and all brought about because of that miserable creep, Winter. I wanted to step forward and say, 'Look, we can settle this another way,' but there was no other way. So Garbou refused. And as a result he has been removed from the *peloton* and been subjected to the final indignity of being expelled from the regiment – back to the infantry.

We are all very sober tonight. The *peloton* is in mourning. Our spirits have been jarred with shock and I think something has died in all of us. Collectively we can always keep going and most of us have the inner strength and fibre to sustain this kind of treatment for a long time. But what happened today was something that we cannot take. It has not frightened us but it has scarred our minds and taken away all the meaning at one blow. When there is no meaning, the spirit dies and when that happens it's all over. There is no will and no force to carry on. We are brooding. I think we are potentially very dangerous at this moment in time. All our thoughts are the same and all our collective feelings are as one. We could be mobilized into total defiance if someone spoke and urged some kind of action. But there is no voice and we each maintain our silence and let our thoughts run their angry course. Violence waits just below the surface ready to spring, but it will evaporate before the morning.

15 July 1963

Loridon I think I like. He appears more relaxed than Mascaro. He allows us to smoke when he is addressing us collectively, which would never have happened under Mascaro. He has a voice that is so quiet that he is sometimes hard to hear even from a foot or two away. But underneath it all there is something deadly. Not necessarily unpleasant, but a ruthlessness, a capacity to do almost anything. Nothing would surprise me about this man. He is quite unlike anybody I have ever met.

We jumped today over the forest of M'sila. Amazing experience descending onto the trees. At first the trees look like a thick pile carpet, but when you get closer it all looks like what it is, a nightmare. There is little evasive action that can be taken, because as you come down you are swinging from side to side like a pendulum and being blown horizontally at the same time. The main thing is to keep one hand over your nuts and the rest is with the gods.

All was well. Acebal landed in a tree and was suspended from the branches like a trussed-up goose unable to move. But no damage was done. After the jump Loridon divided us into groups and said the first complete team back to camp – ten miles – would be allowed a *passe de nuit* in the *bordel*. Never were ten miles covered in such haste. Manbar, Willet and myself won by a hair, although Strobender came in miles ahead on his own. So next week we are on the town. Loridon has moved up in the popularity polls, although I do not think for one second that that is why he did it.

17 July 1963

My boil has come up again. It's like a golf ball. We were in the mountains today digging trenches and I could stand it no longer so I asked Noel, who was with me, to lance it with his sheath-knife. It was quite funny because Loridon came on the scene as Noel was standing behind me with the knife. I think he thought Noel was about to stab me in the back. He came rushing up yelling, '*Arrêtez-ça! Arrêtez-ça!*'

I explained the situation and when he saw the boil he bundled me into the jeep and ran me back to the regiment. It was the same old routine. Beret in my mouth and the big squeeze. I was a wet rag when they had finished, covered from head to toe in sweat, but I felt as though someone had lifted a ton weight off my back when it was over. Half a pint of penicillin up the back-side and a wad of lint soaked in iodine into the crater in my back and I was a new man again, ready to get back on the job.

20 July 1963

There is nothing that will foster friendship faster than the shar-ing of bad times. And so have these last few weeks drawn Vig-naga, Soto and myself steadily and almost inevitably together in a bond of friendship that I think will endure. We have discovered through talking during the many hours of marching that we share common thoughts about things and people. We have similar values. I think it started when we were dropped one night behind the forest of M'sila and we had to get back to Lindless before seven the following morning.

We all set off individually into the night and between us and Lindless there were five companies on the look-out for us. They were using helicopters and numerous jeeps and trucks. Loridon said if anybody was stupid enough to get caught they would automatically be banished from the *peloton*. The following day at dawn I found myself two miles from the camp with one road to cross. And on that road spread in front of me was half a regiment. A detour round to outflank them meant another three hours and I had spent the night walking through rivers, climbing up and down hills and valleys, falling over shrubs and tree stumps. I was dead and I was damned if I was going to go round them.

And then from the bushes nearby came a rustle and a whisper. I crawled over to find Soto and Vignaga sitting in a little ditch under some bushes. Vignaga had some coffee and I was grateful for that. They both looked like skeletons, so drawn were their faces, and I suppose I did too. It was two hours before we got our chance to move and in those two hours we talked the world through. I remember when the sun came up we suddenly noticed a spider's web spread between the bushes like a glistening pearl necklace and sitting at one end was a black monster with yellow hoops round its abdomen and legs on it that would have satisfied a gorilla. A wasp landed on the web and the spider shot across the surface of the net and within seconds had that wasp trussed up unable to even so much as blink. It was fascinating to watch. We were spellbound. I had never seen that before and somehow it was that which started us talking about so many things, things that in the Legion one never got around to.

We decided there and then that when the Legion was all over we would meet up and look back on it all and laugh about that which we could not laugh at now. Belgium was selected as a neutral country and midnight on New Year's Eve in 1966 as the time. Soto will be out in 1964 and I am scheduled to finish in February 1965. Vignaga finishes eight months after me. The rendezvous is to be underneath the statue of the Manneken Pis just off the Grand' Place in the centre of Brussels. It's a long way from today. I wonder if we will ever make it.

We got back to Lindless with six minutes to spare.

Two Days Later

We came into camp this evening having been out for two days and something happened that is rare in the Legion. One of Delgado's favourite forms of amusement is to get us on parade when we return from a march and keep us standing alternately to attention and at ease for half an hour. When we come to the position of attention our left hand is supposed to smack sharply against the thigh so there is a good slapping noise. When we do this together and the timing is right it sounds like a rifle shot. When we are tired and pissed off and the timing is ragged it sounds like a machine-gun. So Delgado just keeps us at it, until our thighs are blue.

Anyway he started on this routine this evening and we had had just about enough over the last two days without this. We were absolutely knackered and nobody was in the mood to be mucked around by Delgado. We hadn't eaten anything since midday the previous day. And after about fifteen minutes of this Noel yelled out at the top of his voice, '*J'ai plein les couilles*,' which loosely translated means, 'My balls are full.' It was dark and Delgado could not see who had called out, but he must have known. We waited in suspended silence for the axe to fall. And then Delgado did a very intelligent thing. He must have realized that we were nearly at the brink – and in spite of his pride which was under pressure, because he knew that some people would read what he was about to do as an act of fear – he dismissed us.

I gave Noel a few marks too. It takes a lot of guts to do what he did. His neck was right out over the block.

And then this evening Baudet, who is a small French fellow, blew his stack. He was given *tenue campagne* at *appel* by Winter. It was too much. His tiredness made him irrational. And when Winter went out Baudet suddenly grabbed a grenade and went charging off to the N.C.O.s' mess. The boys were just getting into their second round of Kronenbourg when Baudet went in, pulled the pin from the grenade and started yelling abuse at them for all they had done to him over the last few weeks. I would have given my arm to have been a fly on the wall to watch them sweat. Apparently the shouting must have eased some of the tension in Baudet and he gradually calmed down until Delgado was eventually able to persuade him to hand over the grenade. The pin was put back and Baudet is now behind bars. Tomorrow he will be transported back to the regiment where he will probably get thirty days' hard labour. His corporal days are over, but I am not sure he isn't better off than we are.

25 July 1963

Some signs of Loridon's recklessness came through today. We were practising throwing grenades. He stood in a gun butt surrounded by sacks of sand with the grenades and we took it in turns to stand about ten yards in front of the butt and wait for him to throw them at us. The only problem was that he pulled the pin out before he threw them. Once the pin is out there is a seven-second time fuse before the bang. If you catch it you don't spend too much time aiming before you throw it. If you drop it you get the hell out of there with a flying dive over the gun butt. It's much more tricky than catching cricket balls.

A Week Later

We are coming up to the halfway mark. More exams. The N.C.O.s keep the pressure on. They still have another nine of us to get rid of before the end.

Three days ago we did a night jump over Cap Falcon and this was followed by a night exercise. In small groups we set off on a given compass bearing and the following morning we were supposed to arrive at a particular spot. We missed it. There wasn't much we could do. We had covered twenty miles by dawn, we'd had no sleep and we just lay at the side of a mountain path and brewed up some coffee.

We had hardly boiled the coffee when Sergeant Dadone, who has only recently joined the *peloton* staff, turned up. He had been sent out to look for us and he asked us what the hell we thought we were doing idling at the side of the road. He worked himself up then and started yelling and pushing us. We were like sullen cattle. There was Vignaga, Kalushke, Manbar, myself and Nalda. Vignaga didn't move and just remained on the ground drinking his coffee. That threw Dadone and he charged across to him and gave him a clout across the ear. It was a mistake. Vignaga sprang to his feet in a second, grabbed his sub-machine-gun, rammed back the breach and shoved it into Dadone's gut. He was trembling with rage, and Dadone was frozen still with his mouth open. All the weeks of tiredness and strain had suddenly boiled over in Daniel in those few seconds and Dadone's life hung by a thread. In hardly more than a whisper Daniel made it clear to him that if he ever put a finger on him again he would be a dead man. Nobody who witnessed the incident had the slightest doubt that Vignaga meant what he said. There was a certainty about it that was total.

Slowly, very slowly, the situation defused itself and Vignaga put his gun up. We gathered our bits and pieces together in silence and Dadone told us to go to the beach at Madahk where the rest of the *peloton* were and with that he drove off in his jeep.

We had five miles to walk. We moved off in a dispirited little band. Nobody had any doubts as to what Daniel might expect on arrival. The sun came up like a sizzling fried egg. It was going to be a long hot day.

Two hours later we were at Madahk. Delgado came forward and told Vignaga to fall out and to begin by digging himself a *tombeau* in the middle of the beach.

We spent an idle day on the sand, swimming and resting. And we ate our tinned rations and we talked and smoked but none of us could take our eyes off the coffin in the middle of the beach for long. There was no room to move in the hole. He could just lie still on his back and over him they had stretched a canvas sheet flat across the sand. The canvas sheet never moved an inch throughout the day and I found myself wondering if he was actually under there at all. It must have been like an oven in there. The sun was lethal that day.

And then the evening came and everybody returned to Lindless in trucks except the group that had failed to arrive on time in the morning; we had to slog it back on Shanks's pony.

It was after midnight when we got back. Vignaga was thrown in the can and the rest of us fell into our bunks. Sleep was elusive. Our minds and bodies are all mangled up and out of step.

The Next Day

Vignaga has been given fifteen days, with four hours' *pelote* each day. If Mascaro were still here I think Daniel would have been given the boot, but Loridon is perceptive and I think he sees the qualities in Vignaga as being too good to waste.

The second round of exams is on. Daniel takes part in between bouts of *la pelote*. The incident will count against him and he will pick up a fat zero for attitude. The competitive spirit is multiplied now. I think Daniel was in many ways head and shoulders above the rest of us but after what happened he cannot possibly come out first. It is not just the fact that the favourite has been eliminated that has intensified the competition. It is more because of what we have been through. We have had to wade through so much shit over the last few weeks that the stripes of a mere corporal cannot really justify it. Only first place can compensate for the indignity we have suffered at the hands of Delgado and his henchmen.

7 August 1963
Pitzer takes the lead. I was second again and Soto moved up to third slot. Daniel dropped to seventh inevitably because of the incident with Dadone. But we are only at the halfway stage so it is early days. Four people were sent back to the regiment.

A Month Later
Much has happened over the last few weeks. The most important development has been the concentration on practical instruction that has taken place under the directorship of Loridon. After the last exams the tone changed and we began to do what we came here for. It wasn't as if they consciously took the pressure off, but deliberately buggering us around became a secondary occupation for the N.C.O.s instead of their main function. There was one lapse, when we did the lavatory-cleaning routine again with toothbrushes. An inspection took place every five hours for about three days. They finally got bored with it and we have had no repetition since.

Much of our time has been spent in practical field exercises, launching attacks on outposts. A lot of planning goes into this beforehand and when it is my turn to prepare the operational assault I must confess that I get tremendous satisfaction out of it. I suppose we are really playing at soldiers because there is no enemy, but the rest of the action is real enough.

Morale is good. We have become well united as a body of men, with very few exceptions. Pitzer is still as competitive as hell in everything he does, which irritates Daniel, Soto and myself. We would rather see anybody than Pitzer pass out first. But he's good, of that there is no doubt, and I fear our wish will not be granted.

We are fit and can cover long distances in the mountains at amazing speeds. We were fit in the old days when we used to go on operations but this is different. We eat less and we drink very little now.

Loridon has introduced a marathon combat course which starts in a helicopter. We go careering across the sea and are flung out thirty feet above the water at thirty-five miles an hour. We are in combat uniform including boots and the object is to swim to shore, assuming you survive the jump. On the beach awaiting each man is his rifle, *sac* and helmet which he hoists aboard and then runs eight kilometres. The stopwatch is on us from the moment we leave the helicopter.

Jumping out of moving helicopters without parachutes is exhilarating and very scary. We have a rubber pad over our chest and back which is supposed to keep us afloat until a boat arrives in the event that we are knocked out when hitting the sea. The impact is like concrete. There's nothing soft about water when you are thrown at it from thirty feet up.

Tomorrow we are going to raid a regular army camp. We have spent the last couple of days spying on the camp checking on the movements of the sentries, observing the exact location of the mines. We have a plan of the layout of the camp so we know the exact position of the magazine, the officers' mess and the sleeping quarters of the men. They have been warned that we are coming some time but they do not know on which night. The sentries have been doubled and there is enough barbed wire round the perimeter of the base to discourage a tank.

Two Days Later

Last night we jumped over a drop zone about four miles from the regular army camp in the hills. There were ten of us and we split into small units of two and three. Everybody knew what he had to do, but first we had to get into the camp. We arrived at about one o'clock to find the lights on all over the place and about a hundred men patrolling round inside the wire. They were obviously expecting us.

We had made posters marked with the emblem of the regiment and it was our intention to penetrate as many places as possible without being seen and leave our signature wherever we went. Loridon had bet the regular army commandant five cases of champagne that his men could get into the camp without being spotted. I was with Delgado and our objective was the officers' mess and the guardroom. It took us an hour to cut through the wire. After that we had to crawl across two hundred yards of open ground. The regs were everywhere but they were blind. At one point four fellows walked along a path chatting away and we were lying on open ground, but in the shadows, two feet from them. There were so many people about that we decided the best ploy was boldness. Two men walking calmly in the darkness would be taken for their own people, but if there was a furtive air in our approach we would be spotted in a second. I was expecting the alarm to go off at any moment.

We got to the guardroom. Three guys were lying on their bunks and a sergeant was reading a comic at a table. Behind him was the rifle rack unlocked. I walked in behind him – icy calm with not the slightest sound. Delgado was crouched at the door ready to spring forward if he moved – but he didn't and I took one of the rifles and walked silently out through the door.

We pressed on to the officers' mess. One of the doors was marked with the name of the C.O. and it was obviously his sleeping quarters and from the sound of snoring from within he was clearly oblivious to the intrusion that was taking place in his camp or that he was about to lose five cases of champagne and more besides. There were several other rooms and under the doors we slipped our calling card. On some of them we had written, '*Le deuxième R.É.P. vous souhaite une bonne nuit*'. They were going to be very surprised in the morning.

We helped ourselves to three bottles of Scotch and a bottle of Pernod and as many beers as I could get in my *sac* and then we scarpered. The regs were still wandering about but in greatly reduced numbers now. It was four o'clock by this time. We got out without incident and made our way to the rendezvous which was about four miles from the camp. Everybody got through. It was a hundred per cent success. We were all in high spirits although fatigue was written over all our faces.

Loridon and Delgado drove off in the jeep and we followed in the truck. And then an amazing spectacle occurred. We had not eaten for a while and with all the energy we had used up in the preceding six hours our bellies could not have been more empty. It was five-thirty in the morning and one thing our systems did not need now was alcohol. But we opened the Scotch and drank it neat from the bottle and the Pernod too. The predictable result was a disaster. Pedro Rodriguez went off his head and staggered us all by breaking the top off the bottle and eating it. He was pouring Scotch down his throat and then taking great bites at the bottle and chewing it. There was blood all over the place and he was bellowing at the top of his voice, totally and absolutely right out of his mind. Never in my life had I seen anything like it although I had heard that Russian Cossacks after knocking back a couple of bottles of vodka usually ate their glasses – but this was the bottle. Somehow we all got back to Lindless. The return journey was like being in a mobile madhouse.

On arrival most of us went to bed and slept until midday, but not Pedro. When I got to the *réfectoire* at lunchtime I thought the whole place had gone stark raving mad. Pedro was standing on a table covered in blood which was pouring from a great gash in his arm, raving and screaming that if we were his brothers in arms we were his blood brothers and should prove it by drinking his blood. Everybody in the room was shouting and yelling, some telling him to belt up and get out, others laughing their heads off and hailing him as a hell of a fellow. It was complete pandemonium. And then he threw the bottle through the window and picked up another and smashed the end of it against the edge of the metal table. Things were beginning to look ugly. Nobody was particularly keen to approach Pedro, he was beyond any reason. And then Delgado came in with three guards. One swing of a rifle knocked Pedro's feet from under him and he crashed to the ground and a blow on the back of the neck laid him cold. He was picked up bodily, thrown under a shower, his clothes ripped off him and then he was driven to the infirmary.

The latest report on him is that he has been stitched up and after a tranquillizing injection has calmed down somewhat. He will return to the *peloton* in a day or two and begin eight days in the clink for damaging Legion property.

Loridon is obviously delighted with our efforts against the regulars, although the regular commandant is apparently very upset that we pinched some of his liquor. Delgado says that he has complained to Colonel Cailloud. I shouldn't think Cailloud gives a damn. I know Loridon doesn't. The only trouble is that it now looks as though he won't come through with the champagne. What a miserable fellow he must be.

11 September 1963

We all went down to the regiment today to get cholera injections and we were allowed to spend the rest of the day there. There was a convoy going back to Lindless in the evening at seven thirty but I missed it. There was no other way back so I decided to go on foot. I had to get back there before *appel* at nine o'clock and the only chance I had was if I could get a lift from Bou-Sfer to Les Andelouse along the coast road. Les Andelouse is about halfway. After that the road to Lindless turns off and climbs into the hills. Only trucks going directly to the *peloton* use it and so I would have to walk the last two miles.

And then I nearly got myself into very deep water indeed. I was walking along the side of the road and a car came along and stopped when I thumbed it. There were four Arabs inside and they said they would give me a lift. It was dark and I could not make out their faces otherwise I might have seen something there that would have changed my mind. I got into the back of the car and that was a mistake that was nearly fatal. There were two fellows in the back with me and as the car sped off in the direction of Les Andelouse one of them casually put his hand behind my neck and reached round and pressed the lock down. They started to jabber away in Arabic and I didn't like the way they laughed periodically.

Alarm bells started to ring inside me and I suddenly realized that I was in terrible trouble. I knew with my every instinct that these guys were making plans that were not in my best interests. They were thugs and the war was still very fresh in everybody's mind. Here was a legionnaire dropped right into their laps and I could expect the very worst.

After the first few minutes of shock and near panic, I got my thoughts under control and started thinking how the hell I was going to get out of this. It was no good jumping out. The car was travelling at fifty miles an hour and by the time I had the door unlocked they would have been on to me.

My best chance would be to make a break for it when the car stopped. The last thing they wanted was trouble before they got off the main road and they would make no move before the car stopped. I had told them I was going as far as Les Andelouse and if they were genuine there would be no need for them to turn off onto the Lindless road at the entrance to the village. So that was to be the testing moment. If they stayed on the main road and stopped that would prove that my instincts were dramatically overdeveloped, but if they turned off onto the hill road which led nowhere as far as they were concerned, then I was in trouble.

As we approached the turning I asked the driver to stop the

car but he said he didn't understand. I repeated the request to stop but he carried on, again pretending he didn't quite know what I wanted. We came to the turning and the car slowed – he took the hill road. I said in the calmest voice I could manage, 'O.K., this is fine; you can drop me here,' and I repeated it several times. Once we were off the coast road it was dark. He drove on for about another fifty yards, all the time gradually slowing down as if he now understood and the only thing preventing the car from stopping was a slight problem with the brakes.

And then suddenly I wasn't scared any more. I knew what had to be done and I was in control of myself completely. The key was to get out of the car while it was still moving. I started to offer my thanks for their kindness in going out of their way and in a very relaxed and natural way I casually lifted the lock on the door. I gave myself five seconds and then I slapped the driver in front of me on the back of the neck and shoved the door open. When I hit the driver he jammed on the brakes and the car gave a great lurch forward and threw the others off balance. In that second I was out and running like hell. I heard a yell. The door slammed and the car roared into life and came tearing after me. I threw myself headlong into the ditch and they sped past. I was shaking like hell. Their headlights went off up the road, but it would only be seconds before they turned round. It was no use going back to the village. There was no sign of life and I could hardly expect refuge from any Arabs that did live there. So I leapt to my feet and ran away from the road and into the hills. While I stayed near the road they would always have an advantage over me with the car. I could see the lights of the car and was disturbed to see that they didn't turn round but kept on going up the twisty road to our camp. They must have guessed that I was heading there and they were going to cut me off. It was an unpleasant thought to dwell on, that they might be between me and the camp. But I know every inch of the hills around Lindless and I know where the mines are. I was back in camp and ready for *appel* with seconds in hand. Camp Lindless felt like home for the first time.

14 September 1963
We are off on a long trek tomorrow to Sassel and back over two

days. We leave at six in the morning. This is a big one, and will count in the point system. The total distance is about ninety miles, and that is a distance that really sorts out the men and the boys.

The Next Evening
We set off this morning in cheerful spirits. By midday very few people were smiling. We had covered twenty-four miles and our backs and feet were beginning to feel the strain. We paused for an hour and then continued. It all reminded me of the long march at Sully. Jesus, that was a long time ago. I gradually got into the rhythm. That's the secret and then your mind can relax. Once your mind wanders you're in business and you forget your feet and back and drift along in a sort of dream.

We arrived at Sassel at seven in the evening. Willet collapsed just before we got there and became the first casualty.

16 September 1963
I had sentry duty last night and when I got up I could hardly move my right leg. There was a sharp pain behind the knee and I knew I was in for trouble this morning. I limped along for the first five miles and gradually the pain eased and I was able to get moving. By this time the *peloton* was in two groups. A band of about six really fit guys including Loridon had gone off at a gallop and the rest of us made up a second wave some miles behind with several people already straggling and showing signs of defeat.

By four in the afternoon I had left the rear group well behind and I was entirely on my own. No sign of the boys in front. And then, with about seven miles to go, I came round a corner of the road and saw the bedraggled figure of Soto. Poor old Soto, he was absolutely done for. His feet were a mess of blood and blisters and he was hobbling along as though he were walking on burning coals. He was in a miserable state. I walked along with him and tried to cheer him up, but he urged me to go on so that I could beat Pitzer.

'You're the only one who can beat Pitzer,' he kept saying, 'you must go on.'

I told him to relax and that as far as the march was concerned, Pitzer was miles behind and we would both finish before him. I

I

couldn't have been more wrong. We came to a village and stopped for a drink and we had hardly started off again when Pitzer appeared two hundred yards behind us.

I think I might have left Soto then, but he was in such bad shape that if I had done, he would probably have come to a grinding halt. He kept pressing me to leave and I couldn't help thinking what a splendid fellow he was. Pitzer gradually overhauled us and went slowly past without a word. He was suffering too. I didn't give a damn whether he passed us or not at that moment. I wasn't being a hero; my God-damned feet were killing me too and Soto was a good excuse to go slowly. So we allowed him to beat us and we toppled into camp ourselves shortly before eleven o'clock this evening. We had covered the best part of a hundred miles. It was an achievement, but it was marred by Pitzer beating us.

18 September 1963
I was corporal of the day yesterday and failed to have the *peloton* ready for *appel* at the appointed hour, as a result of which I was given a night in a *tombeau*. Never slept better in my life!

22 September 1963
We ambushed a regular army unit in the forest of M'sila today. Everybody was charging around firing blanks and throwing grenades. We scared the living daylights out of them. At the end we were face to face and we charged them, shouting and yelling threats of death and torture. They panicked and ran for it. Terrific sport. We rounded them all up and I think they genuinely thought we were going to beat them up and pull their ears off. Poor fellows, I felt rather sorry for them.

Two Weeks Later
We have learned all there is in the programme and we have revised it until we know it backwards and now the final exam approaches which will test this knowledge in each of us and sort us into an order of merit. Over the next four days we will be tried in leadership and movement of troops in combat, knowledge of armaments, weapons, tanks, explosives and mines, radio equipment, drill and medicine. And we will go through all the physical tests, running, jumping, rope climbing, swimming,

press-ups, pull-ups and God knows what, until we have covered everything that we have touched on during the last four months. And then it will be over and we will be able to return to the peace and quiet of the regiment.

Halfway Through
It is difficult to forecast the end result at this stage because one is only aware of one's own errors. I did not do well in the sporting events – I must be getting older – and I made an awful bog of some of the theory on explosives. Loridon runs around like an excited mother hen watching us all do our stuff and making little notes in his book. The atmosphere is tense and serious. There's a lot at stake. In the evening in the *réfectoire* everybody says how badly he has done and is relieved to hear that it is universal. Soto and Vignaga are pressing me to concentrate to ensure that I beat Pitzer. The bookies have got Pitzer marginally ahead in the betting. This might be something to do with the large German contingent supporting him. I have the support of all the Spaniards who are following the lead given by Soto. The chances are that neither of us will win and that it will be an outsider like Manbar or possibly Kalushke. Kalushke beat me in most of the field sports and he is showing great form and is full of confidence.

12 October 1963
It is all over. Tremendous relief coupled with a feeling of satisfaction. We have really been through the mill and we have all of us changed as a result of the experience we have undergone here. That change may not be noticeable in ourselves but it is very obvious to me in others. We have been through a hard school which either makes or breaks. We have made it, and now there is an underlying confidence in each of us and an assurance of our own capability. This confidence has been instilled in us by the knowledge that we can take a lot of punishment. It hammers home our resilience and it is only now when I stop and look back at what has happened over the last few months that the full realization of what we have been through becomes apparent.

But it is not just this ability to take punishment that has moulded us into something stronger, it is more that we are recognized as being such by each other. There is no one here who has come through for whom I do not have a very high regard. There is not one man here who in my opinion is not fit to be a top-grade N.C.O. in the regiment. I have total admiration for each one of them and I would be quite happy to go out against the enemy with any one of them leading the expedition.

We have been stretched to the limits physically and we are stronger because of it. And we have been squeezed mentally so that our senses are sharper, we are more perceptive and there is agility where before there was a numbness because we never had to think. In the past we just obeyed orders like machines, now we will be giving them and that requires some thinking.

We had a great celebration in the *réfectoire* tonight. Everybody, including Loridon and Delgado, got smashed. All ills were forgotten and forgiven in the relief that it was over. It was a release of energy and emotion unequalled. The *réfectoire* was decimated, all the windows in the barracks smashed, the tables and chairs thrown in every direction; the bottles and plates being thrown through the air looked like feathers exploding out of a burst pillow. There were no fights. It was just twenty-odd people getting something out of the system that had been building up for weeks. Psychologically it was perfect medicine, we all felt much better for it.

Tomorrow they will announce the result and the colonel will come and do the honours. I don't think I care who wins anymore, I'm so relieved it's over. And Pitzer has got a sense of humour after all. He's a good man; so are they all – bloody good men.

The Next Day
We did the best we could to clean the place up, or at least to disguise the damage, before the colonel arrived. It was like trying to pretend that Hiroshima never happened. We were due on parade at three o'clock in full kit, red epaulettes, blue cummerbunds and the works. Somehow we got everything in order. We are well trained in repairing damage after the practice we have had at the hands of Delgado and the others.

At half past two we assembled and the order was read out in which we would parade in front of the colonel. This was to be the order in which we had passed out of the *peloton*.

I was first. What to say other than I am amazed and delighted and I am unashamedly proud of myself. This was a great day for the English. Pitzer was second, half a point behind. He was a good loser and in the moment of shaking hands we became good chums. Soto was fourth and Vignaga seventh. And Kalushke came in fifth, Manbar at eight and Nalda second to last.

We paraded before Colonel Cailloud and one by one we ran forward to collect our corporal's *galons*. All the company commanders were there and half the officers and N.C.O.s of the regiment and we had another celebration, although much more sober, with the colonel and everybody else afterwards. Lafont was there, out of his mind with delight and claiming all the credit for it! It was good to see him. I suppose it was a bit like having your father there to see you collect a prize on speech day at school. Congratulations were heaped upon me like confetti but those that came from the rest of the *peloton* were those that mattered. I think they all wanted me to win. They pushed me into it.

PART ELEVEN

Rewards

20 November 1963
Much has changed in the regiment even during the months that
I have been away. There are so many new faces. When I rejoined
the company I was assigned to the 4th Section. Most of my old
chums in the 3rd Section had gone anyway, so it was to be new
faces wherever I went. Nevertheless I would somehow like to
have been able to say goodbye. Old Theo has gone and Decaluve
too and even the dreadful Grueber has finally disappeared. They
must be the last of the old school that were here that day I
arrived so long ago at Rhoufi.

All the sergeants are strangers with the exception of Karos
and Hirschfeld, who is immortal. He is fat now, a very different
man from the one I first met when I arrived. He drinks too much
and he cannot adapt to the new ways of a peacetime army. It is
sad to see the deterioration in him.

All the officers are new. I was sorry to see that Jais had already
left when I got back. He would have been happy to see that one
of his lads was first in the *peloton*. Benoît has gone. I am not
sorry, but I would have liked to see him once more too – not for
any reasons of malice but because maybe he had something deep
down which I missed. I think we both missed and we needn't
have done.

Grandys has gone and that more than anything closes a

chapter. He was certainly the last of the old breed and his departure turns the leaf on the past.

The modern barracks and the macadamed roads throughout the camp complete the metamorphosis. The new faces add emphasis to it and I begin to feel like a veteran, something from the past, out of touch with what is going on around me. My name has changed from 'Johnny' to 'Caporal' and there is a sort of invisible but tangible barrier between me and the fellows in the line. I am no longer one of them.

Guhl and Sot are still here and have adopted a patronizing attitude towards me now that I am a corporal, which I find slightly puke-making. They are nevertheless a reminder of why I went to the *peloton* and I am glad that they can no longer pull rank. I am also glad that I am in a position where I can temper their excesses of leadership and authority when they are misguided.

The regiment is a hive of activity. Everybody seems to be undergoing some kind of specialist training. There is a frogman unit now which appears to be professional in the way it operates and in its results. And we have a team of athletes which trains twenty-four hours a day and will participate in the military pentathlon in France next year. They mean to win. They have already wiped the floor with most of the other regiments in North Africa in various cross-country marathons during the last few months.

Forty men have been sent to France for skiing instruction and will form a special alpine unit when they return. Others are doing mountaineering courses and survival courses. And then there is a guerrilla training school which is being hailed as the best in the French army. It sounds very good indeed.

There is a night warfare school to which we may be sent for three weeks during which we learn to do everything we normally do with the assistance of our eyes, in darkness. We sleep all day and rise at eight in the evening for breakfast. By the end of it we are supposed to be able to handle every weapon we've ever touched, from grenades to rocket launchers, blindfold. We do night parachute jumps into forests as though we are landing on a cricket field on a hot summer day and generally learn to live without our eyes.

There is a considerable amount of marine activity in addition to the frogman unit. Night jumps into the sea over Cap Falcon are a popular form of torture and operational exercises involving submarines and rubber dinghies are all the rage.

There is an anti-tank school where one learns to relax with a bloody great Chieftain tank rolling over you. The form is that you stand facing the tank as it slowly comes towards you and when it hits you, you allow it to push you onto your back and pass over so that you are between the enormous tracks. There is nothing dangerous about it unless you happen to pick an uneven bit of ground, but it is nevertheless quite nerve-racking. Another thing that one learns in the anti-tank school is how to put up a good show against a squadron of tanks coming for you in a line. It requires some foreknowledge of the fact that they are coming. One digs what is called a bottle-hole in the path which the tank is expected to take. This is a hole about four feet deep shaped like a bottle with a narrow neck and a wide base at the bottom. It will hold one man. The neck is just wide enough for a man to lower himself into and once in he sits and waits for the tank to arrive. Visibility from inside a tank is restricted in the area immediately surrounding it and the technique is to let the tank roll over the hole. The narrowness of the neck is supposed to ensure that the hole doesn't collapse. As soon as the tank has passed you pop out, run up behind it, deposit a sizeable mine with a ten-second fuse on the back, and then dive back down the hole. Ten seconds later the tank is on the moon. That's the theory of it anyway.

So the stage is set for the home run. I have peeled my last potato in the Legion and swung a pickaxe for the last time. No more carrying rocks and digging latrines – unless, of course, I go inside again, which is always a possibility around here. Prison sentences in the Legion are doled out like porridge in the British army. It's routine.

In spite of this I don't feel particularly cheerful. Something has gone out of it all that was there before and it is only now that it has gone that I miss it. The atmosphere has changed. The camaraderie that we had has gone, or maybe it's here but I am just not a part of it. Perhaps it's the newness of everything, particularly the faces. One face that is not new but which I am not pleased to see is that of the recently appointed sergeant major, none other than Chief Sergeant Peltzer, the terror of the stockade at Mascara. He is liquid slime as far as I am concerned and when I saw his face on my return to the company, all the stories that I had heard about him at Mascara passed through my mind. Thank God for my little green stripes, they will help keep the bastard at bay.

The new company commander is a rather wet captain called Legrand. This is always a dangerous situation because it means that the N.C.O.s will run the company and in this case that moves the seat of power over to Peltzer. My section commander is a young lieutenant called Mercier. He is either going to be very good or very bad. He has a good sense of humour and he is popular with the men in the section because he is very easy on them. His concept of discipline is out of keeping with Legion tradition and that probably means trouble in the long run. Half the company think he is a pansy and whilst he is undoubtedly effeminate in some of his gestures, I do not think he is. I like him and support him and think his non-conformity is refreshing. He is terribly chuffed at having what he calls 'the best corporal in the regiment' in his section and he thinks I'm a hell of a fellow. This indicates that he is perceptive if nothing else.

24 November 1963
A letter from Nicole arrived asking me when I am coming to France and imploring me to come and see her in Vence. I should be able to get some leave next summer in France. I will have completed four and a half years' service and as a corporal one's application for leave normally receives some attention.

26 November 1963
Pay-day. My first salary as a corporal – thirty pounds. Thirty pounds a month may not be much, but when compared with the fifteen pounds that a private gets, it's a fortune. And when compared to the ten pounds that legionnaires who are not paratroopers receive it sounds even better; and when I finally measure it against the three pounds a month I got when I first came to the Legion I suddenly realize that I have arrived. This is living.

6 December 1963
We are becoming deft hands at landing rubber dinghies on beaches at night in all sorts of weather. These are sizeable craft

that will hold sixteen men and it takes a fair amount of practice in coordination to handle them effectively. We have spent hours and hours practising landings and many times have been mercilessly hurled into the sea by gigantic waves. At night it is particularly difficult and if thirty dinghies are landing on a beach the confusion that can arise is unbelievable. It sounds like fun but it's murder. The water is freezing and when all your kit and yourself are flung into the sea and visibility is nil it's all very wet and nasty.

Six of us are going on a survival course in a few days' time which should put us in the right frame of mind for Christmas when we come back.

A Week Later
We are off tomorrow. Mercier is leading the expedition. In addition to myself and Mercier, there is Schneider, Schick, Galfi, a Hungarian, and Bucholtz. These are in my opinion the best men in the section and I had no difficulty in persuading Mercier to select them. We are leaving tomorrow afternoon in a submarine from Mers el-Kébir which will take us within two miles of a remote island down the coast. Nobody seems to know very much about this island; whether or not it has fresh water for instance. The only thing certain about it, in fact, is that it is on the map. That is to say, it was there when the map was made.

There is a theory that if you drink sea water slowly and regularly in small quantities it will replenish the need for fresh water. Sea water taken in large quantities clogs up the kidneys because of the salt content. I do not think very much of this theory but it is the answer that we have been given in response to the question, 'What happens if there is no water on the island?'

We are supposed to stay on the island for as long as we can and eat birds and fish if we can catch them. Amongst the six of us we will have one packet of cigarettes, a radio, one box of matches, three pistols, three knives, one compass and three fish hooks, each with a nylon line. In addition we will have our rubber dinghy with six paddles and a sleeping-bag each. No water.

Two Days Later
We boarded the submarine *Amazon* yesterday afternoon after we had been searched to ensure none of us were carrying extra

iron rations or tins of smoked salmon, and off we set. The submarine was small, sweaty and claustrophobic but the crew were magnificent. They fed us endlessly on steaks until we could cram in no more and then they poured red wine down our throats until it overflowed out of our ears. We were ready to go and felt that we would have no difficulty surviving a year without food or liquid.

We surfaced at midnight on a bare and rolling ocean. Chilly and totally desolate. The sea never looked so big and so menacing and the night was as black as pitch. We inflated our little dinghy – it was half the normal size, a six man'er – and lowered it into the sea and then one by one we clambered in. We had been given a compass bearing and provided we stayed on it we would hit the island after two miles of paddling. The boys on board the sub gave us a last wave and whispered good luck – everybody whispers at night – and then we were in business. The black shape of the sub gradually merged with the night and we were alone on the ocean. The swell lifted us high and then whisked us down into the troughs. There was nothing regular about it; all movement was at the discretion of the sea. We were like a tiny matchbox tossed around on the water in a vast expanse of black nothing, totally impotent in the grasp of the sea. We began to paddle at first furiously in a sort of panic to get to land, but after half an hour we calmed down as we began to feel the rhythm of the sea and to lose some of our fear of it.

Three hours later we were still paddling and beginning to think we had lost our way when the island leapt out of the night like a huge towering monster looming above us. We were suddenly aware of just how big the swell was as it lifted us towards the rocks and then pulled us back at the last second. As we drew nearer to the island so it became more difficult to control the dinghy. The water just tossed us anywhere. The island seemed to stand straight out of the water on stilts of vertical rock faces and we paddled frantically looking for a gap and found nothing.

Gradually we were sucked into the rock face and each time the swell threw us forward so each time it seemed that we would be splattered on the rocks. And then we were finally picked up in one tumultuous thrust of water and heaved forward onto the rocks. Schneider jumped out into the blackness as the backwash dragged the dinghy back into the swirling water, and grabbed for a hold. In doing so he cut his hands to ribbons on the vicious coral rock but he held for a second with the painter of the dinghy tied to his wrist. Bucholtz leapt off and joined him. I was at the stern of the dinghy where I had been steering and I yelled above the screaming wind and roar of the waves for Schick to go next. Schick had the radio and he was one man I wanted to see on dry land. Mercier was sort of frozen in the middle of the dinghy. And then another huge wave suddenly grabbed us in its wake and crashed us down on the rocks again. The dinghy was full of water and ripped to shreds. Schneider and Bucholtz still had the rope, thank God, and in that final surge of water we were all literally flung onto the rocks. It was like landing on broken glass. There was no time to dwell on that for the sea was rushing in again and we had to get clear. We scrambled up the rocks in the darkness, falling every second step, dragging the remains of the dinghy with us.

Once out of reach of the sea we were able to pause and take stock of our position. Apart from the fact that we had lost half the paddles and the dinghy was a write-off anyway, things did not appear to be too bad. In front of us was a sixty-foot wall of rock which looked more formidable in the darkness than it transpired to be once we started up. Half an hour later we were at the top and thankful to be there. We were all completely drenched and there was no refuge from the wind, so we just lay on the ground, piled our sleeping-bags on top of ourselves, and waited for the morning.

We were up at first light and combed the island for driftwood, so that we soon had a good fire going. When we had got our circulatory systems moving again we set about exploring the ground. The island itself was four hundred yards long and half as wide. The vegetation was sparse dry grass with a few shrubs, and apart from this there was nothing but rock. There was not a drop of fresh water to be found. On top of the island there was a small light for shipping housed in a concrete structure and obviously fuelled by gas. I wondered why the hell it had not been working the previous evening; it would have saved us a lot of agony. At the opposite end of the island to that on which we had been thrown ashore we discovered a small landing stage, so it was clear that people visited the place from time to time. This was comforting, although it did not solve our immediate problem of finding something to eat.

By midday our attempts to catch fish had yielded nothing but we had managed to collect a number of tiny crabs and clams. These tasted delicious after they had been warmed over the fire. We made our first radio contact with base at noon and reported that all was well. Mercier had recovered somewhat from last night by this time and was once more his cheerful self.

I spent the afternoon stalking seagulls with a pistol. This is a fruitless task and I do not recommend it as a sporting pastime. It is impossible to get within range and when you do fire a shot you have to wait an hour and a half for them to settle down again. During the day we all drank regular but very limited quantities of sea water.

It is the evening now. We have a good shelter in a small dry cave and with plenty of grass on the floor I think we will sleep well tonight. We have left several garments outside the cave and spread a canvas ground sheet on the ground in the hopes that we may collect some dew during the night. Schick had the ground-sheet in his *sac* as a cushion against the radio on his back. Schneider is playing a harmonica that he brought with him and the fire is roaring. We have feasted on boiled crabs. Outside the wind is howling and there is a feel of rain. We need rain. The theory about the sea water is not proving to be a success in practice. We are all as thirsty as hell and one can feel the strength of the body ebbing from the lack of water.

The Evening, Two Days Later

We continued our efforts to find some form of nourishment the next day. There was no dew. The tiny crabs were sufficient in number to feed a baby kitten. The fish refused to bite on our hooks and the seagulls refused to sit still while I shot at them. But the real problem was the water. By mid-afternoon we were in a bad way. Tempers were fraying a bit by the time the sun went down. We were expecting radio contact at six o'clock in the evening and Schick and Schneider were all for calling for help. Mercier, surprisingly enough, thought we should try to hang on for one more day and I supported him, although without water I did not see how we could take much more. Everybody looked totally emaciated and we were a sad little group compared to the previous evening. The mouth organ had ceased to play and we were left with the noise of the wind outside and the sea crashing on the rocks.

And then this morning when we awoke with the first glimmer of light, I knew it was going to be the last day. We were in a miserable state. The fact that we had eaten practically nothing since we arrived on the island was not a problem. In fact the pangs of hunger had become considerably reduced during the second day. It was the water, and it wasn't even a problem of thirst. We had all met chronic thirst before. This was a craving for water like oxygen and if we didn't get some soon our bodies would have no energy for movement. We agreed that when we made the midday radio contact we should pull the plug on it and admit defeat.

And then something happened that changed the situation completely. Bucholtz suddenly gave a shout that there was a boat approaching and sure enough a small vessel was chugging towards the island some two hundred yards out. It transpired that it was the local marine department who had finally noticed that the light on the island had ceased to function and had come with a new supply of gas. The men on the boat were Arabs and when they saw us their faces went through a series of expressions starting with panic, through surprise and finally came to rest on humour. We explained our position, helped them get the gas cylinders up to the light and then asked them if they could spare a couple of drops of water. They were absolutely splendid, although they clearly thought we were quite mad. They gave us two bottles of water, which was all they had, two loaves of bread, some dried fish and a tin of sardines. We were new men.

When they had gone, Mercier, who had not been involved, started to become difficult about the whole thing. I was amazed. He said it was against the principles of the whole expedition and ordered us not to touch the food or the water. He furthermore declared that when the radio call came through he intended to ask for help. I had never heard such garbage and we then got into a tremendous argument with him. I was next in command after Mercier and the boys all looked to me for a lead. My view was that on a survival course you use any means that are available to you and if the good Lord decides to send down a couple of bottles of water and some sardines, why then, you eat and drink and are merry. Mercier finally got off his high horse and we plunged in. The pangs of hunger were refired the moment that we had finished but the water was like pouring liquid morale down one's throat. The change in us all was immediate.

The call came through on time and the boys at the other end were amazed that we still held on as we had previously reported the absence of fresh water. They would be heralding the whole thing as proof of the sea-water theory.

19 December 1963

We threw in the towel at noon and two hours later we were taken off the island by helicopter. It was tremendous to shovel warm food down our throats when we got back to camp. We all had stomach cramps immediately afterwards. And then this evening I received a Christmas hamper from Francis Widdrington containing half of Fortnum and Mason's store. What incredible timing.

20 December 1963

The barracks are being decorated, the crèches are appearing and bars are being constructed as the mad scramble to produce the best display heralds the approach of Christmas. Mercier has bought an old piano in Oran. I am the only one who has the slightest idea how to play and I haven't touched a piano in years. Guidon has produced a set of drums from somewhere and Pitzalis has managed to get hold of a guitar with two strings missing. Schneider's harmonica is our wind instrument and a string and a broom and an old plywood tea-chest can produce a sound that resembles a double-bass. We are in the music business!

Christmas Eve

In spite of myself I have become totally engrossed in the preparations for Christmas over the last few days. I'm not sure how it happened, I just suddenly became enthusiastic. Mercier must take the credit for this. He is an enthusiast for everything and this is a quality in him that I admire. It's not easy to be a consistent enthusiast. Our barracks look fantastic. We have created an atmosphere of a cellar and it could not be a better place to throw a party.

Our band has been playing non-stop for three days and nights and we can put together 'Silent Night' and 'Seven Lonely Days' and one or two other little numbers. Guidon on drums would put Buddy Rich out of business and Schneider's harmonica is making sounds that would warm the heart of Larry Adler. Pitzalis with two more strings produced by Mercier from somewhere is now showing wonderful form and I am plugging a few chords on the piano to give the whole thing some body.

Christmas Day
Last night was probably the best Christmas party ever. It was not particularly Christmasy as such but we had a great evening. Our barracks were jammed tight until six in the morning and we played our terrible music until our hands were numb. Everybody loved it. Mercier has asked us to play for the forthcoming officers' dance. I cannot believe it. These people must be musically deaf or something.

In the Christmas honours list I was promoted to chief corporal and was presented with my gold stripes and black kepi by Colonel Cailloud this afternoon. Vignaga and Soto came over later in the evening with a bottle of champagne and we celebrated the event. They are good chums. Everybody is very generous in their praise and congratulations and it promotes a good feeling inside. If I stay around this place much longer I'm going to start liking it.

26 December 1963
There was a party for the children of the officers and N.C.O.s today. Lots of sketches and clowns, and our band was on parade. We are already becoming quite famous.

31 December 1963
1963 goes under the bridge. It has finished well for me personally. I'm getting much more out of it now and I feel that I am ready to make a better contribution and to give a bit more of myself. I think I can do something during the next year. I have some authority now and I can participate in the direction of things. I can make sure that the Sot Garcias of this world do not overplay their hands. I can help some of these fellows like Schneider and Sigi Weiss get more out of it all, change their thinking a little so

that they do not regard their presence here as some sort of prison sentence. I can put some fun into it too. I know how to maintain discipline for the sake of general control and not for the sake of discipline itself. I should like to instil some motivation into the men in the company and beef up morale. I think I am going to enjoy 1964.

1964

6 January 1964

It gives me a lot of pleasure to write '1964'. I began my first day as '*sergent de semaine*' today. A chief corporal acts as a sergeant on the duty roster, so this week I will be responsible for organizing all the various services within the company and for taking *appel* and other things. This morning I had my first shot at getting the company on parade. The various section commanders present their sections to me and then I bring the company to attention and present it to the company adjutant. Seeing the whole company on parade in front of you and watching them spring to attention at your command is a great inducement to megalomania and I was tempted to do a Delgado on them; that is, to bring them to attention a few times until they really got it together like we used to at the *peloton*. I finally decided that it was premature and let it go at one. They came to attention like a pistol shot.

And I took my first *appel* this evening. As I wandered round the barracks and looked at the men ramrod to attention beside their bunks I remembered all the mishaps that had happened to me during the many times I had stood as they were standing now. I remembered all the times at Mascara that our kit had been destroyed and thrown about the room and the antics of Sergeant Winter at the *peloton* – and I smiled to myself. I was on the other side of the fence now and very delighted to be so.

8 January 1964

I was summoned to Captain Legrand's *bureau* this morning. He asked me if I was interested in becoming an officer. It would

mean doing two years at a military academy in Strasbourg. I was
of course very flattered but I requested time to think about it.

He then said he was prepared to send me to the sergeants'
peloton immediately, but that it was necessary for me to have at
least six months to serve at the end of the *peloton*. Since the next
sergeants' *peloton* does not start until the middle of the year and
lasts for four months, it would be necessary to sign on for the
minimum time of six months. I said I would like time to consider that too.

I have not the slightest intention of signing on for ten minutes
to become a sergeant, but the other proposition bears thinking
about. I might seek some advice on the subject from Loridon.

12 January 1964

Mercier came into the section this evening with a couple of regular army officers in civilian gear. Hirschfeld and Sergeant Meyer,
who were both drunk, started complaining about it, saying
regulars had no right in our barracks, and we had a very embarrassing situation. Mercier has been too close to the men for too
long and now he's getting the backwash from it. The N.C.O.s
are openly critical of Mercier and Legrand; there is no respect
at all. What is particularly bad is that they criticize them behind
their backs in front of the men. This would never have happened in the old days. If I am any judge, I think it is Peltzer who
is stirring things up; he has nothing but contempt for both these
officers and doesn't conceal his sentiments from anybody.

We no longer draw on the first six who pass out of the French
military academy for our source of officers as we used to. The
Legion is now open to all French army officers, even those doing
national service. The result has been a marked decline in the
quality. Even so, open disloyalty by the N.C.O.s makes things
worse and can only be bad for morale.

I heard Peltzer discussing Mercier the other day in the *bureau
de semaine* with Sot Garcia. Peltzer was airing the view that
Mercier was a homosexual, '*tapette*', and that in all his years in
the Legion he had never seen anything like it. I joined in the
discussion and came out in support of Mercier and said that
since there wasn't the slightest proof it was premature to judge
merely because the fellow had some effeminate mannerisms.
Peltzer's response to this, without actually saying it directly, was

to insinuate that if that's how I felt about it then I was probably one as well. There is no point in rising to this sort of bait, and anyway I don't give a stuff what Peltzer thinks of me, anymore than he gives a damn what I think about him.

17 January 1964

Kalushke has deserted. I wish him luck. He'll make it. Loridon trained us well and he can look after himself.

A report has come through that out of the first detachment from our regiment that was recently sent to Corsica, where the Legion has established a base, twenty out of thirty-seven have already deserted. That's what I call a real exodus.

20 January 1964

Sot Garcia has been transferred from the third section to my section. The hour of retribution draws nigh. He has but to put one toe out of line and I will blow it off. He knows this and that is already causing him misery. Nobody likes to exist on a tight-rope.

2 February 1964

Mercier has confirmed that I can take thirty days' leave in June. I have written to Nicole to break the good news. Jacqueline suddenly slips into second place. She hasn't written for ages and time must have eroded her feelings and mine too I suppose. I wonder if I will feel anything when I see Jennifer in the summer if I go to England.

Life goes on in the regiment. Operational exercises, night jumps, marches, guard duty (I am the *chef de poste* these days – no more sentry duty), parades for visiting generals, and all the various courses. It's dull routine stuff. I see a lot of Daniel Vignaga and Eduardo de Soto. Vignaga and I are thinking of raising a rugger team in the regiment; there are very few people who have any idea of the game at all, but it might be fun to teach them.

I have had my first salary as a chief corporal – the vast sum of eighty pounds. I'm on a saving jag to get enough to go on leave. My total savings to date amount to precisely nothing.

14 February 1964
Somebody was killed at the anti-tank school today. The tank rolled over him and I suppose the ground was uneven because his head was squashed. His helmet was crushed onto his skull so that it could not be removed afterwards. They had to use a blow-torch to get it off apparently. A general happened to be watching the whole thing, which probably hasn't helped the career of the officer in charge of the school.

1 April 1964
Five weeks have slipped by. Life is routine and more routine. My mind is on June and the present has no meaning.

I was supposed to go on the frogman course a week ago but the dentist is playing 'she loves me, she loves me not' with my teeth so I failed the medical which requires one to have teeth that are impeccable. The dentist himself is a character and confessed halfway through the first visit, just as he was about to go for the needle, that he was still studying dentistry and had asked for a transfer to the Legion so that he could get some practical training. I lost a kilo on the spot and he confirmed my worst fears when he got the drill going. It took three injections to freeze the tooth and the drill looked as though it had been used for road work. There was a second-hand feeling about everything – everything except the dentist. He looked too damned new.

I did the anti-tank course, which was a diversion, but that and the dentist have been the only excitements. Nicole continues to bombard me with letters but God knows what we will feel when we meet – it has been so long.

4 May 1964
Camerone went quietly by. We had the usual stands and every-body got drunk and that was about it. And then last night the peace and the routine came to an end with a paralysing event.

Mercier has finished his two years in the Legion and is due for a posting in a day or so. We had a celebration for him in the section – lots of ale and Scotch and we presented him with a bronze statue depicting Napoleon's victory at Austerlitz. Then at 'lights out' he left with the other sergeants and myself and it was all over. And then the bomb.

Mercier returned to the section and continued drinking there, getting more and more drunk, and suddenly jumped into Legionnaire Schaeffer's bed and literally started to assault him.

The first thing I knew about it was when Sergeant Grau came storming into my room and started giving me a garbled account of the incident and blaming me for allowing Mercier to return to the section. Peltzer was up in arms by this time and storming round the place yelling his head off as though the whole regiment was on fire. He also was blaming me, declaring that since I was in charge of the section I must be held responsible and that I should have been on the look out for it as he had warned me that Mercier was queer weeks before.

Where the blame lay did not particularly concern me at that moment. My first reaction was total disbelief but as Schaeffer and the others responded to questions I realized that it was true and disbelief dissolved in a tide of uncontrollable rage. That this man, my section commander whom I had come to like well and whom I had supported behind his back so many times against all sorts of accusations, had now shown that everybody was right and chosen his farewell party to demonstrate the fact was too much. It wasn't so much that he had let himself down, it was that he had somehow let me down and everybody else for that matter too.

I must have become slightly irrational because I set off for the officers' barracks where Mercier had fled and without any thought at all I went to his room, thrust open the door and blazed in. I flicked on the light and there he was in bed. He came to life in the glare of the naked light bulb and his face was covered with a mixture of guilt and fear as he scrambled out of bed and grabbed his cigarettes. He offered me the packet with his hands trembling, and he kept saying over and over 'What's the matter Johnny? What's happened? What's going on? What's happening?'

I knocked the cigarettes out of his hands so that they all went flying across the room and then I struck him full force across the mouth with the back of my hand. He reeled back against the wall with his hands to his mouth and a look of total amazement on his face. Blood was pouring down his chin and he suddenly reacted and started shouting for me to get out and that he would have me sent to the penal battalions for striking an officer and that I would be shot.

He was hysterical and then I really hit him. I had never hit anyone like that. I just pulled back my arm and with my fist clenched as tight as a rock I swung it with every ounce of force and weight that I could put behind it. It caught him full on the side of the jaw. In that I had never done it before I had never seen or expected the result. His whole face screwed itself up and went sideways and his feet literally took off so that he landed flat on his bed.

I turned round, flicked off the light and walked out. In the corridor doors were beginning to open and officers rudely awakened were making noises of curiosity and anger at the disturbance. Nobody took the slightest notice of me and I walked back to my room and went to bed. I felt sick.

And this morning to my amazement Mercier appeared on parade. He looked terrible. He had been patched up in the infirmary. The side of his face was swollen up so that it looked like the worst case of toothache I had ever seen and he had a bandage round his face, under his chin and over the top of his head. He said nothing to me, nor did he look at me but just stood in the line where he normally stands at the side of the section.

After the assembly when everybody was dispatched in the direction of their various tasks for the day, Peltzer called me into the *bureau* and asked me point blank if I had done it.

By this time I had resigned myself to the fact that I probably would be going to the penal battalions. In the Legion nobody strikes an officer and gets away with it. To lay him out cold demands an even worse punishment. It just does not happen. In the cold light of day my actions of the previous evening, stripped of all the emotion, now seemed incredible and I was trying to convince myself that it had never happened. It could not have happened. But it had and as I faced Peltzer I knew I could expect no support from that quarter. He loathed me. I was a goner this time.

But I was wrong. I told Peltzer exactly what had happened and he said I was mad but he would do everything he could to help. He said the first and immediate thing to do was to see the senior N.C.O. in the company, Adjutant-chef Holemeir (he is also one of the senior N.C.O.s in the regiment), and to make a clean breast of the whole thing. This I did with Peltzer in attendance, and I told him the story from beginning to end. Holemeir said he would look into it and then report to Captain Legrand.

I had a fairly nerve-racking day and then this evening Peltzer told me that Holemeir had made a report to the C.O. completely in my favour and that the incident was closed.

Two Days Later
We had a parade for Mercier. It was a solemn occasion. It was an embarrassing occasion. Everybody was trying to pretend nothing had happened. I felt sorry for Mercier and I wished like hell that I had imagined the whole thing. But he had brought it all on himself and he would have to live with it forever. He shook hands with the sergeants and then he suddenly stepped towards me and said, '*Au revoir, Johnny,*' and put out his hand. I shook hands and said goodbye. I felt no anger any more – mixed feelings. We had had some good laughs and he had some excellent qualities. The situation was more pathetic than anything else. A sad ending. He left in the afternoon.

11 May 1964
Chief Sergeant Peltzer left today after fifteen years of service. He outlived Mercier and I think that was a source of immense satisfaction to him. I said goodbye to him with clouded feelings. He was a tough, ruthless, savage bully, with standards totally foreign to mine – but he had something. If for nothing else, I owe him thanks for taking the line he did over the Mercier incident, although I realize that it was not because he liked me but rather that he disliked Mercier more. At his departure the whole company gave a sort of universal sigh of relief. A great invisible weight has been lifted from the shoulders of one and all.

13 May 1964
I went to Mers el-Kébir to arrange my flight to France. Unbelievable excitement. I am leaving on the twenty-eighth. The whole thing is likely to unhinge my mind. I have been issued with a ticket which I find myself reading over and over again. I called on Soto who is in the infirmary at Mers el-Kébir with an

appendix or something, I didn't register properly. He looked absolutely fine anyway and was in terrific form.

He introduced me to a splendid Frenchman in the regular army, called Patrick Baumann. He is doing national service and is yet another acting dentist. The only difference in him and the one who is murdering people up at the regiment is that Patrick has never done any dentistry before and has no desire to do any in the future. He is involved purely because there appears to be nobody else for the job. He says the screaming when he yanks people's teeth out is having a psychological effect on him which could make him a manic depressive if it goes on much longer. God knows what sort of effect it is having on his patients! I liked him immediately and his great sense of humour. He is '*libérable*' next month and told me to come and see him in Paris. This I will certainly do. Paris – Jesus, I'm going mad.

28 May 1964
The last two weeks have had no meaning.

I took off at midday and two hours later I was in Paris – Europe after four and a half years in the wilderness. It was another planet. My mother, my stepfather Leo and Caroline, my half-sister, were at the airport to meet me. We were complete strangers at first. My mother had left middle age behind her. She looked fifteen years older and I felt a flow of sadness pass through me when I saw her. Caroline had become a little girl of ten. She had been a baby of four when I had last seen her. Leo looked the same. We had a long evening. So much to tell, so much to listen to. It is fantastic to be back.

The Next Day
The first thing I needed to get was a passport as mine was still held by the Legion and I was set on going to England. Officially my leave was limited to France and I required special permission to leave the country as far as the Legion were concerned. Such permission would be automatically refused, so there was no point in asking for it. I went to the British consulate and pleaded my case. I was asked lots of questions and filled in a few forms and they quickly realized that I was a genuine Brit and a gent to boot. After a long wait I was escorted to the back of the building through endless passages and finally brought face to

face with a Colonel Fields – at least that is what he said his name was. He was clearly one of the boys and we had quite a nice little chat. In a nutshell he was prepared to see that I was issued with a temporary passport, which would enable me to travel, in exchange for information on everything I knew about the Foreign Legion, from the numbers in the various regiments and their precise locations to details of the types of armaments we were using and many other things. I spilled all the beans and I made his day. I was given a passport.

A Week Later

What a week it has been. Seven days of freedom like being released after years in a strait-jacket. The trees, the cars, the restaurants, the girls, the people, the colour of everything, the shops with their unbelievable luxuries on display, everything is magnificent. Life is just sunshine and champagne. My parents went back to Holland after a few days and I decided I would see them on my return from England.

I met up with Patrick. He was wild with delight at the excuse to show somebody his beloved Paris and he whirled me through the Crazy Horse, up and down the Sacre Coeur and twice round Notre-Dame. I was always in Legion uniform and from the stares it appears that legionnaires are as rare in France as they are in England. Many times we were accosted on the Champs-Elysées by ex Legion officers who poured beer down our throats and wanted to hear all the news of the regiment. Some of them were ex-para and some of them had been involved in the *putsch*. There is a great camaraderie among all men who have served in the French para regiments and they can talk all night until the dawn about the experiences they have shared in Indo-China and Algeria. Their talk is a private domain with no room for intruders.

8 June 1964

It was time for me to leave Paris. Nicole was waiting for me in the South and so with some reluctance I boarded the night train for Nice. On arrival I checked into a hotel near the station and got on the telephone to Vence. Nicole answered, thank God; I would have dropped the receiver like a hot potato if her mother had come on the line. There was a shyness in her voice and I was a bit pushed for something to say too. She said she would come to the hotel the next day.

A Week Later

She came as she said she would. There was a moment when I thought it was going to work, but it didn't. We went out the first evening but she had to get home by a certain time and then we met again the next day and it still didn't click. It is three years since I have seen her. In that time she has matured into a beautiful young girl. I think she was disappointed in me. She had probably worked up some fairly romantic ideas about her legionnaire in those three years and though it hurts me to admit it, I'm afraid I don't think that I came up to the standard she had set in her dreaming.

She couldn't make dinner the second evening and we were to meet the next day for lunch. She didn't show.

Tonight I am catching the train to Paris and tomorrow I will be in England. I've waited so long for this moment I cannot believe that it has finally come. The Legion is a hazy memory of something that happened long ago.

Ten Days Later

I left Nice the next morning for England. These last few days will stay with me forever. I have seen so many of my old friends and realize once again, now that it is all over, just what fantastic friends I have.

I stayed the first night with Anski. It was after midnight when I arrived and I threw stones up to her window until she finally opened it and looked down into the street. When I yelled up that it was me, she practically fell into the street below. I had told nobody when I was coming. I like surprises.

I spent a couple of days with my brother Anthony and his fabulous wife Caroline and I was given a great party at the McCallums' house. All the famous deerstalkers were there. Everybody was exploding with curiosity and I gave them a few yarns to make their hair curl. It was amazing to see the changes in people. Fellows I had known at school as idle layabouts had now become City gents, lawyers and doctors. They all looked terribly respectable members of society and I was delighted with them all.

Peter Clapham gave me a splendid dinner one evening, and I spent a day or two with Alister Hall and his lovely wife Julia in Shropshire. They have a son called Marcus. Francis Widdrington gave me lunch with his old friend Andrew Grahame at Brown's Hotel. They were worried that I was going to pinch the silver. I saw Cedric Gunnery and Christie and my old friends the Cornwall-Leghs. They were in good heart. And finally I saw Jennifer.

She had been away when I first got back and I called her the day before I left. She said she was going to Spain the next day and having dinner that evening with her grandparents and why didn't I come too. I went. I could not have put up a cooler front or been more indifferent to her. I talked to everybody with enthusiasm except her. To her I was just coldly charming. It was a masterly performance. She gave me a lift back to town, her grandparents live in Wimbledon, and that was nearly that. And then as I was leaving I said, 'How about a little night-club for old times' sake?' After some hesitation and mumbling about Spain the next day she finally allowed herself to be persuaded and we headed for London's night-life.

I don't know when it happened precisely – all I know is that at some stage in the evening we were dancing and suddenly I found myself telling her that after all those God-damned years I was still in love with her, and I think in that moment she was in love as well. We talked all night and the next morning I left for Holland. We left each other with promises.

And last night I caught the train from Paris to Marseille where I am now. Memories flick through the mind of the last time I did the journey. Tomorrow I am catching the good ship *Sidi-bel-Abbès* to Oran. History repeating itself again, but I will have my own cabin this time.

I've got seven months left to do and I've got seven months of thinking about Jennifer in front of me. That just might make it go very slowly.

PART TWELVE

Le Dénouement

Back in Africa

My feet had hardly touched the ground on my arrival back at the regiment before I was posted to the *peloton*. This time it was to be as an instructor. Legrand told me that it was at the special request of Loridon (now captain) and that the request had been made through the colonel. This was good news and it meant that I was going to have an active last few months before I finished.

15 July 1964

I had a long chat with Loridon this evening. He was trying to persuade me to take up the offer to do a year at Strasbourg and then I could probably do the final year at Saint Cyr. It sounds attractive in some ways but the problem is that as a foreigner I would never get beyond the rank of captain and to adopt French nationality is not on as far as I am concerned. I am a son of England and whilst I may at this moment be taking time out to give the French a helping hand, I could never surrender my British nationality voluntarily. So I think the proposition is a non-starter because I have no wish to be a captain in the Foreign Legion for the rest of my life. Besides, after my recent glimpse of England, I want to get back. Life is much better on the outside.

We talked of other things – life, philosophy, people, places, the Legion, the French, the English, the Germans, the future, the past and the present. This is Loridon's third *peloton*. He said ours was the best by far and he had never seen a bunch quite like ours all together in one place at one time. Ours was also the toughest of the courses, in some ways due to our N.C.O.s and in some ways due to the fact that it was something of an experiment: they wanted to see how far the system could go without cracking. One of the essential differences between our *peloton* and the others is that most of the men had seen action, whereas in the *peloton* now this was the exception rather than the norm. We eventually decided that the present *peloton* was too soft and needed toughening up a little so that we could get a clearer view of those that had fibre and those that did not. I said that I would put this in hand.

Ten Days Later
The senior N.C.O. here is Sergeant Westhof. He is as tough as steel and totally impersonal in all his dealings with the men. He is therefore straight and there is no deviation from the path. He is a permanent shit.

We are giving the *peloton* quite a rough time but it is not as rough as we had, for above all else they get a reasonable amount of sleep. Certainly we give them stick and I throw their kit around at *appel* and have them drilling at two in the morning. Indeed on a couple of occasions when their singing has been below standard I have had them marching at knees bend for a couple of hours in the bushes at midnight and I have sent them several times to get sea water in the middle of the night – I am very careful not to taste it when they get back.

Another thing about this *peloton* which I think they recognize is that there is also time for some humour too. We get a lot of laughs and I think they are probably wise enough to appreciate that it is possible to maintain discipline without running the whole thing on concentration-camp lines. They have already improved a great deal since they arrived and collectively maintained their morale in spite of the efforts of Westhof, Loridon, Killiaris and myself to make their lives reasonably miserable. They are potentially a good mob and there is a clear understanding on both sides of what it is all about.

1 August 1964
Loridon inspected the barracks today, and just so that these
fellows really understood the position he awarded a total of
eighty-eight days' prison between eleven men whose gear was
below standard. I took them through the *pelote* in the afternoon.
For the first time I was on the whistling end of this terrible
punishment. Actually they had an easy time of it, because they
did not have the traditional sacks of stones on their backs and
the guy with the whistle determines the degree of torture. I think
I'm a bit soft for this sort of thing. In some ways I would rather
do the *pelote* myself than be the man with the whistle.

A Fortnight Later
The boys are at breaking point. We have had three deserters in
the last few days. It is not because we have been giving them
excessive punishments but because we have been working them
too hard. Loridon is a fanatic for commando training at night,
and as it was with us, life has become devoid of sleep. They are
always on the move marching with their compasses at night in
the hills covering many miles; night after night without rest and
then doing drill, weapon training and all the rest of it during the
day. They look haggard and drawn and Loridon has decided to
send the whole lot down to the infirmary tomorrow to make
sure we are not overdoing it.

Two Days Later
The result of the medical examination has been an outcry from
the senior medical officer in the regiment. The men are out of
their minds with tiredness, they are run down and on the
verge of collapse. I wonder why we didn't have a medical
check during my *peloton* days, I think we could have used
one.
   Anyway Loridon has decided quite rightly to put the brakes
on a bit but has emphasized that this should be done slowly,
otherwise the men will feel that with the support of the medical
officer they can get the upper hand. In order to demonstrate
what he meant by this, the night following the great medical
check the programme was a night jump over Cap Falcon,
followed by an exercise with aerial photographs, followed by

one hour of sleep; then a forced march back to Lindless, a cup of coffee, and three hours' drill.

Three Weeks Later

The training that these fellows have undergone is fantastic. Seeing it now from the other side I appreciate the concentration of it and whilst this puts a strain on the men at all times, the results are impressive. They have learned to handle themselves well and are a different breed of animal from those that arrived here two months ago. They can put together a commando raid that would make Warner Brothers green with envy. They can get themselves up and down a vertical precipice of a hundred feet and more, or rig up pulley systems to swing themselves across a gorge in the twinkling of an eye. They can fire machine-guns from the hip with amazing results, and they can find their way through the mountains at night without the slightest hesitation. Their morale is good and I think their standard is now every bit as good as ours was. Fischer, Vorshtedt, Vallier, Schackt, Pallicke and Tippmann are all first-raters and it's going to be very difficult to pick the winner out of this lot. It is, however, still early days and there is plenty of time for some of them to do a Vignaga.

8 September 1964

Fantastic letter from Jennifer. She's crazy about me.

We are all going on the anti-tank course tomorrow which will be a good break. I think everybody could do with a little diversion.

Two Weeks Later

It's a good course. Everybody now knows about Molotov cocktails and other forms of home-made incendiaries, mines, rockets, anti-tank grenades, booby traps and a hundred and fifty other ways of making life miserable for a tank. In fact I would never volunteer for a tank regiment having seen what I have seen. A tank is a mobile coffin.

26 September 1964

Loridon's fertile mind has devised a new combat course. Instead of jumping out of helicopters as we used to, the start is now at the top of an old fort in the port of Mers el-Kébir and one has to shin down a series of ropes down the walls of the fort, which are about fifty feet high, and then climb up to the top of a transit shed which is sixty feet above the water, jump in and swim half a mile to shore and then do an eight-kilometre jog in full kit.

The jump from sixty feet nearly ended in my demise today. Jumping out of aeroplanes is one thing, because they are moving and there is no contact with the soil; jumping at sixty feet from a stationary object that is in contact with the ground is something quite different and is without any question at all the most nerve-racking thing I have ever faced in my life before.

When I got to the edge of the transit-shed roof and looked down I could feel the blood drain from my face right through my body into my feet. I was absolutely terrified. I do not like heights. I had to go, there were people behind me. I must have felt exactly like that fellow who refused to jump at Blida. This time there was no parachute and there was no choice – and so I jumped. It was like hitting concrete and I left my guts twenty feet above me as I went down.

I was so damned scared that I knew I had to do it again to prove something to myself or I would never master it. That was a mistake and I should have left things as they were. Up I went again. The same sensations of panic – it was all I could do to stop myself peeing in my pants – and over I went. I am not a mathematician and cannot account for the speed of my descent, but it was rapid. I hit the water with the smack of a rifle shot. My arms were stretched out horizontally to help me balance and I must have fallen slightly sideways because as I splattered onto the water my left arm was ripped straight out of its socket. I think I blacked out for a second and then the pain struck. Agony unbelievable, unimaginable, impossible to describe. I thought my arm had been torn right off. I just wanted to carry on sinking down into the water into nothing. Eventually I hit the surface and everybody could see immediately that I was in trouble. They all dived in but I screamed at them not to come near me. One touch on that arm, the slightest movement, sent pain through me that jarred me to the point where I thought the old heart would seize up. I got to the edge and somehow got out of the water. The dislocation was total so that the top

K

of the humerus bone was sticking out at the side. It looked very out of the ordinary.

It was three-quarters of an hour from the time I hit the water until a doctor finally managed to manipulate my shoulder back into position. That's the last time I jump from sixty feet into water. It was a hard lesson in water density. One of our people actually dived off the shed. The Legion has at least one of everything, and this fellow was one of those.

1 October 1964

Loridon is about to go on leave and a young lieutenant called Reppellin has arrived to stand in while he is away. If first impressions are accurate, which they are often not, then we have in Reppellin everything that we do not need. He is brand new and obviously has come with the understanding that the Legion survives on discipline alone. As a result he is behaving like a little Hitler, and whilst I do not think there is anything personal in it, he obviously thinks it is expected of him. Loridon ought to put him right on this, I can't; but Loridon appears not to notice – he's got his mind on leave.

We have added one more sergeant to the staff in the form of Grau. Grau is Spanish and I think that basically he is a good N.C.O., but there is a weakness in the structure somewhere. The night that Mercier went off the rails Grau over-reacted somewhat. Having said that, I suppose I did too. Maybe that's not it, but somewhere I detect a flaw. Grau and I tolerate each other, no more than that.

Two Weeks Later

Reppellin has driven the boys over the brink. During the last two weeks they have been pushed almost beyond endurance. Punishments every night, endless route marches and night exercises, weapon inspections, barrack inspections, lavatory inspections at three in the morning, *tombeaux, tenue campagne*, and all the old favourites.

Reppellin instigated the drive and it somehow gathered momentum, with Grau appearing just too eager to support him. I would have expected Westhof to step in and slow the thing down, as the senior N.C.O., but if anything he has supported it. It makes no sense, because these fellows have come on well during the last few weeks and the stage for giving them hell just for the sake of it has passed. They should be revising for the final exams. The *peloton* is practically over.

There are rumbling noises in the ranks. Killiaris says that there is talk of desertion.

The Next Day
I was in town all day and when I got back to camp this evening I was given the news that the whole bloody *peloton* had run off. Reppellin was in a hell of a state and Westhof and Grau had both lost their cool. It was dark when I arrived and Reppellin had taken the incredible decision to get the mortar out and was in the process of shelling the surrounds of the camp. Apparently the *peloton* had left the camp as a manifestation against the present regime under Reppellin and they were in the bushes about two or three hundred yards outside the wire. Reppellin's intention in firing the mortar was to frighten them into surrendering. But when mortar shells are being fired at random all around you at night it can be scary, you have no idea where the next one may land. There is only one way to run – out of range, and that is what they have done.

It is now midnight and there is no sign of them. Reppellin has put the mortar to bed and that is where I am going to put myself. We will see what tomorrow brings.

16 October 1964
The *peloton* came in at dawn. Their demonstration has not achieved very much. I wish Loridon had been here to handle the situation – Reppellin was clearly not up to it from the word go – and the senior officers at the regiment should have stepped in much sooner instead of letting this young and inexperienced lieutenant make an arse of himself.

Reppellin quite rightly wanted to establish who the leader or leaders of the demonstration were and if he could do this he would be able to reassert his authority – the leaders would be sent to prison and the rest would be punished but allowed to finish the course. But his attempts to do so were embarrassing. The men were formed up on parade in the first instance. They looked drawn and haggard, as well they might. There was much at stake here. They had virtually completed the *peloton* course and there remained only the final exams and here they were about to chuck it all away. As one that has done the course, I knew to a great extent how they must be feeling. If there was one among them who emerged as the leader, then he could be sacrificed and that would save a lot of agony for the rest – not the least being the authorities, who also had no wish to lose the entire *peloton*.

Reppellin addressed the men along these lines and vainly tried to persuade somebody to step forward. He urged them to consider their own positions carefully and warned that if nobody came out then the whole lot would go down the plughole. They stood firm.

It was cold on the parade-ground this morning and the atmosphere made it more so. I had come to like many of these fellows over the last few months. After all we had shared an experience that was unique in many ways. That they had run off was a bad let-down to themselves, particularly so near to the end. It was ill-conceived and whoever had produced the idea should be winkled out and made to carry the can, if that was to be the only way to save the majority. Otherwise it was all going to be a terrible waste. But they were solid as a wall and it did them credit.

We waited for them to make a move. Hour after hour they stood there to attention with Reppellin pacing up and down in front of them, ranting and raving for the culprits to come out. There was never a ripple in the ranks. They were like stone statues. It reminded me somewhat of the Garbou situation when I was doing the *peloton*. The same confrontation with authority, on the same parade-ground. There was only one man then and this time there were many; and yet to me they were as one man again.

Reppellin then crucified himself forever as far as I was concerned. He went up to Koblenz, one of the men in the ranks, and asked him whose idea it had been to run off. Koblenz didn't answer, he just stood there staring straight ahead. And Reppellin asked him again and still he said nothing. It was like talking to a tree. And then Reppellin lost control of himself and started to attack the man by punching him in the face. Koblenz is a big man, not an inch under six feet three inches, and he could have murdered Reppellin with one hand tied behind his back but he remained motionless. It was pathetic to watch and I turned my back. I hoped Reppellin would see the gesture. In a way it would have been better if he had laid Koblenz flat on his back, that would have at least been positive, but as it was it looked like a baby against a grown man. Definitely one up to the men. At last the commandant and some of the senior officers arrived from the regiment. The commandant's first move was to dismiss the men and confine them to barracks and then the officers went into seclusion to debate the situation. I went into the barracks and talked to the men. Apparently the whole episode had been sparked off the previous evening by Sergeant Grau, who had taken them on a fifteen-mile run in the afternoon because the barracks were not up to scratch and then he had ordered them to do the *pelote* on their return. They had refused.

They all poured out their grievances when I went in and it was difficult not to feel sympathetic. They had come a long way and had no desire to throw it all away any more than the officers had. I think if Loridon had been there, he and I could have solved it. The pity of it is that it need never have happened in the first place.

Within half an hour of being in the barracks it was clear to me that the principal agitator was Ambrozetti. He is a Frenchman with an inflammatory tongue and the Germans, who are followers rather than leaders, seemed to be mesmerized every time he spoke. He is a good soldier and is well liked by his fellowmen. He is not a bully and is therefore the sort of natural leader that emerges through a process of general acceptance.

It was Ambrozetti who at this stage appeared to feel that the *peloton* still had a bargaining point, which was that they would fall into line in every way if Grau could be removed from the *peloton* staff. I told him that he was dreaming and that to hold on for that would make a solution impossible because the Legion would never accept it. It would be a precedent with which they could not live. The idea that legionnaires could have a sergeant sacrificed every time he was a bit rough on them was contrary to all Legion traditions of discipline and would be a hammer blow right in the guts of the system.

Up to this point they had still refused to do the *pelote* and I felt that the only way to salvage something from this was for them to now back off and do it, and indeed all the other punishments that would be coming their way after last night's escapade.

This would effectively mean that they were a hundred per cent back in line. There was a glimpse of a face-saver for them if they agreed to do the *pelote* on the condition that Sergeant Grau did not take them through it, but even that would be imposing a condition which I did not think the authorities would accept. When I remember what happened to the fellows who smashed the plates in our section that time, I didn't think it was in the interest of these people to do much more than fall in as quickly as possible without any 'buts'. And I reminded them (for the benefit of Ambrozetti) that if they did cooperate, even though this meant that they were backing down, it could save the ultimate sacrifice of one of them, because as sure as hell, the officers were set on finding a leader or some leaders. Somebody had to take the knock to prevent total loss and to enable a rationalization to be made of the incident. One bad apple in the barrel contaminating the others would be acceptable and could be explained. The alternative was total capitulation, which would mean that the incident had never happened. To the authorities there could only be these two alternatives.

The *peloton* eventually accepted the second.

Four Days Later

Even by Legion standards they have had a rough time. They cannot have had more than seven hours' sleep in the last four days and when they have not been doing thirty-kilometre route marches, they have been on night exercises, or doing the *pelote*. Each man has a sack of sand strapped to his back at all times during the day, even at mealtimes, and they have lost a month's pay to correspond to the effective loss they would have suffered if they had been given fifteen days' prison. They begin their final exams in two days' time.

Tippmann has been thrown out for falling out on one of the night marches and going to sleep in the bushes. That is the loss of a good corporal.

The morale of the boys is at rock bottom as might well be expected, and coming right at the end of the *peloton* this could have a major impact on their future roles as corporals. If they leave here anti the establishment the long-term damage to the regiment could be serious. Loridon comes back next week – I wonder if he can salvage anything.

22 October 1964
It was Soto's last evening and we took him out for dinner in Bou-Sfer, just Vignaga, Killiaris and myself. Sad to see him go – he has been a good friend and we have seen some bad times together. Bad times make fertile ground for good friendships. We gave him some gold cuff-links, reminded him that we all had a date for the first day of 1966 at the Manneken Pis and sent him on his way. He is one man who will not be back.

24 October 1964
It has been decided to put the *peloton* through the guerrilla warfare school and to delay the results of the final examination until after this is over. This makes sense to me as if things go well it will lift morale, which is currently on the floorboards, and it will give the men a break before returning to the regiment. I am keen to go through the school myself. The man who runs it is Captain Maidec. He learned his trade during the Second World War when he was attached to the Special Air Service of the British army. There is very little he does not know about explosives and the use of them for sabotage work. He is as tough as oak and expects everybody else to be the same. He is slightly mad and his guerrilla training school is the best there is anywhere.

Six Weeks Later
The six weeks have flashed by and we have crammed a lot into them. All the stories I had heard about Maidec are true. He is brilliant at his job.

We began with theory – a lot of it – until we knew the characteristics of all the explosives that we were likely to come across: the chemical construction and the physical properties and, more important, the behaviour characteristics. We learned when to use which explosive for maximum effect and precisely how much of it was required for a particular job. We learned how to calculate with various formulae the precise charge of different explosives for concrete pillars under a bridge or a steel pipeline or a high-tension cable pylon. There is a great truth in the much used saying that people work well at subjects they like. This for me was a duck-to-water experience. I have dived into this course with an enthusiasm that I have not felt in years, if ever. And because of this complete fascination and total interest that has eclipsed all else, I find the retention of information has been easy.

Maidec started by giving us two things: first, the knowledge of explosives and what could be done with them, from which we learned respect; secondly, endless practical use, particularly at night, so that we were constantly handling explosives, and this gave us confidence. These two elements of respect and confidence are the beginnings and essentials of a successful career in sabotage.

On the first day Maidec made us lie flat on our stomachs five feet from a couple of kilos of T.N.T. which went off like a bomb blast. No damage to us because the blast goes up and out in a V shape so that we were in the shadow of it. That was an impressive start and from that moment on we were in business. Each night we were shut into a darkened room and would spend hours tying the various knots required to link an explosive fuse (used to blast several separate targets at the same time) and handling different explosives so that we could identify by touch. And in the daytime we were memorizing the appearance of many different fuses, explosives and detonators of German, French, British and American manufacture.

We learned about T.N.T., tetryl, plastic, dynamite and what could be done with them. We learned how to make 'home-made' explosives from ammonium nitrate and a little bit of diesel oil and what could be produced from aluminium powder and potassium chlorate. We could run up snowballs, gas bombs and Molotov cocktails the way my mother can run up a martini. We learned how to make plate charges and fill them with bolts and nuts so that when they exploded the bolts and nuts would penetrate the side of a tank at four hundred yards. We learned about booby traps and the devastating effect that plastic can produce in experienced hands; how to fix a ball-point pen so that it would blow your wrist off when used; how to make lethal death traps of the mundane like door handles, a book, a drawer, or a motor car. We learned to set up an innocent gramophone so that when switched on, bolts and nuts would spray out of the speakers and be hurled across the room at three thousand feet per second – great potential if you want to wipe out a few hundred people in the city hall when an unattractive politician is addressing his followers.

We know how to modify hand grenades so that when the pin is pulled the grenade will explode immediately and how to alter a case of cartridges so that when they are fired the gun will explode and blow off the head of the man firing it. We can make rockets and incendiary bombs from elements found in the shops at the local village and we can shape explosives to do special work because we are able to capitalize on their very special characteristics.

All this information was fed to us in a very professional manner indeed and with an incredible amount of detail. The detail of all the different devices used in the field of pyrotechnics would cover a full university course in advanced physics.

And then we had some practical training at last. We worked in teams at night and blew disused tracks of railway, deserted farmhouses, old pylons and bridges. Each time we went off to do a job, it was preceded by hours of planning. We would build a mock-up of the target, calculate the charges we were going to use and precisely where they would be placed for maximum effect. Each man in the team would know exactly what he had to do. Nothing was left to chance. There is nothing more dangerous than confusion at night when you are playing with explosives. There is no room for fooling. When the charges are set and you disperse, it needs one man to step on a detonator and you're all on the moon.

We work quietly and efficiently because we have been well trained and we have confidence in ourselves and what we are about. In this game there is much that is documented and with concentration and with time it can be learned in theory. But there is much that is not documented which is the province of experience and in this field Maidec is the master. He has seen everything in the business and it is his little tips, advice and sometimes unorthodox techniques that distinguish the training we have had here from that which one would receive in a more conventional army. Maidec is lethal and so devious that the mere thought of him working for the other side brings me out in a cold sweat.

And during the last two weeks we have studied the details of clandestine guerrilla operations. How to set up a base and a network of cells, a communication system and codes, interrogation of prisoners, and above all how to plan an operation and execute it.

Loridon has been back for a week. Reppellin has gone, so have Grau, Westhof and Killiaris, who has finished his five years and disappeared with great plans for the million he is going to make in civvy street. Westhof and Grau have returned to the regiment. That leaves Loridon and myself as the only remaining staff with the *peloton*. He and I have a tremendous rapport. I talked to him one evening about the prospects of becoming an officer and told him that I had decided against it, particularly after my leave; there were a lot of things to be done on the outside and I think he understood what I meant.

7 December 1964
I did my last jump today – number 73.

8 December 1964
The *peloton* is over. Twenty-one of them finished and passed out in the final parade out of the thirty-eight that started. I was glad to see them get their stripes and felt proud of them as they did so. Volstedt was first with Fischer right behind him and Schack at number three. They are all good men and they have come down a hard road that I have come to know well and I have respect for each of them. They made speeches and said nice things about me and Loridon and they gave us each a silver paper-knife. I will never lose it. And then they got into their trucks and drove out through the gates of Lindless waving their arms off and cheering their hearts out. I know how they felt.

Tonight Loridon and I had dinner together and over brandy we talked it all through. We discussed them all and all the men of the previous *peloton* and the shadow of each one of them passed in front of me as I walked across the parade-ground to my barracks. The night held the echo of their voices in the wind and I felt for the first time a sadness that it was all coming to an end. My five years are nearly over and it is my turn at last to go home.

31 December 1964
It is the eve of a new year and for me a new beginning. Christ-

mas passed almost unnoticed. There was nothing for me in the company when I returned. I have spent so little time here during the last two years, ever since that first day when I went off to shoot with old Lafont, that I have no friends here. Those that I did have are long since gone. Young people in the company look at me as though I were a complete stranger, which I am – but there is something else in their faces too. Legionnaires respect length of service and I have done my time and come through. They are just starting the climb and they will soon learn that the road is long.

I am leaving for France on 4 January. Now that the hour of departure is at hand I cannot help feeling a certain apprehension. The Legion adventure is nearly over and I am about to start a much longer one for which I am not prepared. On the other hand I was not prepared for the Legion either – and yet I obviously was in a way because here I am at the end of the course. So it may be that the Legion has prepared me for what is to come next even though this cannot be translated into tangible certificates of worth. 1965 is a step into the unknown and, if nothing else, that is intriguing.

1965

4 January 1965

I left Algeria this morning in a military aircraft and I might have said 'never to return' before but now I hope that I may some day. Today it is a sad country. Its new-found independence has yet to bring it happiness; it is moving to the left rapidly and the signs of repression and rigid conformity are already very much in evidence in the towns. But it will always physically be a beautiful country of mountains and wildness. It contains massive areas of total silence and huge tracts of land where Nature has been left alone to run its course. I would like to return one day for this and to travel some of the old paths under different circumstances.

Last night some of my friends gave me a farewell party. I said goodbye to Daniel Vignaga and this time it was his turn to remind me that we had an appointment at the Manneken Pis. Old Sigi Weiss was there in good form, and Kenny and Bob Wilson. It was good to see them – I haven't seen so much of them in the last few months. They gave me a splendid watch as a souvenir of it all. Pedro Rodrigues was also there. He has just returned from the sergeants' *peloton*, having been thrown out for losing his temper once too often and hitting somebody over the head with a hot iron. He's been busted down to private but he doesn't seem particularly worried about it. I think I'll remember old Pedro always for the time he chucked his rifle at Schmidt and the occasion when he ate the bottle of Johnny Walker. Schreiner was there and some of the guys from the second *peloton* came and said goodbye. I said my adieux to Loridon over a cognac. I hope I'll see him again some day. And then this morning I bade my farewell to the colonel. He is not exactly a buddy of mine but he's a man I like and respect. He presented me with an album of photographs and inside he had inscribed:

> *Au Caporal-chef Murray,*
> *pour lui dire ma joie de l'avoir connu, ma*
> *gratitude pour ce qu'il a fait au régiment*
> *et la place qu'il a tenue, mes voeux pour*
> *son avenir et mon éspoir de lui rencontrer*
> *à nouveau plus tard.*
> > Cailloud

I think that must be nearly the nicest thing anybody has ever said to me.

Two hours later I was in the air and Algeria became history for me. As I passed across the coast and saw the sea below I finally knew that it was over for keeps this time and I felt a strange sadness.

24 January 1964

Churchill is dead. The last stone of the Empire crumbles. I listened to the radio all day. The French could not have paid greater tribute to him.

I am in the transit camp at Aubagne just outside Marseille. This has become the Sidi-bel-Abbès of the Legion. The great Monument aux Morts stands gloriously at the end of the enormous parade-ground. Everybody is here. It is a sort of combination between a burial ground for oldies, a starting place for new recruits, and a finishing line for people like me. Killiaris has turned up. He has signed on and is going to Djibouti. He was a bit embarrassed when I met him. I wonder what happened to those millions he was going to make. And Strobender appeared yesterday. He has spent four months on the outside and that was enough for him to realize that he didn't like it.

*To Chief Corporal Murray,
  To express my pleasure in having known him, my
  gratitude for what he has done in the regiment
  and the place he has held, my best wishes for
  his future and my hopes that I will meet him
  again some time.
                Cailloud

There is a man here who is just starting again after a break of eighteen years. He deserted from Morocco after six months' service eighteen years ago and the other day he was picked up by the police for drunken driving and somehow it was discovered that his name was on a wanted list. Poor devil, that's a really bad start to 1965.

Old Chief Corporal Kroll is here. I was delighted to see him and glad to see he had got his rank back. I thought he was given a bad deal after the plate-smashing episode. D'Église is also here.

There are many other familiar faces. Half the people who did instruction with me at Mascara are here waiting to get out. They all seem to remember me but I have lost the names of many of them. It's an amazing sensation to be here. Somehow it's like a summary of the five years, a sort of parade of characters at the end of the film.

There is nothing to do all day except drift around Marseille and wait for the end to come. I rang Jennifer today and told her D-Day is 12 February and she is coming to Paris to meet me.

3 February 1965
I ran into Volmar last night. That is the most marvellous thing that could have possibly happened to me. I was absolutely delighted to see him. This really was the end of the road. He's an adjutant now and is permanently attached to the base here. It was one of the great pleasures of my life finally to get that dinner that I missed in Mascara so many years ago and I think the whole five years in the Legion have been worth it for that alone. We talked all night and his fabulous wife kept pouring coffee for us. I told him about my five years, every step of the way, and how it has all ended where it started in meeting him.

12 February 1965
The great day finally came. Those leaving paraded at seven in the morning before Commandant Vadot. He presented us each with the colourful certificate of 'good conduct' which states that we have served for five years with '*honneur et fidélité*'. We then received our demob suits – mine is a long way in quality from the one in which I arrived! There were eight of us leaving. None of them was of the seven who joined with me on that first day in

Paris five years ago. I wonder what happened to that Spanish fellow with whom I had a fight on the train.

And then we went to the Deuxième Bureau at Fort Saint Nicolas. That really did set the old memory ticking. I was given a small brown envelope and it was all I could do to prevent the tears rolling down my cheeks as I opened it to find my lovely old passport and my little address book that they had confiscated when I arrived.

I walked out through the gates into the crisp morning sunshine and turned to face the sentry in his box. I saluted him and I saluted the old fort and I saluted the Foreign Legion. It was all over.

And then I raced to the station and caught the fast train to Paris.

EPILOGUE

Well all that happened a long time ago. I was twenty-four when I left the Legion. I spent a couple of years wandering around Scandinavia undertaking commissions while I toyed with a job offer from a department in the Foreign Office and then I finally decided it was time to settle down. I married Jennifer – she would wait no longer – and at the end of 1966 I joined the great house of Jardine Matheson in the Far East. Today I am running the Jardine Engineering Corporation in Hong Kong – A long way from the Foreign Legion – but it has its excitements.

The Manneken Pis? I made it. There had been no contact with Vignaga or Soto, according to Legion tradition, since we had gone our separate ways, and when the time came I spent hours persuading myself that it would be a fruitless journey to go all the way to Belgium on that New Year's Eve. But finally my pride and my curiosity won through. I could not bear the thought that I would spend the rest of my life wondering whether they showed up or not and so off I set in my little car and Jennifer came with me.

We drove to Dover and then took the ferry to Ostend and from there we drove on to Brussels. It poured with rain every inch of the way.

Eventually we got to the Manneken Pis. It is in a tiny little back street off the marketplace. The streets were deserted, the rain continued to fall in bucket loads, and I knew the whole thing had been a mistake. Opposite the Manneken Pis there is a small scruffy bistro which was miraculously open and we sat in there and supped red wine for two hours. There was no one else in the bistro, it was like a morgue. Outside the bells of Brussels chimed the New Year in and clanged their old hearts out. The rain never ceased for a second.

One o'clock came and went and finally I accepted the inevitable truth. I took a table napkin and wrote on it, '*Je suis venu – Simon*,' and I staggered outside into the rain and stuck it on the railings round the statue and then as I turned a voice hailed, 'Johnny', out of nowhere.

And down the dimly lighted street through the rain came Soto. It was a magnificent sensational moment. Yet another of the truly great meetings of history. An experience that everybody should feel once in a lifetime.

We put Brussels on the map that night and the next day we parted. Daniel didn't show and I have never seen him since the day I left the Legion. Soto I see every year in Paris. He was fired from his job when he came to Brussels (he told me this years later) and he started polishing floors when he returned. He now has a small but profitable business cleaning windows. He employs ten people and operates a number of sophisticated lifts on the outside of tall commercial buildings from which his men clean the windows. He has a fabulous wife and two children and when I go to Paris we take off into the country, light a fire, grill some lamb and steaks and over flagons of red we recount stories of our Legion days and sing the old songs. We share something of immense value.

I met Captain L'Hospitallier, my old company commander, who was axed after the *putsch*, at Bangkok airport one day right out of the blue. I had just returned from a trip to Laos and I was waiting for my bag to come through when suddenly there he was standing ten feet from me. I could not believe that it was him and for a full minute I just looked at him, telling myself that it was someone else. And finally I approached him. '*Capitaine L'Hospitallier?*' I asked.

'*Oui, c'est moi*,' he replied and we both looked at each other completely amazed. He didn't recognize me at first and his amazement was due to the fact that someone knew who he was.

I said, in French, 'I was in your section in the Legion in 1960,' and his mouth dropped open.

'My God. You're the English one, aren't you?' he said.

He had gone into voluntary exile in Cambodia after the *putsch*, and had been there ever since as an adviser to the Cambodian army on parachute training techniques. And he was catching the S.S. *Vietnam* from Bangkok to Paris that night. The ship was actually due to sail the following morning. We had a splendid dinner on board, just the two of us, and that was another evening that I slotted in amongst my many memories as one of the greats of my life.

We talked it all through, particularly the *putsch*, and he gave me his view of the action from the officers' side of the fence and I gave him mine. We both learned much. When I remember the rigid discipline that used to exist in the Legion, and the enormous gap between the officers and the men, it was totally incongruous for us to be sitting there like old friends meeting for the first time in an age. He sent a cable on my wedding day which I still have but I have not seen him since. He was one of France's greatest sons.

There was yet one more coincidence that brought me into contact again with history. When I lived in Bangkok for a while I used to travel regularly for Jardines to Laos, and on one such journey the British Embassy in Vientiane were having a party to celebrate the Queen's birthday. I was invited. So was everybody else: the French, the Vietnamese, the Chinese, the Russians, the Americans and anybody who was anybody in Vientiane. In those days there were a lot of those in Vientiane. There was a Frenchman whom I knew quite well through business and at some point in the evening he came up to me and said he wanted to introduce me to a French general who had been in the Legion.

The party was taking place on the lawn in the embassy garden and at one end next to the house was a raised dais. On the dais slouched in an armchair was a French general, fat as a walrus, in a white uniform, scarcely visible through an array of brightly coloured medals, and he was talking to the Prime Minister, Prince Souvannah Phouma. My friend dragged me onto the platform and said to the general, '*Mon général*, I would like to introduce Mr Simon Murray who used to be in the Foreign Legion.'

The general leapt to his feet and shook my hand until my arm practically fell off. He introduced me to Souvannah Phouma and then started a barrage of questions.

'What regiment were you in?' – 'My God. Who was your commanding officer?'

'Colonel Cailloud,' I said. He started getting enthusiastic.

'Yes, yes, and before him?'

'Before him it was Channel.'

'*Mon Dieu*, old Channel, and before him?'

'Before Channel it was, let me see now, I think it was Damusez.'

'Yes, and before Damusez?'

'Before Damusez it was Colonel Lefort.'

'*C'est moi*,' he roared, thumping his chest, '*c'est moi, Lefort.*'

And my God it was. He was suddenly recognizable as the man he had once been. Without more ado he grabbed me by the arm and dragged me down the garden to where a Laotian military band was making a tremendous effort to get the party moving. By this time we were the focal point of attention and I was wishing the night would close in and swallow me up.

The band was obviously French trained and looked splendid in white uniforms and red berets. Lefort drew them to attention and ordered them to play '*Le Boudin*', the traditional march of the Legion. And play it they did, for their lives. I was horrified to see Lefort throw himself to attention with even more enthusiasm than the band had done. face me and salute. Everybody had gathered round to watch by this time. There was nothing for it but to spring to attention myself. The general looked as though he was going to start crying his eyes out at any minute.

At last the music stopped and the general with his arm over my shoulder staggered back to the platform; I staggered along with him. He had had about two bottles too many. He shook my hand some more and said I was welcome at his house any time I was in Vientiane; and that was that. He was a magnificent general in his time, and now he was a splendid character in semi-retirement.

I have met but these three ghosts from the Legion days and now Soto is my only link with the past. They were rough days and we saw some hard times, but looking back on it now I do not regret a single second. It was a magnificent experience, we had a camaraderie that was unparalleled and the world was a much freer place in which to move than it is today. There was more time to wander off the path then, so that a boy of nineteen could run off and climb a mountain if he wanted to. The corridors of life today seem narrow by comparison and the materialistic ends we seek require a constant progression along the path from the moment we take our first examination. There is no allowance for time out.

But there is. And to those that totter on the brink, my advice is go, and do so while you are young, and you will be happy at forty.

APPENDIX

'CAMERONE'

The story of the battle of Camerone goes something like this:

When Maximilian, the new Emperor of Mexico, landed in that country in May 1864, the military position was that a French force, consisting of about forty thousand Europeans, held Mexico City and a corridor from it to the sea at Vera Cruz. Opposed to this was the Mexican leader, Juarez, who with some twenty thousand troops continually harassed French activity, persistently attacking supply lines along the corridor coming to and from the capital city. At the beginning of April 1863, two battalions of legionnaires had arrived to assist the French military forces.

Towards the end of the same month, an escort was needed for a convoy which was carrying bullion to French troops in the interior. The Third Company of the 1st Battalion was allocated to the task. Its effective marching force had been reduced to sixty-two legionnaires – the rest, including the officers, were sick with yellow fever. Three officers volunteered to go with the escort; they were Captain Danjou, Lt Vilain, the pay officer, and 2nd Lt Maudet. Danjou was a French officer of some experience who had fought in Italy, Algeria and the Crimea, where he had lost his left hand and he now wore a false one in its place.

News of the pending convoy of bullion filtered through to

the enemy and the Mexican sector commander, Colonel Milan, began mustering a large force of guerrillas with the object of capturing it. Milan managed to assemble about two thousand men, eight hundred of whom were mounted cavalry armed with Remington and Winchester rifles. Early in the morning of 30 April, the 3rd Company set off along the corridor ahead of the convoy to ensure the way was clear. The company moved off in two platoons marching in extended lines, with Danjou in the centre with a couple of mules carrying rations. A small rear guard followed behind – French intelligence was poor and they had no idea that a large enemy force was watching their every move. Just before 7.00 a.m., Danjou's company passed through the deserted hamlet of Camerone, near a stream noted for its excellent crayfish. The hamlet consisted of a farmhouse and out-buildings, together with a few other ruined hovels, all enclosed in a courtyard. A mile or so past Camerone, Danjou called a halt for *casse-croûte*. Fires were made and coffee was boiled – it was never tasted, for at that moment Colonel Milan and his cavalry attacked. The legionnaires formed a square and pre-pared to meet the Mexicans in best Algerian fashion. They were caught in the open but, fortunately for them, it was not good cavalry country owing to the plentiful clumps of tropical vegetation and waist-high grass. Continuous volleys from the Legion rifles kept Milan at a distance and, unable to charge directly, he manoeuvred his men closer and began to surround the French company. Danjou, seeing the vulnerability of his boys caught in the open and appreciating the enemy strength, decided to fight a running action back to the farmhouse at Camerone, over a mile away, and hold out there. His mules had broken loose in the first mêlée and galloped off with rations and reserve ammunition, a fact which did not improve his prospects.

The legionnaires, in a wide square, began to move back to Camerone and as they moved Milan and his men sniped at their flanks. Moving painfully slowly through the tropical under-growth, Danjou eventually made it to the farmhouse, arriving with a pitiful handful of forty-two men, many of whom were wounded. On arrival, they immediately set about improving the defences by barricading the openings and reinforcing the walls.

Up until this point Milan had only his cavalry with him, and it was towards 9.00 a.m., two hours after the action had started, that his three battalions of infantry arrived, comprising some twelve hundred men. Several charges and forays were tried by the Mexicans and, though repulsed, the legionnaires without food or water began to suffer. Towards eleven, the sun high in the sky poured down a fearsome heat and the continued volleys from rifle and musket began to take their toll.

Colonel Milan called on Danjou to surrender but he refused and made his men swear to fight to the end. Shortly afterwards the Mexicans penetrated the upper storey of the farmhouse and Danjou was shot through the head by a musket ball fired from the roof. Vilain took command and continued to direct the defence.

As time wore on and the Legionnaires fell, the enemy assaults became deadlier and more telling. The heat increased and the men were tortured with thirst. At 2.00 p.m., after seven hours of continued fighting under fantastic pressure, Vilain was killed and 2nd Lt Maudet took command. Wave after wave of attack was launched and repulsed, but the final result was inevitable – yet still the survivors resisted.

Another call to surrender was yelled by Milan but he received words of defiance in return. The dead and dying now lay sprawled all over the courtyard; both legionnaires and Mexicans, with the stench of death and cordite in the nostrils and a thousand flies relishing the filth. They fought on through the long hot weary afternoon and at 5.00 p.m. Maudet was left with twelve men. The Mexicans fired the main farmhouse and Maudet and his men dashed across the courtyard to a last small outhouse. Again Milan called for surrender and again he was refused.

After a brief lull towards 6.00 p.m., the Mexican infantry massed and moved slowly in – Maudet was left with himself and five others to fight. Seeing it was hopeless, he gave the order to load and fire, and then the final order to fix bayonets. Tearing aside the barricades, the six men charged into the mass of Mexican infantry and were completely absorbed by it. Yet by some miracle Colonel Milan was able to call a halt to the ultimate massacre. Three legionnaires survived the final charge. Milan appears to have been much impressed with the legionnaires and gave them their lives and allowed them to keep their rifles and bury their dead.

Danjou's wooden hand now rests in the Legion Hall of Honour in Aubagne. It is a symbol of Legion durability – for the Legion never surrenders.

Thus ended the battle of Camerone – Napoleon III ordered that the word 'Camerone' should be inscribed in gold on the walls of Les Invalides in Paris. Of all the scores of battles fought by the Legion, this is the one most highly regarded and celebrated annually with all the pomp and ceremony that the Legion can muster. Camerone Day, 30 April, is without doubt the most important day in the Legion calendar.

GLOSSARY

coupe-coupe: knife shaped like a machete

douar: Arab village

fellagha: name given to Algerian 'rebels'

F.L.N. (Front de la libération nationale):
originally an Algerian group which started to bid for independence from France and later became the official voice of the Algerian freedom movement

fouillage: a search

mechta: Arab dwelling

O.A.S. (Organisation de l'armée secrète):
secret army founded by French civilians in Algeria with the aim of preventing Algerian independence

voltigeur: front-line infantryman